PUTTING WOMEN IN PLACE

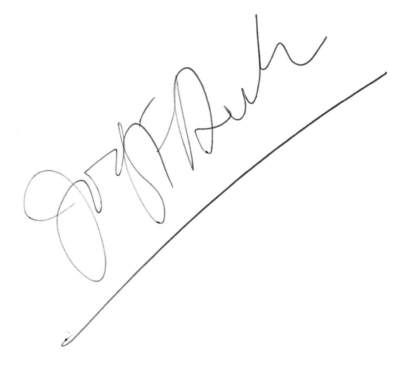

PUTTING WOMEN IN PLACE

Feminist Geographers Make Sense of the World

Mona Domosh
Joni Seager

THE GUILFORD PRESS
New York   London

© 2001 The Guilford Press
A Division of Guilford Publications, Inc.
72 Spring Street, New York, NY 10012
www.guilford.com

Printed in the United States of America

This book is printed on acid-free paper.

Last digit is print number: 9 8 7 6 5 4 3 2 1

Library of Congress Cataloging-in-Publication Data

Domosh, Mona, 1957–
    Putting women in place: feminist geographers make sense of the world /
Mona Domosh, Joni Seager.
        p. cm.
    Includes bibliographical references and index.
    ISBN 1-57230-668-8 (pbk.)
    1. Women—Social conditions. 2. Sex role—History. 3. Spatial
behavior—History. 4. Feminist geography. I. Seager, Joni.
    II. Title.

HQ1150 .D65 2001
305.42—dc21

                                                                    2001023878

To our parents, with love

Natalie Frankel Domosh
Stanley Domosh

Joan Seager

CONTENTS

FIGURES AND TABLES

FIGURES

TABLES

ACKNOWLEDGMENTS

We owe thanks to many friends for their support through the various stages of writing this book. In particular, we want to thank Julie Abraham, Gilda Bruckman, Ellen Cooney, Walter Delaney, Madeline Drexler, E. J. Graff, Gail Hollander, Barbara Hutchings, Melissa Hyams, Amy Lang, JoBeth Mertens, Rod Neumann, Judy Wachs, and Ellen Winchester, for their friendship, companionship, and comic relief.

We also want to recognize and thank colleagues who provided institutional assistance at the University of Vermont, Florida Atlantic University, and Dartmouth College, particularly Mary McBride, Joan Smith, Charles White, Kelly White, and Richard Wright. Thank you to our friends in the Geography and Women's Studies departments at the University of Vermont and Dartmouth College for their ongoing intellectual and collegial support. Our colleagues in the Association of American Geographers' feminist caucus ("Geographical Perspectives on Women") provide a national and international network of intellectual camaraderie, support, and sense of shared purpose essential for a work of this kind. We intend this book to be a testament to the intellectual liveliness of this network of feminist scholars; we hope they are not disappointed.

Anna McCall-Taylor was invaluable as our research assistant, tracking down prints, photos, maps, and permissions from across the globe. Without her persistence and creativity we would never have been able to include such a wide array of photographs and images. We are forever grateful.

Our thanks to the tireless production team at the Guilford Press and to our editor Peter Wissoker. The anonymous reviewers who read the manuscript in various stages made important and useful comments and suggestions. We thank them for their guidance and direction.

Some of the research for this book was supported with funds from the National Science Foundation, grants 9422051 and 9911232.

We also want to acknowledge the often unspoken but nonetheless important influences of those brave women who first dared to mention gender, feminism, and geography in the same breath. Their experiences, their scholarship, and their audacity created what we today call feminist geography. We would like to note, in particular, Mildred Berman, an unheralded feminist pioneer, who is much missed.

And to Frank and to Cynthia, with thanks for their love and endurance.

We gratefully acknowledge permission to reproduce the following illustrations from their original sources as detailed below:

Figure P.1: Baroque sideboard from the New York Exhibition, 1853–1854. From *The World of Science, Art, and Industry, illustrated from examples in the New York Exhibition, 1853–1854* edited by Professor B. Silliman, Jr. and C. R. Godrich Esq., aided by several scientific and literary men (1854). By courtesy of the Dartmouth College Library.

Figure P.2: Diagram of a prototype Navajo hogan. From *Native American Achitecture* by Peter Nabokov and Robert Easton. Copyright 1989 by Peter Nabokov and Robert Easton. Used by permission of Oxford University Press, Inc.

Figure 1.1: A medieval houseplan. From *The Village and House in the Middle Ages* by Jean Chapelot and Robert Fossier and translated by Henry Cleere. Copyright 1985. Reproduced by permission of Chrysalis Books, Ltd.

Figure 1.2: King's Square in Soe Hoe (now Soho Square), London, early eighteenth century. Reproduced by courtesy of the Westminster City Archives Center.

Figure 1.3: Parlor view of a New York dwelling house from *Gleason's Pictorial Drawing-Room Companion* (1854). By courtesy of the Dartmouth College Library.

Figure 1.4: Trade card for the Mason & Hamlin Organ Co., c. 1890. By courtesy of The Winterthur Library: Joseph Downs Collection of Manuscripts and Printed Ephemera.

Figure 1.5: Part of a parlor suite, from the Phoenix Furniture Company catalog, c. 1878. From Grand Rapids Public Library Furniture Catalog Collection (232) Lon M. Neely, with Phoenix Furniture Co., Grand Rapids, Mich. [catalog], ca. 1878. By courtesy of the Local History Department, Grand Rapids Public Library, Grand Rapids, MI.

Figure 1.6: Diagrams of unplanned and planned cleaning "orders," from Christine Frederick's *Household Engineering*, 1919. Originally published by the American School of Home Economics, Chicago, IL.

Figure 1.7: Victorian bathroom interior, from J. L. Mott Iron Works illustrated catalog, 1888. From *Mott's Illustrated Catalog of Victorian Plumbing Fixtures for Bathrooms and Kitchens* by The J. L. Mott Iron Works (1987). Reproduced by permission of Dover Publications, Inc.

Figure 1.8: "Modern" bathroom fixtures, from Standard Sanitary Manufacturing Co., 1905. Reprinted with permission of American Standard, Inc.

Figure 1.9: A woman hanging wallpaper, from the Montgomery Ward catalog, 1910. From Montgomery Ward's, *Wallpaper at Wholesale Prices: Newest Styles for 1910* (1910). Reproduced by permission of the Montgomery Ward's.

Figure 1.10: Photograph of Hull House, c. 1905–1910. Reproduced by permission of the Chicago Historical Society and Barnes-Crosby, negative no. ICHi-19288.

Figure 1.11: M. P. Wolff's plan for a public kitchen, 1884. From M. P. Wolff, plan for a public kitchen, 1884.

Figure 1.12: Advertisement for Levittown houses, 1950. Reproduced by courtesy of Levittown Historical Society and by permission of Levitt and Sons.

Figure 2.1: Cartoon of census enumeration. Cartoon by Terry Hirst, commissioned by the International Centre for Research in Agroforestry for *Agroforestry Today*, Vol. 1, No. 2. Reproduced by permission of Terry Hirst, *Agroforestry Today*.

Figure 2.2: Photograph of women on the assembly line. Reproduced by courtesy of Gary Massoni/AFSC.

Figure 2.3: Brochure about women in the global economy. Brochure reproduced by courtesy of Press for Change.

Figure 2.4: 1910 Riis photographs of home-based production. *National Consumers' League, Finishing Pants* Photograph c. 1900 and *Organized Charity. Family Making Artificial Flowers* Photograph, c. 1910 from The Jacob A. Riis Collection, Museum of the City of New York 90.13.3.173 and 90.13.4.64.

Table 2.1: Real Work versus Census-Defined "Work." Reprinted from "What Counts? Critical Analysis of Statistical Indicators" by Janice Monk in *Encompassing Gender: Integrating International Studies and Women's Studies*, edited by Mary M. Lay, Janice Monk, and Deborah S. Rosenfelt, New York: The Feminist Press. Copyright 2001 by Janice Monk. Reproduced by permission of The Feminist Press, *www.feministpress.org*.

Table 2.2: Workday of a Rural Woman, Eastern Uganda. Reprinted from "Agricultural Production and Women's Time Budgets in Uganda" by Victoria Mwaka in *Different Places, Different Voices*, edited by Janet Henshall Momsen and Vivian Kinnaird, New York: Routledge, 1993. Reproduced by permission of Routledge and the editors.

Figure 3.1: The ideal, planned Renaissance city of Palma Nuova, designed by Vitruvius. From *Civitates Orbis Terrarum* by Georg Braun and Franz Hogenberg, originally published between 1572 and 1618. Photo courtesy of Edward E. Ayer Collection, The Newberry Library, Chicago, IL.

Figure 3.2: A 1569 depiction of Paris. From *Civitates Orbis Terrarum* by Georg Braun and Franz Hogenberg, originally published between 1572 and 1618. Photo courtesy of Edward E. Ayer Collection, The Newberry Library, Chicago, IL.

Figure 3.3: View inside a London coffeehouse, c. 1650. Detail from *A London Coffee-House* c. 1705, Anon. Copyright the British Museum. Reproduced by permission of the British Museum.

Figure 3.4: An etching of a woman walking in Cornhill, by W. Hollar, 1643. Copyright the British Museum. Reproduced by permission of the British Museum.

Figure 3.6: A Winslow Homer drawing, *The Drive in Central Park, New York, September, 1860.* From *Harper's Weekly: A Journal of Civilization*, Vol. IV (1860). By courtesy of the Dartmouth College Library.

Figure 3.7: Photograph of T. E. Fitzgerald's bar, 1912. *T. E. Fitzgerald's Bar* photograph, 1912 from the Museum of the City of New York, The Byron Collection.

Figure 3.9: Photograph of women working in a laundry room, 1902. *Downtown Club, Laundry Room* photograph, 1902 from the Museum of the City of New York, The Byron Collection.

Figure 3.10: Photograph of the bargain counter at Siegal Cooper Department Store, New York City. *Siegel Cooper Company Bargain Counter* photograph, c. 1897 from the Museum of the City of New York, The Byron Collection.

Figure 3.11: Photograph of women parading along the Boardwalk, Coney Island, c. 1897. *The Boardwalk, Coney Island* photograph, c. 1897 from the Museum of the City of New York, The Byron Collection.

Figure 3.12: Exterior view of Stewart's 1851 department store in New York City. *Christmas Parade of the Expressmen of NY* engraving by J. A. Bogart. Reproduced by permission from the Collection of the New-York Historical Society, negative no. 41435.

Figure 3.13: Inside view of Stewart's 1862 department store. *A. T. Stewart's Astor Place Store*, c. 1880s, interior, engraving by unidentified artist. Reproduced by permission from the Collection of the New-York Historical Society, negative no. 70132.

Figure 3.14: Lithograph of a woman "walking the gauntlet" on Broadway. *Running the Gauntlet*, drawn by J. N. Hyde, from *Frank Leslie's Illustrated Newspaper*, May 16, 1874. Reproduced by permission from the Collection of the New-York Historical Society, negative no. 74255.

Figure 3.15: The title page of *Good Homes Make Contented Workers*, 1919. Title page, *Good Homes Make Contented Workers*, Industrial Housing Associates, 1919.

Figure 3.16: Aerial view of a portion of Levittown, Long Island, New York, 1947. Photo courtesy of Levittown Public Library.

Figure 3.17: Photograph of a festival in the "Village" of Manchester, England. Copyright News Team International Ltd.

Figure 4.1: "Our Best Society." *Our Best Society–A Scene on Fifth Avenue*, from *New York Illustrated News*, January 31, 1863. Reproduced by permission from the Collection of the New-York Historical Society, negative no. 70510.

Figure 4.2: Photograph of a woman with a baby carriage. From the photo series "Urban Obstacle Course" in *Making Space: Women and the Man-Made Environment* by MATRIX, London: Pluto Press. Copyright 1984 by Pluto Press. Reproduced by permission of Pluto Press.

Figure 4.4: Pleasure Park. *Kake Pleasure Park* by Tom of Finland, c. 1969–1970. Courtesy of the Tom of Finland Foundation, Los Angeles.

Figure 4.5: Road map image of a woman driver. Road map cover from the John Margolies Collection.

Figure 4.6: Map of global women migrants. From *The State of Women in the World Atlas, New Edition* by Joni Seager (1997). Reproduced by permission of Myriad Editions and Joni Seager.

Figure 4.7: Map of the global sex trade. From *The State of Women in the World Atlas, New Edition* by Joni Seager (1997). Reproduced by permission of Myriad Editions and Joni Seager.

Figure 5.3: Photographs of Amelia and Lena Brennon in front of their sod homes in North Dakota. From *Land in Her Own Name* by H. Elaine Lindgren. Reproduced by permission of the North Dakota Institute for Regional Studies and University Archives.

Figure 5.4: Photograph of Mr. and Mrs. David Hilton and their children, Custer County, Nebraska, 1887. Reproduced by permission of the Nebraska State Historical Society, Solomon D. Butcher Collection.

Figure 5.5: The MacNab family, posed in front of their bungalow in the hill station of Ootacamund in Madras, India, c. 1910. Reproduced by permission of The British Library, MACNAB 752/4 No. 58.

Figure 5.7: A depiction of a Native American-themed "historical corner." From *The Decorator and Furnisher*, Vol. 31 (1898). By courtesy of the Library of Congress.

Figure 5.8: Photograph of Annette Ackroyd with her pupils in India, 1875. Reproduced by permission of The British Library, MSS EUR C 176/244.

Figure 5.9: Family of seven Afrikaners on and around a covered wagon. From *Gedenboek, Eeufees: 1838–1939* by H. J. Klopper, originally published by Cape Town: Nasionale Pers (1940). Reproduced by courtesy of Tafelberg Publishers.

Figure 5.10: Photograph of Billy Byrne Memorial Statue, County Wicklow, Ireland. Reproduced by courtesy of the National Library of Ireland, Lawrence Collection, Cab3959.

Figure 5.11: Cradling Wheat by Thomas Hart Benton, 1938. Reproduced by courtesy of The Saint Louis Art Museum, Museum Purchase.

PREFACE

Sometimes the most everyday and seemingly unimportant facets of our lives can turn out to be profound and provocative. The way we arrange our furniture, for example, tells a lot about our economic situation, our ideas of good taste, perhaps even our ethnic or national identity. It can also tell us about gender relationships. We see this in typical middle-class homes in the United States, where the garage, basement, and barbecue pit tend to be men's spaces, while the kitchen and living room are women's domains. In Victorian times, the dining room was thought to be a masculine space: fine dining was associated with meat eating and, by implication, with the violence of the hunt. Victorian sideboards, such as the one shown in Figure P.1, were decorated with the depictions of dead animals, while the pictures that hung on dining room walls often celebrated the killings.

In some other cultures around the world, domestic spaces are more formally divided between women and men. In traditional wealthy Muslim homes in Iran, for example, the female area of the home is located in the rear, near the family living room, while the male area is located in the more public areas of the home close to the entrance. The traditional circular home of the Navajo in the U.S. Southwest, the hogan, is divided into male and female areas, both lived-in and spiritual (Figure P.2). Thus, the floor represents the female earth, while the roof symbolizes the male sky. Women occupy the south side of the hogan, while the men occupy the north side.

Examining how people organize their most everyday spaces,

FIGURE P.1. Baroque sideboard from the New York Exhibition, 1853–1854. Decorating this extremely ornate sideboard are carved depictions of dead animals, which link this dining room piece with masculinity and the violence of the hunt.

then, is often related to how they think about and relate to each other in terms of gender. For many of us (Euro-Americans), the most obvious gendered space is our home. Is there a large chair in the living room that is usually occupied by the "man of the house"? Who is in charge of arranging the furniture and decorating the rooms? Who keeps the home clean and in order? We don't often think to raise these questions because the answers seem so obvious. It is precisely the taken-for-grantedness of roles and behaviors in our homes that makes their embedded gender politics so powerful. Most people don't stop to question whether (or why) the man of the house needs (or deserves) his own chair. Yet we can raise similar questions about a whole range of issues: Why do women and men tend to work in different jobs, in different ways, and in different spaces? Why are the suburbs supposed to embody a certain ideal of family, while the city represents a more masculine, public world? Why is nature often represented in feminine form?

In this book, we raise these types of questions about some of the most basic ways we organize our everyday lives, and the ways our lives

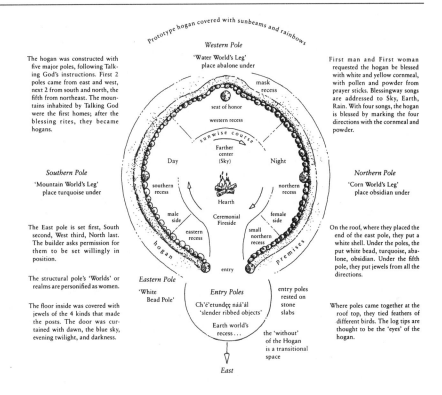

Prototype hogan covered with sunbeams and rainbows

Western Pole
'Water World's Leg'
place abalone under

mask recess

seat of honor

western recess

sunwise course

Farther center (Sky)

Day   Night

Hearth

Ceremonial Fireside

southern recess

northern recess

male side

female side

eastern recess

small northern recess

hogan

premises

entry

Eastern Pole
'White Bead Pole'

Entry Poles
Ch'é'etundęę náá'ál
'slender ribbed objects'

Earth world's recess . . .

entry poles rested on stone slabs

the 'without' of the Hogan is a transitional space

East

The hogan was constructed with five major poles, following Talking God's instructions. First 2 poles came from east and west, next 2 from south and north, the fifth from northeast. The mountains inhabited by Talking God were the first homes; after the blessing rites, they became hogans.

Southern Pole
'Mountain World's Leg'
place turquoise under

The East pole is set first, South second, West third, North last. The builder asks permission for them to be set willingly in position.

The structural pole's 'Worlds' or realms are personified as women.

The floor inside was covered with jewels of the 4 kinds that made the posts. The door was curtained with dawn, the blue sky, evening twilight, and darkness.

First man and First woman requested the hogan be blessed with white and yellow cornmeal, with pollen and powder from prayer sticks. Blessingway songs are addressed to Sky, Earth, Rain. With four songs, the hogan is blessed by marking the four directions with the cornmeal and powder.

Northern Pole
'Corn World's Leg'
place obsidian under

On the roof, where they placed the end of the east pole, they put a white shell. Under the poles, the put white bead, turquoise, abalone, obsidian. Under the fifth pole, they put jewels from all the directions.

Where poles came together at the roof top, they tied feathers of different birds. The log tips are thought to be the 'eyes' of the hogan.

FIGURE P.2. Diagram of a prototype Navajo hogan. As symbolic representations of the cosmos, hogans are divided into male and female spheres, each of equal importance.

are often organized for us by society. As feminist geographers, we engage these questions through our understanding of place and gender. Three interlocked observations serve as our departure points: (1) that the design and use of our built environment is determined in part by assumptions about gender roles and relations—or, as we like to say, space is gendered; (2) that spatial organization and relations are not simply a neutral backdrop for human dramas, but instead help to shape them; (3) that gender is an important interpretive lens that influences human relationships to and perceptions of both built and natural environments.

The story we tell, then, extends from our understanding of the terms *space*, *place*, *gender*, and *sexuality*. "Space" and "place" are words that, like "time," seem so commonsensical as to not require definition. Yet as geographers (whose raison d'être is often thought to be the exploration of space and place), we will be using these words in particular ways. When we use, for example, the word "space," we are not referring to planetary exploration! What we mean is that all of our actions take place in particular locations. In this sense, "space" refers to the three-dimensionality of life—to its material form. We often think of material forms, such as houses and communities and cities, as organized in certain ways. Their patterning and organization, as well as their relative locations (as measured on a map, for example), are central to our understanding of the role of spatial organization in social life. For example, we feel it useful to ask questions about the significance of the proximity of shopping malls to middle-class residential areas; the reasons for the internal arrangement of the shops within the mall; and the importance of the daily social interactions that occur there.

"Place" has a different connotation. We use it to refer to spaces that have been invested with meaning. An appropriate illustration is found in the words *house* and *home*. "House" is a drier term that refers to the physical structure—and perhaps to its relative location, its arrangement of rooms, and so on. A "house" becomes a "home" when we invest it with our personal meanings and associations. So we might say that "spaces" become "places" when we have some personal association with them. Because of this, we might study place in a manner different from space; instead of numerical measures, we would probably use more personal methods designed to understand particulars instead of generalities. For example, examining the shopping mall as a place would include analysis of shoppers' experiences of it, and of the relationship of those experiences to the history of shopping, and to the forces in society that operate to reinforce the association of women, femininity, and consumption. We don't mean to suggest here that there is a clear and certain difference between the terms *space* and *place*, only to point out that each term tends to represent different aspects of geographical curiosity.

Which brings us to gender. In this book, we use the term *gender* to refer to a culture's assumptions about the differences between men and women: their "characters," the roles they play in society, what they represent. Scholars used to differentiate "gender" from "sex." They argued that "gender" referred to the attributes assigned by culture, attributes that therefore were variable and unfixed over time and space. "Sex," on the other hand, referred to those attributes assigned by biology, attributes that were fixed by nature. Yet that conceptual division is eroding as we have come to see the variabilities of biology, and as we have examined how cultures assign bodies particular meanings. We will be using "gender" as an inclusive word to refer to all the literal and metaphorical ways that cultures mark differences between women and men. We will use "sexuality" to refer to the sexual behavior and actions of women and men.

This book will show how intimately connected these terms are. Readers will see the relationships between common assumptions about the roles, actions, and portrayals of men and women (gender), the patterns and organization of how we live (space), and the particular locations in which we invest meaning (place). Our scale of analysis will range from the home to the world, from our intimate connections with local environs to global concerns over environmental issues, and from individual lives to those represented only by dots on maps. Using examples and case studies drawn primarily from the research of scholars in geography, we will provide the evidence for our main argument: that the gendering of space and place, and the role that space and place play in the making of gender, matter. In other words, we argue that it matters that shopping malls are designed to fit middle-class notions of femininity; that secretaries rarely have private offices, but instead are assigned spaces that can be seen by others; that it is "masculinist" institutions that have precipitated global environmental crises. It matters because the decisions that are made about our everyday lives, based in outmoded ideas of gender, are fixed in our everyday places and spaces. The maintenance of these outmoded ideas serves the people who have the power to make the farthest reaching decisions in our society. Feminist geography helps us see that power concretely, and by so doing, gives us an important entry point for challenging it.

Chapter 1

HOME

The association of home with women and femininity is so commonplace that it is often considered natural. Let's think for a moment of the two images of women that have dominated popular media in the United States during the past fifty years: the "happy homemaker" of the baby-boom years, presiding over her new suburban home, and the "working woman" of the 1980s and 1990s, running between her demanding job and her 'perfectly styled home. These two stereotypical images of womanhood are powerful: they have fueled political rhetoric on both sides of the arguments about the "progress" of the women's movement, and they have come to epitomize the values and lifeways of particular generations of Americans: the "stay-at-home mom" represents "traditional" family values and harks back to the purported stability of the U.S. postwar years; the "working woman" speaks of the breaking down of gender boundaries and of the challenges of new family roles for both women and men. Both these powerful images of women rely on the home as the basis for definition: in the case of the "traditional" women by her literal attachment to home, in that of the "working" women by the fact that her activities take place at a distance from home.

So home, both literally and metaphorically, is intimately involved in popular definitions of contemporary womanhood. And this association is not just an abstract concept: women themselves seem to derive more of their identities from their domestic life than do men. When guests arrive for dinner, it is usually the woman who worries about what judgments they make: Is her house tidy? Are there clean towels in the bathroom? Will her planned menu please her guests' trendy taste buds? Although it is certainly true that women still shoulder the lion's share of housework (a recent survey estimated that married women spend forty hours a week on household chores, compared to seventeen for men; *Health*, 1999), there seems to be something more than work invested in their homes—some intangible connection to self and identity. Geographers Susan Hanson and Geraldine Pratt (1995) found in their study in Worcester, Massachusetts, that women almost always live closer to their place of work than do men, no matter if they are married or single, have or do not have children. For reasons that were left unspecified, because seemingly so "natural," it was just more important for women than for men to have their homes close to where they spent their days working. Men may take pride in the greenness of their lawn, or in the barbecue grill in the backyard, but for the most part it is women's identities and women's interests that are bound up with the idea of, and the literal form of, the home. As geographers, we are certainly curious about this most "feminine" of spaces. What is the history of this powerful association between the home and women? Have women always been defined in relation to the home? And what are the implications of such a deep-seated and seemingly "natural" association?

THE SEPARATION OF SPHERES

To start, we need to think historically about the home, and to consider when and how it became a place that was separate from "work." We know that prior to about the sixteenth century in Europe, this separation was not complete. In medieval Europe, for example, most people were engaged in some form of agriculture, and their houses served as both living spaces and work spaces. Both men and women were involved in productive labor, though there was a differentiation between the tasks usually assigned to men and those to women. Women, for example, did most of the food preparation (including, interestingly enough, the brewing of beer!), as well as spinning, weaving, and sewing clothing. Women also shared the agricultural labor with men, including planting, plowing, harvesting, and tending to animals.

The houses of these agricultural workers were usually small and spare (Figure 1.1). Eating and sleeping areas surrounded a central hearth. Indeed, many peasants shared their roofs with their farm animals—a separate building to serve as a barn was an expense most

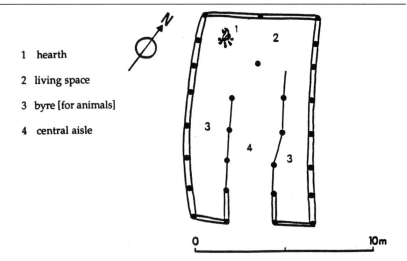

1   hearth

2   living space

3   byre [for animals]

4   central aisle

FIGURE 1.1. A medieval houseplan. Most agricultural medieval homes were simple in design, with spaces undifferentiated by use, or by gender.

could not afford. Except for this division between living spaces and animal spaces, the medieval European "commoner's" house itself was generally not divided into separate rooms. These spaces were undifferentiated by gender, and were used interchangeably for the wide range of activities necessary to support agricultural life. In these circumstances, it is difficult to think of the house itself as the domain of one sex, although it was probably true that women spent more time in it, given their work in food preparation and clothing manufacture.

Massive socioeconomic and geographical changes occurred in Europe throughout the fifteenth, sixteenth, and seventeenth centuries. These centuries saw the transition into the modern period, marked in part by the emergence of early capitalism. It is difficult, if not impossible, to pinpoint what led to the changes that ushered in the modern age, or to say exactly how and when these changes began, but we do know that the economic, social, and geographical realities of people living in the 1700s were qualitatively different from those living in the 1400s. One of the most significant of these changes, at least in terms of our discussion here, is that work spaces and living spaces became separate. This certainly did not happen all at once, nor in all cases. But the rise of urban life, the consolidation of capitalism as the dominant economic system, and the increase in local and long-distance trading during this period led to the removal of jobs from the home. Making beer, for example, went from being a job that was done in the farmyard by women, to a job that was done in the cities by men. Brewing developed into a commercial enterprise that was located away from the home and funded with capital. The "manufactured" beer was sold to the taverns of the growing cities. Historian Judith Bennett notes the consolidation of brewing in the hands of a few men: "In 1300 many villages boasted numerous female brewers who supplemented their households' income by selling ale to friends and neighbors; in 1700, those same villages often hosted only a handful of male brewers" (1994: 59).

For the emerging European middle classes, the changes of the fourteenth to sixteenth centuries often meant that the home was increasingly defined by its separateness from work. Women continued their work within the home, such as child care, food preparation, and sewing, but increasingly their jobs came to be defined as qualitatively different from the jobs men did outside the home. The role of "production" was separated from that of "reproduction," and men became the productive wage earners, while women carried on the reproductive tasks for the family.

We need to emphasize here that the reality of women's lives during the early capitalist period often did not conform to this stereotype. Many women of the working and middle classes toiled for wages because their families required the income. They were engaged in a variety of jobs, including manufacturing, and their work was not punctuated by time-out for child rearing. As historian Margaret Hunt points out, eighteenth-century middle-class women in England "were most likely to have jobs outside the home during the prime childbearing years. Women were heavily concentrated in occupations that were heavy and dangerous both for them and for their children, . . . that demanded that they spend a considerable amount of time away from home, and that left them little additional time for household tasks" (1996: 136).

Nonetheless, even though many members of the working and middle classes couldn't afford the luxury of having only one wage earner in the family, they were not immune from the powerful ideology that separated the male world of work and the female world of home and family. This ideology associated certain values with these two "worlds." The masculine realm was portrayed as one of equal individuals going out into the world to prove themselves through economic competition. In distinction, the feminine world of the home was portrayed as one of people joined together in a communal structure (but one that was importantly hierarchical). The husband was in charge of the family, the wife had her subservient but complementary role as caretaker and spiritual center, and the children followed instruction in order to take over future care of the family. Individuals in the family, therefore, in principle related to each other through the bonds of familial obligation and compassion (Nicholson, 1986).

In other words, by the eighteenth century throughout much of the Western world, men worked to earn money, women worked for "love." It is important to recognize that the development of this ideology of "separate spheres" served very particular purposes; the separation of a masculine world of work and production from a feminine world of family and reproduction was essential to the ideology of the emerging capitalist system. This system required a commitment to hard work and competition in the marketplace, and at the same time required the behind-the-scenes care and nurturance of family and children, and the unpaid maintenance of the physical (and psychological) needs of the workers.

This formation of feminine and masculine spheres of life became more entrenched with the industrialization of the eighteenth and nineteenth centuries in Western Europe and North America. One of the main features of industrialization was the transformation of cities. For the middle and upper classes, spaces in the city became segregated as home and work moved further and further apart. Let's look at the case of London more closely since it is often considered a prime example of an early industrial city. In London, industrial areas began to concentrate to the east of St. Paul's Cathedral, while the area to the West, closer to Westminster, the court, and the nobility, became home to the middle and upper classes. These residential sections, such as Soho Square and Covent Garden, represent the first spaces devoted exclusively to residential land use, and to one group of residents: the middle and upper classes (Figure 1.2). In these elite residential enclaves, the idea of a home as a preserve distinct from the world of work came to fruition. These elegant townhomes were meant as spaces for leisurely activities, for entertaining guests, and for displaying wealth, while the competitive world of men's work took place in the office or the factory, far removed from these domestic enclaves.

Such a differentiation of the use of urban space was carried across the Atlantic, so that as early as the late eighteenth century cities such as New York and Boston developed their own distinctive middle- and upper-class residential enclaves. The massive industrialization of the nineteenth century brought this segregation of land uses to most cities in the United States. New York's Upper West Side, Boston's Back Bay, and Chicago's Gold Coast are all known as exclusive residential areas for the upper classes.

It is important to recognize that this elaboration of a feminine, private sphere of home and a masculine, public sphere of work was articulated much more clearly at the level of ideology than it was on the ground. In other words, even though the eighteenth and nineteenth centuries witnessed segregation of urban land uses, and the separation of areas of work from areas of home, that separation was never complete. For one thing, most middle-class women considered

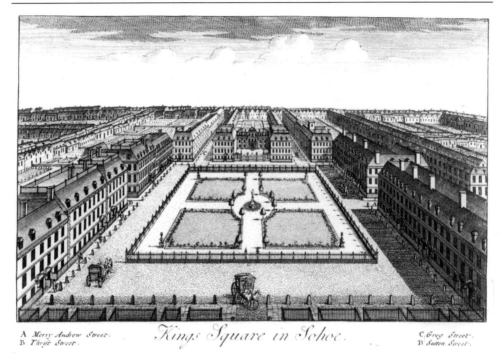

A *Merry Andrew Street*.   *King's Square in Sohoe*.   C *Greg Street*.
B *Thrift Street*.   D *Sutton Street*.

FIGURE 1.2. King's Square in Soe Hoe (now Soho Square), London, early eighteenth century. Soho Square was one of the first homogenous residential squares, designed for the new bourgeois classes as a residential "retreat" from the areas of work further east in the City of London.

the home a site of work, while places of men's work were often also sites of their leisure activities. But as a set of ideas about how middle-class families should govern their lives, the articulation of separate spheres was quite powerful. Proper Victorian women were meant to stay at home, raise children, decorate their homes, and tend their gardens.

AT HOME WITH THE VICTORIANS

The association of Victorian home interiors with notions of feminin-ity is enduring. Even today we still associate Victorian style—rooms stuffed with goods and fabrics, draped in laces, decorated with curios—with women and femininity. A quick scan today at the maga-zine rack of most U.S. bookstores reveals scores of magazines about home decorating, with many issuing directives about how to re-create Victorian interiors or restore Victorian homes. In fact, several magazines are devoted exclusively to this type of information, such as the magazine *Victorian Homes* published in California, a recent issue of which contains articles on "The Victorian Garden," "Victorian Lifestyles," and "Decorating with a Victorian View." Similarly, the name of the popular U.S. lingerie catalog and chain of stores, Victoria's Secret, resonates with an image of the Victorian. The design of these stores carries through the Victorian motif: deep colors of red and gold, dark wood, a profusion of lacy and silky feminine lingerie.

Why the continuing importance of the Victorian period to notions of home and of femininity? Design historian Penny Sparke (1995) argues that the Victorian home set the tone for the contemporary U.S. and British gendered relationships with the home. The Victorian "cult of domesticity" served an important social role. It set up a women's world that complemented, but did not supersede, the world of men. The feminine world of home was intended to be the seat of moral, aesthetic, and cultural stability—qualities not furthered in the male world of waged work. The important job of maintaining these values, while at the same time expressing the status of their families, fell to women. Their taste in designing their homes became a most important representation of social status and cultural values. As Sparke states:

> The mid-Victorian, middle-class home was a highly feminized phenomenon: within its walls women had a major responsibility both to ensure that it was an appropriate moral milieu for the family and that it displayed the "proper" sense of taste. This is not to say that the domestic ideal was solely a middle-class affair. In spite of the fact that working-class women (and indeed single middle-class women) were more likely to participate in the wage economy at this time—many of them working in the textile factories, for example—the cultural ideal of domesticity penetrated their world as well. (1995: 19)

In the Victorian ideal, women were in charge of creating in material terms a sanctuary from the masculine, public world. And this sanctuary was more than an escape; the home was meant to be an environment that actively shaped character and behavior. Just as women were supposed to play vital roles in Victorian society by providing moral and spiritual guidance, so a proper home and its furnishings were thought to provide everyday and active reminders of appropriate bourgeois behavior. According to historian Katherine Grier, "This 'domestic environmentalism' conflated moral guidance with the actual appearance and physical layout of the house and its contents" (1988: 6). For example, the importance of home furnishings was proclaimed in an 1873 essay published in a London-based trade journal called the *Furniture Gazette*:

There can be no doubt that altogether, independently of direct intellectual culture, either from books or society, the mind is moulded and coloured to a great extent by the persistent impressions produced upon it by the most familiar objects. . . . That a carefully regulated and intelligent change of the domestic scenery about a sick person is beneficial is obvious, and yet there are few who correctly apprehend to how great an extent the character, and especially the temper, may be affected by the nature of ordinary physical surroundings. (Quoted in Grier, 1988: 7)

In other words, the correct selection of home furnishings was far from a trifling matter. Not only did the tasteful and well-arranged parlor suite express status and character, it was presumed to actively shape that character. The ideas of "domestic environmentalism" were popularized through conduct manuals addressed to women, women's magazines such as *Godey's Lady's Book*, popular novels, and trade journals relating to home furnishings. In Victorian ideology, home decoration, then, was a matter of great consequence. Women were involved in making decisions that not only provided material comfort, but that also expressed the status, taste, and moral character of their families. We can begin to see here why the home and home decorating have been so important for women's identities: during the Victorian era, the home was one of the few sites of women's prerogative. Home decoration expressed not only a woman's taste but her moral standing in the family and the community. This has left a lingering after effect: even today it is usually the woman of the house who is most concerned about how "her" home appears to others, because that appearance (whether it is clean, well organized, and tasteful) resonates as a marker of a woman's so-called inner character!

Reading the Parlor

Of all the public spaces in the Victorian home, the parlor was perhaps the most important marker of a family's socioeconomic and moral status (Figure 1.3). Each element in the parlor could be read for its symbolism—it was as if home furnishings constituted a type of visual vocabulary, one that if read correctly could tell the story of its occupants. Certain items were standard, such as "carpets, draperies, a parlor suite, fancy chairs, a centre table, a piano, a mantle" (Grier, 1988: 47). It was the variations in their arrangement and design that indicated the cultural position of the family. For example, homemakers were told by the tastemakers of the time that center tables draped with expensive carpets expressed wealth and communicated religious belief: draped tables evoked images of the Last Supper, and

FIGURE 1.3. Parlor view of a New York dwelling house. This 1854 engraving from *Gleason's Pictorial Drawing Room Companion* illustrates the importance of the parlor to Victorian life—both as a status symbol and as an expression of the taste of the "woman of the house."

were reminders of the types of tables located in Anglican churches that were used for the sacrament of communion (Grier 1988: 98). Having the knowledge to correctly "read" these complex codes of the parlor was difficult—thus the importance of domestic guidebooks and manuals that proliferated throughout the nineteenth century.

In *Death in the Dining Room and Other Tales of Victorian Culture* (1992), historian Kenneth Ames provides detailed readings of certain key elements of the material culture of Victorian homes. For example, Ames argues that the parlor organ, a distinctly Victorian middle-class furnishing, was an important social marker of class and gender. Developed in the 1840s and popularized throughout the century, parlor organs served in the first instance as ornamental pieces of furnishing, with their top portions often architectural in form, tracing out in carved wood stylish designs (Ames, 1992:155). Cheaper and easier to play than the piano, the parlor organ became a symbol of the cultural aspirations of the middle and working classes. Yet the organ, and organ music, of course, was traditionally associated with the church, unlike the secular music generally associated with the piano. The parlor organ, then, merged the material and the spiritual in the Victorian home.

In the Victorian cult of domesticity in the United States and Europe, women were in charge of both the cultural and the religious spheres of life. So it was the Victorian woman who played the organ, combining religious duty with the feminine gentility associated with playing a musical instrument. In almost all advertising images for the parlor organ, it is the woman who presides over it. As an 1890 organ advertisement suggests (Figure 1.4), under the paternal gaze, the organ-playing Victorian woman expresses her gentility, bourgeois good taste, and cultural refinement. Ames remarks:

FIGURE 1.4. Trade card for the Mason & Hamlin Organ Co., c. 1890. Parlor organs were signs of bourgeois respectability and proper gender roles. Under the paternal gaze, women expressed their spirituality and gentility by playing the organ for their families.

With the self-consciousness typical of the age, she could watch herself—sometimes literally, in the mirror in the upper section of the parlor organ case—and hear herself, just as literally, being a genteel lady, enacting the role written for her by the larger society. By playing the parlor organ, she brought beauty into the home. She sensitized her family and friends to accepted episodes of the world's music. By playing the organ, she could set the tone of the household, establish its mood, its character. In short, the parlor organ enabled her better to embrace the role of the bourgeois Christian lady. (1992: 166)

Similarly, other furnishings in the parlor were dictated by gender ideology. In most middle-class Victorian homes, the parlor was furnished with a suite that consisted of a sofa, a gentlemen's chair, a lady's chair, and four small chairs, all unified by coordinated style and fabrics. As the advertisement in Figure 1.5 shows, the gentlemen's chair was of course the larger of the set, more comfortable, with larger arms and padded armrests, whereas the lady's chair was smaller, less comfortable, with lower arms without armrests. The

FIGURE 1.5. Part of a parlor suite, from the Phoenix Furniture Company catalog, c. 1878. These three chairs, together with a sofa, formed a suite of furniture appropriate for the Victorian family. The center chair is for the father, on the right is the "lady's" chair, and at the left is a wall, or parlor, chair.

message of male dominance and prerogative was clear, and lingers today in contemporary notions of "father's chairs"—usually the largest and most comfortable chair in the house is reserved for "father."

Even the style of sitting in chairs was gendered. Ames (1992) points out that the idea of sitting in a chair and tilting slightly back in it, a style that came into vogue in the United States as an alternative to formal European conventions of sitting, was a distinctly male posture, since it indicated a purposeful breaking of the rules. It also indicates a distancing from the scene, allowing the sitter a degree of aloofness. In Ames's words, "Tilting backward allows one to survey a situation better, to assume the role of spectator, of voyeur. . . . All this is congruent with what we know of conventional male patterns of thought and behavior" (1992: 202)

On the other hand, rocking was a distinctly feminine activity. Women rocking in rocking chairs conformed to the chair's function, and engaged in an activity thought suitable for infants. The rocking chair, then, became a symbol of nurturance and femininity. The humble historical roots of the rocking chair also reinforced its association with femininity, as the rocker was initially a folk invention, while the more formal, straight chairs that men could tilt were derived from more aristocratic, courtly models.

Hence, we can think of the British and American middle-class Victorian parlor as spaces that reflected and reinforced gender norms. In one corner sat the decorative parlor organ, presided over by the woman of the house, representing the family's stylishness and morality, and reinforcing the association of women with religion, culture, and fashion. The formal parlor suite clearly marked out the relative positionings of men and women in society, with the comfortable and large man's chair and the diminutive lady's chair. If a rocking chair was allowed into the formality of the parlor, it symbolized the nurturing and passive role of women, while a man tilting one of the formal chairs back expressed his distance from, and power over, the scene in front of him.

Cleaning the Parlor

The Victorian parlor and home were also spaces that reflected and reinforced socioeconomic class. Although working-class women aspired to have the perfect parlor with appropriate furnishings, very few had enough resources to do so. And they certainly didn't have enough time and energy to keep up such grand pretenses. Much of the housework in most middle- and all upper-class households was done by domestic workers—maids, nurses, cooks—who were employed on a visiting or live-in basis. Almost all domestic employees were women; in the United States, they were often new immigrants.

It was their labor that enabled the bourgeois woman to keep her home an expression of her good taste and moral character. For example, the diaries of one Mrs. George Richards, an upper-middle-class women living in New York City, detail her constant search for and employment of women (and sometimes men) to serve as cooks, laundresses, seamstresses, and nurses. Some lived in for periods of time, some came on a daily or weekly basis. For example, on May 5, 1884, she wrote in her diary that she had "engaged Lilly Corbet, cousin Delia's old cook, and her husband to come here for the summer. They are to have the front basement and their own furniture." Then, on October 2, she wrote that "Mary Bagley came as cook, laundress," and on November 26, "The Misses Campbells dressmakers came to be here every day this week except Thursday." The servant women, of course, were engaged in domestic labor in two houses: they were responsible for maintaining their own homes in appropriate order and taste, before making their way on the streetcars of the city to the upper-class enclaves where they worked for other women, "keeping up the appearances" of others' homes. Unable to afford the labor of others, working-class women scrubbed and cleaned their own, less elaborate, homes, dividing their time between waged work and housework.

Keeping the parlor and the rest of the Victorian home clean and in order was more difficult in rural areas, where farmhouses often served as places of productive work for women. Sewing, baking, canning, and quilting were conducted right in the center of what were often fairly small houses, precluding the possibility of owning furniture "just for show." However, as scholars of the U.S. home have shown, even the crudely built farmhouses on the western frontier contained elements that would have resonated with middle-class urban Victorian women. Parlor organs, for example, were often hauled long distances and installed as the primary object of pride in sod houses on the Nebraska frontier, as Figure 5.4 in Chapter 5 depicts. The introduction in the late nineteenth century of catalogs that sold furniture and home decorating items through the mail gave farm women access to a range of affordable domestic objects that echoed their more fashionable sisters living in large cities. Meanwhile, popular women's magazines such as *Godey's Lady's Book* and *Ladies' Home Journal* (the first U.S. magazine to reach one million subscribers) dispensed advice on proper styles and arrangements.

In the plantation south, the "big house" (a colloquial term for the slaveowner's home) was kept stylish and clean thanks to the labor of black slave women. According to historian Elizabeth Fox-Genovese, most domestic labor in the slaveholder home was done solely by black women, except, interestingly, for the job of sewing, which was often shared by both white and black women: "Whereas slave women cleaned their mistresses' houses, prepared their food, nursed their children, and seconded their efforts in the care of gardens and the preservation of fruits and vegetables, mistresses frequently sewed for their slaves, or at least cut their clothes" (1988: 120). Slave women were responsible for the spinning and weaving of cloth, and slaveholding women for the cutting and sewing of this into wearable clothing, a division of labor that kept up racial barriers, while maintaining an important product of the plantation. In general, nineteenth-century middle-class gendered assumptions about work were played out on plantations, although slave women on many plantations did heavy labor, including field clearing and plowing. Since plantations often functioned as self-sufficient communities that were distant from urban markets, domestic duties included a far wider range of jobs than were necessary in urban households. In addition to housework in the big house and in their own cabins in the slave quarters, slave women typically tended fruit and vegetable gardens, canned and pickled the harvest, collected eggs, and stoked the fires for and maintained the smokehouse.

Yet despite all the productive labor associated with the plantation, the house itself, and particularly the parlor, still maintained its symbolic role as the spiritual hearth of the family and, by extension, of society. Within the four walls of the parlor, whether in the big house or in the slave quarters, the rural west or urban tenement, the Victorian woman acted out her proper domestic role.

TASTEMAKERS AND HOME ENGINEERING

As the major consumers within Victorian society, women did gain a certain control over their home environments. Women's tastes were taken seriously by manufacturers and retailers of home furnishings and clothing. So in most senses, women truly were responsible for creating those elements of interior design that we today call "Victorian." However, women's control was not enduring; the power of Victorian women as tastemakers and consumers was soon reined in by the emergence of male "experts" who distinguished good taste from bad.

In the United States and Great Britain, the development of the modern design industry removed women and femininity from the design process. By the early twentieth century, corporate economic power began to dominate most aspects of U.S. society, including domesticity. The values of mass production were joined with an aesthetic sensibility that valued function over ornament and the universal over the particular. This new design aesthetic, called "modernism," fit the needs of the United States's new rationalized and bureaucratized economic structure. "Taste" was a judgment of the consumer, and thus was based on feminine culture; "design" was a creation of commercial producers, and was derived from masculine culture. In modernizing early twentieth-century America, design superseded taste, which as Penny Sparke suggests, removed "aesthetic autonomy and authority from the hands of women" (1995: 10).

And yet this new rationalization of home design did not entirely leave women out of the picture. In fact, many leading advocates of the modernist design movement were women who saw the new sensibility as a way to eliminate the drudgery of housework. Many of these women strove to make the private home more like public workplaces, with the goal of diminishing the distinctions between women's work and men's work. These "domestic reformers" brought efficiency management and "workmanlike" principles into the home. Household management books (such as *Mrs. Beeton's Book of Household Management*, first published in 1861) proliferated in the latter part of the nineteenth and early twentieth centuries. Efforts to professionalize housework led to the introduction of domestic science courses in girls' curriculums in schools and colleges, as well as to the establishment of cooking schools in many U.S. cities. Reformers such as American Ellen Swallow Richards promoted the introduction of home economics courses for girls as a way of training them "professionally" while not necessarily removing them from the home.

Other efforts focused on the scientific management of the kitchen. In such books as *Household Engineering: Scientific Management in the Home*, published in 1919, Christine Frederick, for example, applied scientific management strategies to the organization of the kitchen, and offered new organizational schemes to minimize cleaning efforts in the home (Figure 1.6). In effect, she was recommending a form of home engineering, bringing to the home the rational schemes for greater productivity worked out for the factory. For example, Frederick systematized the activities associated with cooking a simple meal and cleaning up afterward, and then created what she thought would be the most efficient arrangement of sink, countertops, refrigerator, and stove. Her designs for the efficient kitchen had a significant impact in Europe, particularly in Germany, where many of her ideas were taken up by design experts and architects.

These efforts to "scientifically" manage the household filtered down to commercial designers of kitchen and bathroom fixtures and appliances. Ellen Lupton and J. Abbott Miller (1992) have shown how early twentieth-century sinks, stoves, and toilets were designed and arranged to be more hygienic and functional than their Victorian ancestors. The toilet, for example, was originally designed to

look like a chair, and was often enclosed in elaborate cabinetry
(Figure 1.7). But an obsessive concern with hygiene in the 1920s led
experts to repackage toilets in a way that distinguished them from
parlor furniture. Similar concerns led to the redesign of bathtubs,
sinks, and stoves from pieces of furniture to modular units (Figure
1.8).

Most of the design and hygiene experts, both men and women,
formed profitable relationships with industry. Even though the style
of "true" modernism called for a stripped-down, bare aesthetic, man-

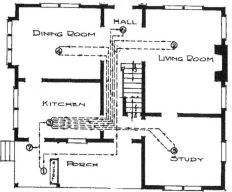

DIAGRAM 1—UNPLANNED CLEANING ORDER
Method.—Worker gets tools from tool closet (1), and walks down hall
and begins on living room (2) ; returns with trash to kitchen (3), and
walks to dining room (4) ; after cleaning it, again returns to kitchen with
trash, and proceeds to clean the study (5) ; she walks back to kitchen
again, and last cleans hall (6), ending by bringing back tools and last
refuse to kitchen again, before taking the final walk back to tool closet (1).
This is not an exaggeration, but the method used by a so-called "good
worker."

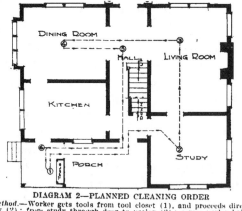

DIAGRAM 2—PLANNED CLEANING ORDER
Method.—Worker gets tools from tool closet (1), and proceeds direct to
study (2) ; from study through door to parlor (3) ; across parlor hallway
to dining room (4) ; she then begins at upper end of hallway (5), and
cleans its length back to the door opening on rear porch, carrying all
waste and tools back directly to service porch (6). Note that this method
eliminates *all tracking to kitchen* and results in about two-thirds less
unnecessary steps and walking.

FIGURE 1.6. Diagrams of unplanned and planned cleaning "orders," from Christine
Frederick's *Household Engineering*, 1919. Frederick applied scientific management
strategies to the organization of the home, in this case using those strategies to minimize labor for cleaning.

FIGURE 1.7. Victorian bathroom interior, from J. L. Mott Iron Works illustrated catalog, 1888. In the Victorian era, bathroom fixtures were built to resemble other pieces of furniture. The toilet, for example (at the left, foreground) could be mistaken by a modern viewer for an elaborate chair.

FIGURE 1.8. "Modern" bathroom fixtures, from Standard Sanitary Manufacturing Co., 1905. The concern for hygiene in the first decades of the twentieth century led to the redesign of bathroom fixtures so that they could be more easily cleaned. Their redesign distinguished them from pieces of furniture.

ufacturers and advertisers of household goods continued to cater to the tastes of middle-class women, who wanted color, texture, and comfort in their homes. As a result, modernism in U.S. house design was rarely the stripped-down, pure functional type of modernism; rather, it was tempered by women's concerns, as consumers and style watchers, to beautify their homes. Throughout the Progressive era (1895–1930s), magazines such as *House and Garden* exhorted women not only to keep their bathrooms clean, but to make them tasteful. For example, a 1932 article in *House Beautiful* about the bathroom begins with the following scenario:

> When Mr. and Mrs. Jebediah Jones built their brand new house some five years ago, their bathroom—white of tile, glistening as the inside of a new refrigerator—was the acme of hygienic perfection. . . . But when [her] sister Jessie displayed her new house the other day, the bathroom turned out to have fixtures of Copenhagen blue, . . . a dark green lacquered floor, . . . and a shower curtain of apricot. (quoted in Lupton and Miller, 1992: 33)

Clearly Jessie had the more stylish home.

This tension between pure modernism (an elite, male-led, architectural movement), and the populist feminized sensibility of making homes cozy is evident in what Jan Jennings has called "the turn-of-the-century wallpaper dilemma" (1996: 243). By the 1880s, decorative wallpaper had become an affordable and necessary means for middle- and working-class women to display their status and taste. In accord with the many revival architectural styles of the time, and the eclectic approach to home furnishings, wallpaper manufacturers produced a diverse range of wallpapers with bold designs (particularly florals) and often bright colors. Yet many domestic reformers favored a more simple approach to home design, arguing that elaborate wallpaper was not only immoral ("wild" patterns could produce "wild" behavior) but also too sensual. These reformers "expressed worries about the sensuousness of wallpaper as a material, the problems in making proper choices amid an abundance of hundreds of tempting designs, and the lure of the salesman's pitch" (Jennings, 1996: 252–253). Jennings argues that it is no coincidence that Charlotte Perkins Gilman, in her classic short story "The Yellow Wall Paper," published in 1892, used wallpaper to express the malevolent forces of the domestic on women. The wallpaper almost comes alive: "it slaps you in the face, it knocks you down, and tramples upon you" (quoted in Jennings, 1996: 259)! However, despite the constant and often forceful advice of experts on the dangers of ornamental wallpaper, most middle-class and many working-class women continued to choose it to decorate their homes throughout the first decades of the twentieth century (Figure 1.9). Wallpaper was a fairly inexpensive and powerful tool for home decorating, and most women were loathe to give up an opportunity to create and control feminine spaces.

So despite the rise of professional design experts for the home, and the influence of their more masculine cultural message of control and functionalism, the association of women, taste, femininity, and the home was never completely severed. The contemporary success of Martha Stewart, the ultimate tastemaker for the home, illustrates the limited hold of masculine modernism in the home. Stewart's success is attributable, at least in part, to the appeal of combining "traditional" women's skills, such as handicrafts, sewing, and cooking, with the technological wizardry and style hubris of a design expert. Many women find the Martha Stewart "lifestyle" ludicrous

FIGURE 1.9. A woman hanging wallpaper, from the Montgomery Ward catalog, 1910. Despite the advice of some "experts" who warned of the dangers of ornamental wallpaper, many woman continued to control the design of their homes by ornamenting their homes with floral-designed wallpaper.

because few women have any extra time to engage in the time-consuming, elaborate domestic "arts" she promotes. However, Stewart's success indicates the appeal that such ornamental, individualized, and remarkably Victorian home projects still have. Most women may have neither the time nor the skill to handcut wallpaper, for example, but that does not mean they do not value it as a sign of good taste and concern for the family.

In many powerful ways, then, we still live within frameworks that were rooted in Victorian times. The modern U.S. middle-class home is simpler in design than its Victorian predecessor, but its look and function are more often than not considered the responsibility of women. The Victorian cult of domesticity was carried forward into the twentieth century, transformed but still active as an ideology that strongly associates women with the home.

SOCIAL ENGINEERING

Victorian ideas about taste and modern visions of home engineering were primarily products of a middle-class imagination. However, in both the United States and Great Britain, middle- and upper-class women reformers were active in spreading the home "gospel," bringing domestic doctrine to working-class women. In cities such as London, New York, Chicago, and Boston, prominent women reformers established "settlement houses" as a type of outreach program for working-class and immigrant women. Numbering only six in 1891, settlement houses grew to over four hundred in the United States by 1910 (Sklar, 1995: 174). These settlement houses were located in or near working-class areas of the city. They were intended to present models of what was considered modern and proper forms of domesticity, including housework, interior design, and child care.

One of the most famous of the settlement houses, Hull House, was built in an inner-city immigrant neighborhood in Chicago by Jane Addams and Ellen Gates Starr in 1889 (Figure 1.10). Funded by local philanthropies, and inspired by the work done at Toynbee Hall in London (founded in 1884), Addams set out on a program to bring democratic reforms to the social sphere—to bring to working-class and immigrant families the advantages that could be derived from hard work, attention to domestic affairs, and participation in a democracy. Hull House had its own kindergarten and nursery, as well as a labor bureau that trained young women in domestic science to prepare them for domestic work in the houses of wealthy Chicagoans. In this way, Hull House combined a pragmatic and conservative message of how working-class women could "fit" into middle- and

FIGURE 1.10. Photograph of Hull House, c. 1905–1910. Hull House was one of many settlement houses established by middle- and upper-class women to bring the ideas of the home "gospel" to working-class and immigrant women. Reproduced by permission of the Chicago Historical Society and Barnes-Crosby, negative no. ICHi-19288.

upper-class norms, with a more radical message that the domestic sphere, dominated by women, formed the central core of the public realm of a democracy. In other words, because creating the correct home was seen as integral to creating good, moral citizens, teaching immigrant women to be "good" housekeepers empowered them as important shapers of U.S. democracy.

Middle-class notions of proper domesticity were often considered essential to the "Americanizing" project, not only in American cities but also on the recently established reservations for Native Americans in the West. In the last decades of the nineteenth century, United States policies focused on the assimilation of Native Americans. Integral to these policies was the introduction of Western, Anglo notions of Victorian domesticity to Native American women. Reflecting the dominant ideology of the time, policymakers believed that if Native American women adopted Western ideals of femininity and domesticity, this salutary influence would ripple throughout Native American societies, creating more "malleable" populations. In 1888 (and lasting until 1938!), the government established the "Field Matron Program" that employed hundreds of white women to live on reservations to instruct Native American women about "correct" forms of domesticity.

According to historian Cathleen Cahill (1998), the program drew on the idea that Native American culture could be transformed by reshaping the home. The matrons were instructed about the proper spatial form and ownership patterns of the homes they were to promote—for example, land ownership was to be individual, and on that land should be found enclosed gardens, single-family houses, cultivated fields, and enclosed areas for animals (Bannan, 1984). This "ideal" form ran counter to most Native American practices of communal property, mobility, and extended kinships systems, and the program was less than successful in "assimilating" Native American populations. Nevertheless, it illustrates the importance of nineteenth-century notions of home and domesticity in shaping U.S. political and social policies.

While settlement houses targeted immigrant women at home, and model homes were established on Native American reservations, many overseas missionary settlements attempted to "civilize" women through the channels of proper domesticity abroad. For example, women comprised sixty percent of the U.S. missionary volunteers to China in 1890 (Hunter, 1984: 3), and their explicit goal was to spread the "social gospel" of domestic responsibility and moral refinement to "heathen" women. The spatial focus of the "gospel" was the home: it was through proper attention to the home that "heathen" women would both become "civilized" and in turn spread that civilization. In the words of historian Jane Hunter, U.S. women missionaries in China "taught that women's nurturing responsibilities included education, culture, and public morality, but that the ultimate center of their lives should be the home, where they would act as a stabilizing force for the tides of change and the currents of history" (1984: 176).

The ideals of Euro-American Victorian domesticity, therefore, were mobilized in these multiple efforts to "reform," "Americanize," and "civilize" other women. Although many of these professional activities were in the hands of women, they were not necessarily driven by forces that were liberating—although an often unintended effect of such efforts was that many women working in these public areas did indeed find their work liberating. The overarching political effect of programs such as settlement houses and model homes was to solidify the conservative ideal of the home as a separate, complementary, but not equal sphere of social life.

In the early twentieth century, a more radical version of the domestic reform movement emerged in urban America. Dolores Hayden (1983) calls the women who looked to collectivist solutions to household work "material feminists." They believed that transforming the conditions of labor within the household—or removing some of that labor altogether—was the key to women's liberation.

One of their leading figures, Charlotte Perkins Gilman, proposed the establishment of public laundries and kitchens that would utilize all the latest technological advances to create efficient work spaces. In addition, she believed that child care should be "professionalized" and removed from the private home to community social centers. By sharing housework and raising children in "modern," scientific ways, women could be liberated from the daily chores that regulated their lives. This utopian vision of collectivizing homework and professionalizing childcare was seen as a way to free women to participate in other parts of life beside the domestic (Figure 1.11). Ultimately, however, this radical movement was no match for the powerful U.S. vision of privatized family life within the confines of a single-family home.

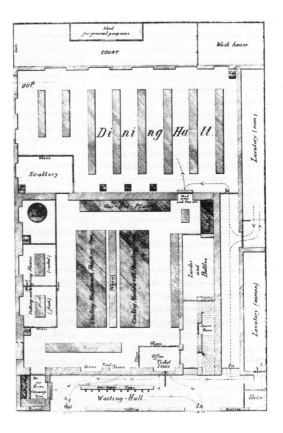

FIGURE 1.11. M. P. Wolff's plan for a public kitchen, 1884. Material feminists believed that creating such facilities as shared public kitchens and professional child-care centers were keys to women's liberation. In this design, people could buy food "to go" in the waiting hall or could eat in the dining hall.

THE SUBURBAN HOME

That vision of single-family home ownership became attainable for many in post-World War II Great Britain and the United States. In the United States, as many scholars have pointed out, little new housing was constructed during the Great Depression and World War II years, so that when the GIs returned, there was considerable pent-up demand for housing. Access to automobiles and the construction of new highways opened up agricultural land on the edge of cities to development. In addition, the single-family home ideal and the allure of escaping the city made suburban housing appealing to many families. Governmental policies provided affordable housing to many families who previously lived in apartment buildings in the city. These policies included the "GI Bill," and Federal Housing Authority mortgaging and financing schemes that gave preference to single-family home construction over multiple-family housing, and to new construction over the renovation of older dwellings. As a result, a huge growth in the construction of single-family homes occurred in the United States, from only 114,000 houses in 1944, to 937,000 in 1946, to 1,183,000 in 1948, to 1,692,000 in 1950 (Jackson, 1985: 233).

In many ways, the renewed emphasis on domesticity and its association with femininity in the 1950s echoed Victorian times: in both time periods, the family was seen as a refuge from the competitive workplace, and domesticity as the source of social stability. U.S. women, who during World War II had worked in factories, offices, and shipyards—the "Rosie Riveters"—were now encouraged to leave their paid work so that their husbands or sons returning from overseas could be steadily employed. Government propaganda insisted that their new "jobs" should be as wives and mothers, so that they would create the stable family and community that their men had fought to maintain. Armed with new appliances to remove the purported drudgery of housework, as well as books and magazines filled with experts' advice on everything from decorating cookies to educating children, the 1950s housewife was seen as more liberated than her Victorian predecessors. Her time could now be spent on beautifying the home and garden, nurturing her family, and consuming new products.

This post-World War II return to domesticity came to be symbolically associated with the suburban housewife and the suburban lifestyle—typified by a married woman, perhaps with small children, living in the new suburban developments ten to twenty miles out from urban areas. Though often maligned by culture critics as representing the worst of mass-consumer culture, these new suburban developments nonetheless were made meaningful by and gave meaning to the women and men who lived out much of their lives there. Men acted out their new domestic roles outside the four walls of the house by maintaining a perfect green lawn, tending to the barbecue, and doing the duties associated with the family's new automobile. Women acted out their roles inside the house decorating with the latest style of furniture, cooking healthy meals, tending children, and, as Marilyn French made famous in her novel *The Women's Room* (1977), chatting to the neighborhood women about their families and their lives.

In Victorian times, as we have mentioned, women were meant to represent society's commitment to morality and spirituality: the Victorian home both literally and figuratively symbolized these values. In postwar America and Great Britain, however, women's roles had shifted. Morality and spirituality were still important, but increasingly those values were molded to fit the demands of the postwar economy: women were to act as "correct" consumers and as community builders. Both of these new duties were viewed as distinct from the masculine world of work, and both were seen as a continuing commitment to a type of moral economy. In the 1950s, shopping in the new shopping centers became one of the key traits that defined femininity (see Chapter 3). But it was also women's role to create community in their new suburban locations, places that were removed from the ties of older neighborhoods in the city. Cocktail parties, barbecues, PTA meetings, and leisure activities were under the control of women, and were the sites in which suburban women could act out new forms of femininity. Tupperware parties, for example, combined both roles: their primary function, after all, was as a sales pitch for plastic kitchen objects, but they also served an important social function, providing reasons for suburban women to talk to each other not only about the upkeep of their homes and families, but also about their own personal lives. As design historian Alison Clarke (1997) suggests, Tupperware parties were one of the few formalized sites for women to meet each other outside their family circles. And for some, these all-women gatherings were important catalysts for political action, offering women a forum for discussing public issues: "Whilst the pretext of the gatherings was domestic this did not preclude women from directing the conversation and interaction towards other concerns" (Clarke, 1997: 145).

The center of the new suburban domesticity and femininity was the mass-produced home—those "little boxes" immortalized by Pete Seeger. Indeed, as the song suggests, these "little boxes" did look "all the same": the assembly-line approach to home construction necessitated standardized plans and construction materials, but it was the very same mass-production techniques that made these homes affordable for many middle-class Americans. The result was that in many suburban communities the choice of house types was limited, with perhaps four or five variations from a standard plan (Figure 1.12). The "Cape Cod" style, a one-and-a-half-story dwelling, was popularized by the Levitt company, a pioneer in mass production of housing (and the company that was responsible for building three new towns under the principles of mass production: Levittown, Long Island; Levittown, Pennsylvania; and Willingboro, New Jersey). The "ranch" style, the "split level," and the "colonial" styles followed in time, spreading quickly across the suburban U.S. landscape in waves.

Most of these houses incorporated modern design elements, particularly the notion of the open plan. The open plan was in sharp contrast to Victorian interiors, where each social function was meant to have its own space in the house. In modern, suburban homes, elements of living and dining, or of cooking and dining, were combined into one space. According to many architectural historians, the open plan was meant to foster family communication, an ingredient that the new wave of experts deemed vital to the nurturing of children. It also allowed a mother to watch the activities of her children even if she was in the kitchen cooking dinner. Rooms now deemed unneces-

FIGURE 1.12. Advertisement for Levittown houses, 1950. There were no more than four or five variations to the standard house plans that were originally built in Levittown, Long Island, New York.

sary, such as the formal parlor, were eliminated from the design, while others, such as the "family room" were added (Wright, 1981).

Within the 1950s suburban home, women usually had total responsibility for arrangement of the furniture and all details of the decor. Even the modern design ethos that we have previously suggested was dominated by men and masculine values was softened to accommodate women's tastes. After all, it was women who were making the consumer decisions: manufacturers of appliances, furniture, and drapes could ill afford to ignore them. In the living room, the "contemporary" style became popular; this style was based on modern design elements, but these elements were "softened" with playful colors, fabrics, and more rounded shapes. In contrast to the harsh lines and monochromatic color schemes of avant-garde modernism, the contemporary style appealed to traditional feminine tastes. "And above all," according to Penny Sparke, "in its appeal to the senses with its soft pastel colors and sensuous textures rather than to the intellect, it was unashamedly 'feminine' in nature" (1995: 191). Women wishing to express their new, modern, good taste could find in contemporary furnishings the right combination of aesthetics, comfort, and traditional elegance.

This feminization of modern home design wasn't limited to the living room. In the 1950s, even the bathroom, the site of the first modernist hygienic, streamlined design, was again opened to ornament. Colored fixtures in the bathroom became common, as did knickknacks, toilet covers, and matching rugs. The kitchen too was often decorated with matching color appliances, and was transformed into an important living/dining space.

This feminization of modern design and the modern home was of course never totally complete, nor did it apply to all homes. But it does suggest that women did have design influence within their homes, and in turn, helped to shape U.S. manufacturing processes. In this sense, the association of women with material goods and consumption, an association that was strengthened in the postwar years, was potentially liberating for some women. It certainly was one source of women's power. Yet that power was always nested within layers of powerlessness, since women's roles outside the home were heavily circumscribed by societal norms. Betty's Friedan's shattering 1963 book *The Feminine Mystique* brought attention to the circumscribed suburban life: "We can no longer ignore that voice within women that says, 'I want something more than my husband and children and my home' " (1983: 32).

At the same time that women's authority over design and decoration was being exerted, it was also being eroded. America's new taste critics of the 1950s and 1960s judged feminine taste to be "bad" taste. Exponents of "high" culture deemed pink refrigerators and household gadgets signs of the "middle-brow" tastes of the masses. Women who attended Tupperware parties were ridiculed for their middle-brow tastes and for the apparent meaningless chatter that was thought to comprise women's conversation. In effect, design experts were critiquing "feminine" influences on the home, but were voicing that criticism in terms of a critique of "mass culture." Women's design decisions were marginalized by aligning those decisions with those of the masses, and the results were denigrated as "low-brow" tasteless design. By delegitimizing women's taste, the male design "experts" hoped to maintain their authority and control over the household design industry. Colorful appliances, patterned wallpaper, and small decorative objects were relegated to the realm of kitsch—that is, "inferior" objects that appeal to mass culture. So we can see that although the increasing commodification of the home in the postwar years gave women some power in the public world of manufacture and design, that power was challenged by aligning women's tastes with kitsch.

THE POSTMODERN HOME

The more recent "postmodern" (1970s–) home continues as both an important site of women's authority and of their oppression. In fact, one could argue that very little has changed in terms of home design and gendered relationships to the home. Women's identities still seem to be tied to home design and style, particularly the interiors of homes, while men, at least in the suburbs, align their manliness with the green lawn, the barbecue grill, the garage, and the basement—the "manly" spaces. A recent article in the *New York Times* (July 18, 1999: 2) summarizes the renewed interest on the part of men in "perfecting" their suburban lawns: "In the waning summer evenings of the millennium, suburban men seem as devoted to their lawns as their fathers were in the golden age of lawn maintenance, the 1950's, the era of suburban migration, the crew cut and conformity."

Much of the rhetoric of postmodern architecture is an outright rejection of the modernist aesthetic. Since modernism was predominantly associated with notions of masculinity (as we have previously argued), postmodernism could be interpreted as a retrieval of feminine tastes (Figure 1.13). Postmodern design is defined by a renewed attention to ornament, color, pleasure, and comfort—which can be seen as a return to Victorian sensibilities and to the tastes of middle-class women. This does not mean, however, that women's tastes are given cultural legitimacy. Postmodernism originally aligned itself not with feminine domesticity, but with the rough-and-tumble "popular"

FIGURE 1.13. Photograph of a postmodern home in Hanover, New Hampshire. As a postmodern design, this house uses color, ornamentation and references to historical styles (the neo-palladian doorway and window/gallery above) to achieve a rejection of modernism, and perhaps a retrieval of "feminine" tastes.

culture of the streets, and its practitioners were almost exclusively men, operating within masculine institutions.

Yet the reaction to, and reassessment of, modernism has opened "spaces" for women and feminine tastes, both at the professional level (there are an increasing number of architects in the United States who are women, but still women comprise only 9.1 percent of the American Institute of Architects membership), and at an every-day level (Coleman, 1996: xi). If we look closely enough, we might see a feminized postmodernism in new urban designs. For example, the planned community of Seaside, Florida, was designed to re-create the closeness of small-town living. Zoning in Seaside mixes residential and commercial uses. The houses in Seaside are located close to the street, within walking distance of commercial and public services, and were designed with front porches in order to facilitate social communication between neighbors. The new Disney town of Celebration in central Florida was designed according to similar guidelines, but its ethos was more family-oriented. According to Andrew Ross (1999), those who benefit most from the spatial layout of the town, a layout that makes services such as schools and daycare easily accessible by foot, are single parents, most of whom are women.

Much of the theory behind this type of "new urbanism" is derived from Jane Jacobs's hallmark 1961 book *The Death and Life of Great American Cities*, a book that advocated neighborhoods characterized by mixed uses of land and informal interactions on the street and between the street and residents. Scholars such as Mary McLeod have argued that Jacobs's book, although preceding the advent of modern feminism, was written clearly from a woman's perspective:

> A domestic perspective is critical to Jacobs' development of the idea of mixed use. This proposal is not only an attack on modern architecture's functional segregation but an implicit challenge to the traditional split between domestic and public life. Jacobs deliberately rejects theoretical models and relies on empirical observation to examine how space is actually used. (1996, 23)

Jacobs's highly influential book continues to shape contemporary planning in the United States and Canada. Her vision points the way to the creation of environments that will accommodate diverse communities and that will bring women's traditional concerns for the domestic into the public realm.

HOME–WORK RELATIONS

Changes in how we design residential neighborhoods are slow to occur, however, and do not necessarily portend major changes in how we think about the relationships between women, work, and home. Today's "supermom" who picks up her children at daycare on her way home from work, and then prepares dinner and cleans up after her husband and kids, participates in the public world of work to a far greater degree than did most middle-class women before her, in addition to doing her private work of cleaning and cooking, tending kids, decorating, arranging, and consuming. The new and often financially necessary entry of women into the public world of paid labor is rarely accompanied by any lessening of responsibility in the private world of home. As a result, many women are left with a double burden of work: they work full time at the office, and as close to full time as possible at home.

In a recent study of the relationships between gender and the locations of workplaces and residences, geographers Susan Hanson and Geraldine Pratt (1995) found some surprising results about relationships between women and home. In the United States women live significantly closer to their places of work than do men—and this applies to all women, whether married, unmarried, divorced, or cohabiting. Hanson and Pratt's original assumption was that women with children and heavy household responsibilities would be the only ones constrained in their job opportunities since they would be the most likely to seek employment close to home. But their in-depth study of three different neighborhoods in Worcester, Massachusetts, revealed this not to be necessarily the case. Even women living in what they term "nontraditional" households—that is, households where women are not married, or are married but don't have children—"tend to find employment close to home" (1995: 153). Thus it would appear that working close to home is important to women in amorphous and myriad ways. Home seems to be a geographical anchor for many women—their identities are bound up with their homes in complex ways. So even as women move into the workplace and gain new sources of self-identity, these are not replacing the private identities shaped by a symbiosis with home.

And yet, of course, the form of women's identification with the home and the domestic is changing. Many middle-class women in North America and Western Europe, faced with the pressures of two full-time jobs (at home and at work) have turned to hiring nannies and cleaning women to assist them at home. In essence, they are bringing the rationale of the public workplace—that is, hiring laborers to perform discrete tasks for money—into the private home. This juxtaposition of these two types of work (public, for money, and private, for love) presents interesting dilemmas that seem to echo (although not to replicate) those faced by the "wages for housework" movement of the 1970s.

One of the ideas behind the "wages for housework" movement was to make men aware of the amount of work women did in the home by putting it in the terms they understood: an hourly wage. But what was the appropriate value, for example, of the making of a soufflé? Could work done for "love" be broken down into discrete units that could then be assigned a "fair" hourly wage value? And, perhaps more importantly, should work done for a family be rewarded in the same way as work done in the factory?

Similar questions are raised when considering the payment to live-in nannies. Are they waged laborers, or "members of the family"? Most paid laborers ("domestic servants") in the home are women, and many are of different ethnicities than their employers. The relationships, then, between employer and employee are complex, not only because the relationship crosses the public/private divide (paying wages for jobs previously done by women out of "love"), but because of the explicit hierarchies established by employer–employee relationships, and the hierarchies implicit in ethnicity and class. Most of the live-in nannies that geographers Bernadette Stiell and Kim England (1997) interviewed in Toronto felt that at some point they had been exploited in their work—most often due to the imprecision of employee–employer relations that take place "at home," and that claim to treat workers "like one of the family." As one nanny said, "You're supposed to feel so privileged to be part of their family that you overlook everything else" (quoted in Stiell and England, 1997: 350).

However, the nannies who felt the most exploitation were those who were the most "different" from their employers: women of color and immigrants from developing countries. Afraid to complain about their working conditions because of the fear of deportation, or because changing jobs looks bad on their records, these women often felt compelled to put up with conditions they find unsuitable. A nanny from Jamaica working in Toronto put it this way: "Each time you have to change jobs, you pay Immigration $100. . . . It doesn't look good on your record—that's why a lot of people take the abuse, you can't be bothered changing this and that" (quoted in Stiell and England, 1997: 349). In Canada and the United States, immigration and tax policies for domestic workers are different from other forms of labor. This, in combination with the inherent ambiguity of being *in* a family yet working *for* a family, creates perplexities that both employers and employees may find hard to negotiate. As a nanny from Jamaica says:

> What I can't deal with is the idea that because I mop their floors, [they think that] I'm stupid. . . . They don't have to respect you, but they come with this disguise, "Oh, you're part of the family." They hug you. I don't want to be hugged! For God's sake, I'm your employee! . . . You're meant to think, "This nice white lady, she's hugging me." Then I'm supposed to take everything they dish out. I don't want that. I just want to be respected as a worker, with an employer–employee relationship. (quoted in Stiell and England, 1997: 351)

These unequal and complex work relationships in the home are apparent also in the situation of women who come to "service" the home, usually to clean. Women in the cleaning industry often are employed by companies that provide housekeepers. These women are paid a wage, and "go" to work, albeit work in someone else's home, instead of living with work. And, more often than not, these women conduct the same work in their own homes as "at work," meaning that they are responsible for cleaning other people's homes during the day and then they come home and clean their own. We know little about the experiences of these women. Does it mean something different to clean for your family than to clean for a job? Do these women experience a blurring of the distinction between home and work?

That blurring of distinctions is explicit in the increasing numbers of women and men who are employed in waged labor that they conduct at home—from their computers, fax machines, telephones, sewing machines, and so on (see Chapter 2). In fact, I'm sitting at a computer myself, in a room in my house, engaged in paid (I hope) labor. "Homework" is particularly complicated for women with small children at home. It is difficult to conduct paid labor at the same time and in the same place as child care. The one form of homework that we hear most about involves the telecommuting professional, working out of home in jobs such as publishing, design, and advertising. But as Ann Oberhauser (1997) has shown in her in-depth studies of homework in Appalachia, many women, particularly those living in rural areas, engage in productive labor at home by sewing, quilting, knitting, or providing daycare and catering services. For these women, working at home versus at the office was not a choice but a necessity, given scarce job opportunities. These Appalachian women are using their "traditional" feminine skills to add to their family's income. On the one hand, this is a less apparent crossing of boundaries between work and home, and yet on the other, a far more radical challenge to our notions of the home, since in this instance traditionally feminine skills have been transformed into waged labor.

So the physical and ideological separation of work and home that began in the early modern period seems to be eroding—well, at least in certain ways, and for certain people. And yet, as Sherry Ahrentzen (1992) reminds us, most Americans live in homes constructed out of the traditional ideology of separate spheres—that is, our houses reflect the beliefs that home is a space of leisure, nurturance, love, and not a place of productive work. Despite the fact that over four million women in the United States work at least eight hours a week at home, our homes are still ideologically and physically constructed as if work did not exist (1997: 80).

Thinking about new forms that homes can take, however, requires understanding the complexity of relationships to them. In Ahrentzen's (1997) study of some one hundred homeworkers in the United States, she found that women attached a diverse range of meanings to their homes. For some, home was a place that represented their "integrative" selves—that is, their roles as mothers, wives, and workers. For others, the home was a trap that isolated them from the rest of the world. Many women separated out particular spaces within the home as refuges. If they had a separate office in their home, it served as a refuge from the family. For some women, the bedroom served as a refuge from work. Ahrentzen's study convincingly demonstrates that it is imperative to understand the diversity of meanings that women have concerning their homes if we wish to consider redesigning them.

Recent studies suggest that even the most taken-for-granted meaning of home as a sanctuary and place of privacy is far from universal. Geographers Lynda Johnston and Gill Valentine's study of lesbians living in their parental home draws attention to the extent to which most homes are imbued with notions of heterosexuality: "Its overwhelming presence seeps out of everything from photograph albums to record collections" (1995: 102). Because of this, many lesbians who are not "out" to their parents find that home is in fact a place where they feel "out of place" instead of "in place" (103), a place where they must hide their identities and pretend to fit into the norms of heterosexuality.

Yet home can also be the most important place for lesbian identity expression and formation, particularly for lesbians living in their own home. The public world of work is often the site where lesbians must disguise their sexual identity, so home is one of the few places they can experience true freedom of expression. And in many rural areas or small towns, where there are no public lesbian spaces, homes are often the only sites where lesbians can comfortably socialize. As Johnston and Valentine suggest, "Informal networks of private homes fill the entertainment gap created by a complete absence of lesbian institutional spaces" (1995: 108).

So again we can see just how complex and multivalent are the meanings of home—as the site of privacy and freedom of expression, but also as a site of oppression. Indeed, what we often forget is that it is within the home that most violence against women is committed. In 1990 in the United States, about forty percent of all female murder victims were killed by their husband or boyfriend (Sapiro, 1994: 259). For many women, home is a battleground, not a sanctuary.

What these varied stories tell us is that the distinction between the private and the public is constantly shifting and blurring, and that women have diverse relationships with and meanings invested in their homes. But these stories also deepen our understanding of the historically constructed association of women, femininity, and home. From the bourgeois townhouses of the West End of London, to the 1920s model kitchens, to the suburban houses of the postwar era, the form of housing has both been shaped by and in turn helped to shape changing definitions of femininity. Formal parlor suites and rocking chairs, pink refrigerators and chintz curtains, family rooms and home offices—these are sites of living that are not simply backdrops to the enactment of gender roles. Instead, these places both create and reflect cultural notions of femininity and masculinity.

Chapter 2

WOMEN AT WORK

In December 1999, in the last session—of the class, the year, the century—of my "Gender, Space, and Environment" course, I (J. S.) cajoled my students into a free-flowing discussion about the future. All of these (then twenty-something) university students recognized that for them, as for their parents, working out their marital or partner relationships would mean that they would have to come to terms with gendered expectations regarding relationships to home and work. In a sign of the times, all the women assumed they would work in the waged workforce, and all the men assumed they would have female partners who would do so. Almost all of them who imagined themselves with an opposite-sex partner also imagined an egalitarian future, in which they and their partners would be *equally* responsible for work, income, home, and children. But when I pressed them for specifics about how they thought they might achieve this parity, the mood turned surlier. Well, they proclaimed, they simply would not settle for/with a partner who didn't share this vision. (I refrained from pointing out that this rosy path had turned into a blind alley for millions who had gone before.) And then I asked the men in the class a pointed question: How many of them would feel uncomfortable with a female partner/wife who earned more—perhaps much more—than they did? Two or three men in the class openly scoffed and said that would be just fine with them, they would have no problem with a "power wife"; another two or three were brave enough to admit that the prospect was discomfiting; the remaining handful shifted uncomfortably in their seats, not committing themselves one way or another.

This discussion was probably broadly representative of how the twenty-first century opens for middle-class North Americans: with high hopes for a harmonious gender future, and for an egalitarianly balanced work–home relationship, yet with a limited understanding of the structures that stand in the way, and—lingering just beneath the surface—a nagging ambivalence about women's place (and success) at work.

Issues about "work" occupy a position at the center of gravity of cross-gender relationships. There is relatively little controversy about *men* working—it is widely recognized that men do, "should," and always have "worked." (Indeed, to the extent that there is controversy about men and work today in North America, it is about men *not* working. The stay-at-home Dad is still viewed as an odd cultural hybrid, and men who choose this role often struggle for respect.) The relationship between "women" and "work" is more complex and controversial, and is often a flashpoint for personal and social conflict between women and men.

Even the most cursory historical and global surveys suggest that when men and women "work," they do so under different conditions and constraints, they tend to work at different jobs, and they work in different places. Such differences are the result of a carefully constructed social calculus—but one that varies over time and from place to place. For example, the "gendering" of particular jobs reveals some of the complexities and contradictions about the social construction of work. Currently, in the United States, clerical work is women's work, while in India most office clerks are men. In Canada road building is men's work, while in Nepal it's women's work. On Sri Lankan tea plantations, most tea pickers are women, while almost all of the tea tasters are men. On commercial banana plantations in Costa Rica, the banana harvesters are men, the banana washers are women. In the United States when the telephone switchboard was first developed, the switchboard operator corps consisted almost exclusively of young men and boys. Within fifty years, switchboard operator had become an entirely feminized occupation; by the 1990s, it had switched again, so that now both men and women work as telephone operators. Similarly, typewriting at first was a male job in the United States, but then quickly became defined as women's work. Computer programming followed the reverse course: at first it was a woman's job, now it is deeply masculinized. Cooking in the home is women's work, but the most highly valued and highly paid restaurant chefs everywhere in the world are men. In the late 1990s in the European Union, women comprised more than eighty percent of all secretaries, nurses, and elementary school teachers; in the United States at the same time, women represented ninety-eight percent of secretaries, ninety-two percent of bookkeepers, and ninety percent of nursing aides.

How do we make sense of these seemingly capricious and chaotic gendered identifications? Sometimes we can't. But if we look closely, we can see common presumptions that weave throughout the differences and that paint a broad picture of the ways in which "work" is so often different for men and for women:

- ♦ Some version of a sexual division of labor appears to be evident in virtually all societies throughout the historical record; the Industrial Revolution, however, codified "work" (and "nonwork") in distinctive and enduring ways that were then replicated around the world with the spread of industrial capitalism.
- ♦ Relatively few jobs are gender-neutral: *most* work is defined as either "men's work" or "women's work" (although the particulars of these designations can and do change).
- ♦ Only work for wages (or within the cash economy) is defined as "work."
- ♦ Much of what women do to contribute to the economy is defined as "not-work."
- ♦ Men are seen to have the primary prerogative (or "need") to undertake work for wages; and/or it is men's prerogative to control the money that comes into the household from participation in the cash economy. Women "shouldn't" earn more than men, nor "take jobs away from" men.
- ♦ Assumptions about "natural" affinities (temperamental, biological, cultural) of men and women—or of *some* men and women of a particular age, race, class—shape the definition of men's and women's work.
- ♦ Men occupy the best paying, highest prestige jobs; almost by definition if women are doing it, it's neither.

By focusing on the *spatial* conveyances or containers of ideologies about women's and men's "place," a geographical curiosity illuminates particular dimensions of the gendering of work. For example, in the preceding chapter we explored the separation of public and private spheres; this division is the primary organizing principle and vehicle for much of the gendering of work. In Chapter 4, we will explore the role of mobility—literally and metaphorically understood—which is gendered in ways that can inhibit or facilitate women's full participation in the public sphere. *Where* work occurs has considerable influence on whether it is considered to be "work" or not and on whether it is counted as work or not. Finally, a gendered geography of work focuses our attention on the ways in which certain work*places* are defined as appropriate or inappropriate places for women to be.

WHAT IS WORK?

The emergence of industrial capitalism and the ideology of "separate spheres" (see Chapter 1) assigned women, at least in principle, to the private home sphere, and men to the public work sphere. The definition of "work" as an exclusively waged activity that was to be complemented by a nonwaged household support system was central to the ideological—and actual—development of industrial capitalism. The benefits of this system to capitalism are myriad, and one can see how this work/nonwork dichotomy evolved as a powerful new economic system that generated considerable profits for the capitalists. Among other things, for the payment of one wage the employer got a wage earner plus an entire unpaid support system.

But economic imperatives alone don't fully explain this work/ nonwork dichotomy. Why it is *men* who came to be associated with work and workplaces and *women* who come to be associated with nonwork and the household is not explained solely by capitalism. Feminist analysis suggests that the configuration of work in this *particularly* gendered way is so universal and so enduring because it suits not just capitalism, but patriarchy. Simply put, this dualism creates an economic dependence of women on men—which enhances the power and privilege of men, even of relatively ordinary and not very powerful men.

Feminist geographers add to this analysis by drawing attention to the spatial system that makes "patriarchal capitalism" possible: the geographic separation of work from home, city from suburb, (paid) workplace production from (unpaid) household production, and the myriad zoning laws, property laws, mortgage systems, and transportation networks that facilitate these arrangements. In a key article, Ann Markusen (1980) outlined the ways in which both patriarchy *and* capitalism benefit from the spatial arrangement that separates men's work from women's nonwork. For example, she argues that defining an ideal home by the absence of waged work ensures that the economic well-being of the home depends on male wages; this positions men as the "natural" heads of households. Confining women to homes in residential locations isolated from work opportunities ensures their economic and social dependence on individual men. The ideal of a nonwaged (female) worker supporting the individual material needs and desires of each waged (male) worker is an inefficient use of the woman's labor, but it maximizes the comfort of the male in the household—that is, providing meals to order, on an individual schedule, makes life comfortable for men but squanders women's labor and time. The single-family, suburban dwelling discourages extended family or community sharing of housework, and advances the interests of capitalism by maximizing consumption and the purchase of goods for the household. (It is no coincidence that feminist and socialist utopias almost always reconfigure the spatial separation of work and home. Noncapitalist and feminist designs for reimagining urban spaces almost always feature collective living of some kind, and designs that allow for the integration of work and residential activities. They also reorder household support systems by promoting, for example, collective child-care or cooking arrangements, and shared household technology.)

However, the convergence of capitalism and patriarchy on particular configurations of work and home, while ideologically powerful, is imperfectly executed. On paper, capitalist patriarchy may look good, as it were, but in real life it's not so easy to pull off. There are gaping contradictions between the ideology (of how women and men are "supposed" to relate to work and to each other) and the reality. For example, the removal of women from waged work is, in fact, not practical; the assumption that a single household should be supported by a single (male) wage is largely unachievable given other priorities in capitalism (such as paying workers the lowest possible wages). In addition, the assumption that most people do or will live in nuclear families in individual households is erroneous. Further, the benefits to men of the patriarchal division of gendered labor, of the subordination of women to their needs, and of the banning of women from waged work are easily overstated. Many men chafe at the roles that this ideology assigns them; being the breadwinner and stoic standard bearer is wearing. The confinement of women in households dominated by men, removed from wage-earning possibilities, has social, cultural, financial, and emotional limits for *both* men and women.

Even the central prop of capitalist patriarchy, the assumption that women don't, won't, or shouldn't "work," is flawed. In fact, what women do in the home is in most instances quite "work-like." Most women need to (and want to) participate in the public sphere, and a substantial proportion of women do now and have always worked for wages. When viewed in terms of the ways that people really live their lives and what they do inside and outside the home, rather than through ideology and rhetoric, the dividing line between "work" and "home" appears more fuzzy than sharp.

However, while this "ideal" system in its purest expression may be unattainable in the real world, economic and cultural elites have invested too much in the ideology to let it go. Instead of giving up the game, they focus considerable attention on papering over the gaps. The biggest gap between rhetoric and reality is the fact that most women, like most men, do "work" most of the time. But because so much of the modern Western social order has been predicated on sustaining the myth that women don't work (or *shouldn't*) work, there has been energetic ideological maneuvering to define away or minimize women's work. The success of this effort is evident in the fact that, almost everywhere, women's work is defined either as less serious than men's or simply as nonwork. The rhetorical and ideological devices deployed to minimize or "domesticate" women's work include:

- ♦ Defining "work" only as those activities that involve cash or other wage exchange, and simultaneously defining work in the home as an act of loyalty, duty, or "love" (and thus as nonwork).
- ♦ Defining waged work as a temporary stage for women: it is fine for young women to work, but once they marry they should stop. Or, in times of crises such as "manpower" shortages during wars, women's work is acceptable, but once the crisis is over women should return the jobs to the men and themselves to the home.
- ♦ Diluting the reality of women at work by defining certain jobs as "naturally" feminized. Sewing, for example, is often defined as a natural extension of women's feminine affinities, so when they do this they remain cocooned within a realm of acceptable female activity.
- ♦ Defining some women—by race, ethnicity, or national origin— as "naturally" suited to some work, thus liberating and protecting the femininity of other women from the necessity of engaging in that work. The black mammy in 1920s America, the Jamaican nanny in 1980s Toronto, and the Filipina maid in 1990s Hong Kong are good examples of this process.
- ♦ Defining work (for wages) as defeminizing and coarsening, and/or defining women who undertake certain work as defeminized and coarse. Calling into question the femininity of women who defy social norms by actively seeking and enjoying certain work (for example, driving trucks, reporting on sports, building bridges).
- ♦ Defining the necessity to work as a misfortune, one that all women of all classes could aspire to overcome, and construing the nonworking wife as a sign of successful upward social and class mobility.

- Prohibiting *some* kinds of women (e.g., pregnant or married women) from waged "public" work.
- Prohibiting *all* women from some kinds of work (such as military combat or mining or airplane piloting).
- Keeping women in the home by bringing work for wages inside; most industrial economies depend on "homework," such as home sewing or light assembly.
- Creating cultural angst about the extent to which the psychological and physical well-being of children requires them to be raised by a full-time stay-at-home mother.
- Constructing social policy to support this angst—through tax systems, maternity leave policies, provision (or lack thereof) of publicly funded child care.

But how is "work" really made into "nonwork"? It would not be possible to define away women's work as nonwork by ideology or rhetoric alone. Indeed, the ways in which work is made into nonwork are more tangible than that—large bureaucratic, cultural, and spatial structures are brought to bear to sustain this deceit. Among the most important of these are national and international systems of economic and demographic accounting: censuses and "national accounts" systems.

WHAT COUNTS?

Every country in the world has an internal national accounting system by which economic activity is tallied. The total value and nature of goods, services, and economic "productivity" are measured annually, monthly, weekly, even daily. Most of these national systems closely resemble one another: they are often developed by literally the same people (international economic consultants, for example, who devise tax codes, or advise governments on accounting systems), and they generally conform to international norms. International agencies such as the United Nations, the World Bank, and the International Monetary Fund (IMF) also independently tally economic activity, as well as exert an influence on how such accounting is carried out.

The ways in which economic activity are counted matter a great deal. Governments use data from "national accounts" to shape economic and social policies. International lending and investments are determined by the results of these accounts. But for our purposes, how nations count economic activity especially matters because it makes invisible much of what women do (Waring, 1988; Samarasinghe, 1997).

Feminist economist Marilyn Waring details some of the activities rendered invisible by conventional national accounts systems:

> Consider Tendai, a young girl in the Lowveld, in Zimbabwe. Her day starts at 4am, when, to fetch water, she carries a thirty-litre tin to a borehole about eleven kilometres from her home. She walks barefoot and is home by 9am. She eats a little and proceeds to fetch firewood until midday. She cleans the utensils from the family's morning meal and sits preparing a lunch of sadza for the family. After lunch and the cleaning of the dishes, she wanders in the hot sun until early evening, fetching wild vegetables for supper before making the evening trip for water. Her day ends at 9pm, after she has prepared supper and put her younger brothers and sisters to sleep. (1988: 15)

According to the accepted international economic system, Tendai does not work. Because she is not part of the labor force, she is considered unproductive and economically inactive. In industrial economies, a similar sleight of hand makes women's work equally invisible:

> Cathy, a young, middle-class North American housewife, spends her days preparing food, setting the table, serving meals, clearing dishes and food from the table, washing dishes, dressing and diapering her children, disciplining children, taking the children to daycare or to school, disposing of garbage, dusting, gathering clothes for washing, doing the laundry, going to the gas station and the supermarket, repairing household items, ironing, keeping an eye on or playing with the children, making beds, paying bills, caring for pets and plants, putting away toys, books and clothes, sewing or mending or knitting, talking with door-to-door salespeople, answering the telephone, vacuuming, sweeping, and washing floors, cutting the grass, weeding, and shovelling snow, cleaning the bathroom and the kitchen, and putting her children to bed. (1988: 15–16)

Economists would record Cathy, too, as unoccupied and economically inactive. Figure 2.1 illustrates the "reality gap" in classifying work.

Geographer Janice Monk (1988; Lay, Monk, & Rosenfelt, 2001) compiled a teaching exercise that demonstrates the gap between the work that women actually do and the census categories that are supposed to record "work." Using the Venezuelan census as a case study, Monk found that trying to match the actual work that women do with the categories of "work" that are allowed by the census is almost impossible, as Table 2.1 shows.

FIGURE 2.1. Cartoon of census enumeration. Much of women's work is made invisible by conventional labor accounting systems.

In every national economic tallying system in the world, and in virtually every demographic census, unpaid labor and reproductive labor (the time and effort devoted to bearing, nurturing, and raising children) are invisible. Household work, volunteer activities, reproductive activities, subsistence activities, and bartering are entirely absent from national accounts. Of course, all these arenas of activity are dominated by women.

The spatial organization of women's work is the key to its invisibility. Hidden away in the household, out of the "public" sphere, it is easy to (literally) overlook the economic contributions of women. Thus, it is not so much *what* women do that makes their work invisible, but *where* women do it. Housework done inside her home by a woman does not count as productive labor, but if that same woman does the same kind of work in someone else's house, then it *does* count as "productive labor." Cooking is "*active* labor" when the cooked food is sold, but economically "*inactive* labor" when it is cooked in the home for home consumption. Those who care for children in an orphanage are "occupied," while mothers who care for their own children at home are "unoccupied."

TABLE 2.1. Real Work versus Census-Defined "Work"

Village Women's Work, Margarita Island, Venezuela (1982)

Housework
Housework/seamstress (makes clothes)
Sells clothing on street in nearby town
Cleaner (in government offices)
Laundress (operates from home)
Housework/works in small family store/makes parts of shoes
Weaves hammocks/ seamstress (repairs clothes)
Teacher
Sells shoes
Street drink-stand operator
Sells clothing in store
Housework/sells rabbits
Housework/sells corn
Clothing store operator
Shoemaker in home
School cook
Maid
Housework/makes and sells corn bread
Housework/operates small general store in home
Revendedore: retails clothing and housewares (purchased duty free) in streets and
    to private customers
Housework/takes in male boarder
Chambermaid
Raises chickens and sells direct to consumer
Housework/operates small fruit and vegetable store
Housework/crochets portions of hammocks for small manufacturer
Housework/rents space in home for small general store
Housework/sells soft drinks from home
Housework/weaves hammocks
Housework/baby sitting
Local government official

Occupational classifications in the 1970 census of Venezuela

Professional/technical workers
Transport and communication workers
Agents, administrators, directors
Artisans and factory workers
Office employees and kindred workers
Service workers
Salespersons and kindred worker
Agricultural, livestock, fisheries, hunting, forestry etc. workers
Others, not identifiable
Unemployed (identified according to categories above)

Source: Lay, Monk, and Rosenfelt (2001).

Feminists have been active in raising challenges to conventional economic measuring systems and in constructing alternative models that would capture more accurately the total labor performed by both men and women. These include "wages for housework" campaigns, time-budget economic accounting, and an emphasis on making visible the "informal sector" in economies.

Although no national economic accounting system yet counts housework, in a handful of countries, including Canada and New Zealand, where feminist reforms have made the greatest inroads, housework is at least now registered as a recognized activity in the national censuses. Standardized formal systems have yet to be developed for assessing the economic value of housework, but estimates in industrialized countries suggest that counting women's unpaid household labor would add about one-third onto the total value of economic activity. In 1998, the then-new Labour government in Great Britain made a formal estimate of the value of housework; it was one of the first governments to do so. Researchers found that its wage-equivalent value would be about £340 billion, more than the value of the whole manufacturing sector of the economy, and the equivalent of half again the total gross domestic product. It is interesting to note that having made this estimate, the government did nothing with it: they didn't revise the formal portrait of the nation's economic activity, nor did they include the estimate in the formal valuation of total economic activity. To formally include housework in economic valuation would require a thorough reconceptualization of the entire economic accounts system, a prospect that will take a truly bold and visionary government.

Both men and women do more total work than conventional measurements suggest. One way to assess the extent of "hidden work" is to look at how people use their time. Geographers use "time–geography" studies to illuminate interactions across and through everyday space, by mapping people's movements and activities across space and through time (see, for example, Palm and Pred, 1974; Thrift and Pred, 1981; Dyck, 1990; Mackenzie, 1989). The equivalent in labor studies is time-use (also called "time-budget") analyses, which are especially useful at revealing the actual work that goes into sustaining households. No government in the world uses time-budget studies as part of its formal economic data collection efforts, and as a result, time-budget data are only spottily available and often based on very small samples. However, enough data is available (including several dozen studies done by feminist geographers) to draw some broad conclusions. Worldwide, about two-thirds of women's total labor time is in unpaid work; for men, unpaid work accounts for one-third or less (Seager, 1997a; United Nations, 1995). Much of women's unpaid labor is spent in the home or in activities to sustain the household and family. A recent field study in Uganda paints a picture of a grueling workday for rural women (see Table 2.2).

In the United States, women do one-and-a-half more hours of "housework" a day than men; in Japan, for every hour of housework that men do, women do ten (United Nations, 1995; Folbre, 1995). The male–female time-use gap starts at an early age. Girl children are much more likely than boy children to be expected to make productive contributions to running the household. The gap is sometimes extreme: a 1990 survey in rural India of children aged six to nine, for example, showed that girls spent an average of 1.4 hours a day in household chores and boys 0.7 hours, and conversely that boys spent 2.5 hours a day reading while girls spent only 0.4 (United Nations, 1995: 119). Table 2.3 shows several dimensions of these boy–girl time-use differences.

In many countries, men are taking more responsibility for household work, but the pace of change is slow. By the late 1980s, for example, married men in the United States were only doing six percent more housework than they were in the 1960s.

The biggest conceptual block to counting women's work is the definition of what constitutes the labor market. Conventional economic and demographic statistics count only what is known as the "formal" sector, that is, jobs for which wages are formally earned. In the formal sector, a record of employment is created, and jobs are "officially" registered through the payment of taxes on income

TABLE 2.2. Workday of a Rural Woman, Eastern Uganda

Type of work	Duration	Time spent
Preparing breakfast for household	6:00–7:00	1 hour
Working on the farm	7:00–11:00	4 hours
Sundrying harvested crops	11:00–11:30	30 minutes
Fetching water/firewood	12:00–12:30	30 minutes
Taking goats to graze/feeding pigs	12:30–14:00	90 minutes
Preparing and serving lunch	14:00–15:00	1 hour
Working on the farm	15:00–18:00	3 hours
Fetching water/firewood	18:00–18:30	30 minutes
Preparing dinner and bathing children	18:30–20:00	90 minutes
Boiling water for bathing for adults	20:00—20:30	30 minutes
Serving evening meal	20:30–21:30	1 hour
Tidying the house	21:30–22:00	30 minutes
Total working time		15.5 hours

Source: Momsen and Kinnaird (1993).

TABLE 2.3. Time Use of Children in Rural Areas: Number of Hours Spent per Day in Different Activities

| | India, 1990 | | | | Nepal, 1989 | | | |
| | Ages 6–9 | | Ages 10–14 | | Ages 6–9 | | Ages 10–14 | |
	Girls	Boys	Girls	Boys	Girls	Boys	Girls	Boys
Work	3.0	1.9	5.4	4.0	3.2	1.7	7.7	4.4
Household labor	1.4	0.7	2.3	0.6	2.2	1.0	4.0	2.0
Reading/ studying	0.4	2.5	0.2	1.1	2.1	4.8	3.8	0.3
Leisure	1.3	1.5	0.8	1.2	na	na	na	na

Source: United Nations (1995: 119).

earned, through licensing, or through other means by which governments keep track of who is getting paid for what. The paid domestic servant, the university teacher, the self-employed lawyer, the secretary—these are all jobs that exist in the formal sector. These are jobs that the government knows about and "counts."

In most countries in the world, the "informal" sector is at least as large (and in some cases *much* larger than) the formal sector. A significant share of the world's "working" population support themselves through the informal sector. The informal sector includes activities such as unregistered street vending, bartering, selling goods informally (at flea markets or small farmstands, for example), work for which wages are paid in cash and never recorded, reciprocal-help networks ("I'll mow your lawn today if you'll fix my leaky faucet tomorrow"), volunteer activities, prostitution, criminal enterprises, and black market activities. Both women and men work in the informal sector, but it looms larger in women's lives. Indeed, in some economies, including countries as diverse as Nigeria and Russia, *most* work done by *most* women (and sometimes by most men) takes place only in the informal sector.

FOOTLOOSE FACTORIES AND NIMBLE FINGERS: THE NEW INDUSTRIAL ORDER

One might think that the prevailing ideologies of "appropriate" femininity would keep women out of factory work. Work in an industrial factory is often dirty, dangerous, and may involve heavy machinery.

The factory is usually a place where men are found in great numbers. All of these factors "should" exclude women from such workplaces. However, industrial production brings toe to toe the competing demands of patriarchy ("Women 'should' stay at home to provide the support system for their working husbands") and capitalism ("We need workers who will do tedious work without complaint and to whom we can pay the lowest wages"). These competing impulses are reconciled by defining *some* factory work as "naturally" feminized.

Industrial production, from its start, has depended on women's labor. Women have been a significant part of the industrial labor force from the time of the very first factories in 1700s Great Britain. In the early British industrial model of textile mills, which was also adopted in the United States, whole families were hired by mill owners. Typically, families moved into mill villages and lived in tenements owned by the company; all members of the family, including children over about age six, worked in the mill (Spain, 1992). Women were the preferred workers in certain parts of these factories—for example, in the sorting, weaving, and spinning rooms of textile mills.

In the "Lowell model" of industrialization, developed in Massachusetts in the early 1800s, women—without their families—were even more central in the industrial labor force. In rural New England at this time, there was virtually no "surplus" male labor: immigrants were few, and most U.S. born men were engaged in agriculture or commerce. To fill their factories, Lowell and his partners instituted a system that brought in a rotating workforce of young, unmarried women from rural New England. To overcome the prejudice against women undertaking factory work, Lowell provided company-run boardinghouses, overseen by matrons who enforced the company's paternalistic policies of strict curfews, mandatory church attendance, and abstinence. The "Lowell mill girls" have become an icon of early industrialization. By the beginning of the nineteenth century women's labor was firmly in place at the core of factory production. By the late nineteenth century, mills became less dependent on female labor as a male immigrant labor force became available.

More than a century later, the new industrial economy at the end of the twentieth century seems far removed from the mills of Lowell and Manchester. But the geographies that define, contain, and shape the new economy—global production sites, homework venues, sweatshops—and the ways in which these geographies are gendered are simultaneously very old.

The geography—literally, the distribution—of industrial production has changed dramatically over the last forty years or so. Perhaps the single best defining characteristic of the new economy is that production is now scattered around the globe: industries have become "footloose," and production sites are fluid. While the brilliance of the "original" Industrial Revolution was in bringing together company headquarters, research, and production all under one roof, success in the "new" industrial revolution depends on constantly shifting production in search of the cheapest labor. The map of production and consumption is now complex and dense with labels from around the world. U.S. car manufacturers produce cars in Brazil and Mexico; Japanese computer companies farm out chip production to factories in Malaysia; the French soccer team kicks around balls sewn in Pakistan. In the 1980s, most Americans were wearing sneakers made in South Korea; by the 1990s, they were made in China. Most Europeans are wearing clothes stitched in Sri Lanka, Vietnam, or Indonesia. In the new industrial system, the headquarters and research-and-development side of business typically stays in the corporate home country in the First World, while assembly and production has been shifted to the Third World.

One of the most distinctive features on the new globalized industrial landscape is the "export processing zone" (EPZ). EPZs are industrial zones—literal, demarcated areas, typically fenced off and gated—put aside for production by foreign companies. More than sixty countries, mostly in the Third World, have established EPZs. Host governments encourage foreign companies to locate in EPZs by offering a range of inducements, such as tax holidays, or waivers of labor laws for factories inside the zones. EPZs (and their Mexican and Central American equivalents, *maquiladoras*) are the entryways for industrial development in countries at the periphery of the global economy. EPZs are the heartlands of the global economy. As zones where the host government has an explicit commitment to and a vested interest in providing a cheap, placid labor force for foreign investors, they are also sites of considerable exploitation and labor repression.

Geographers have been prominent in mapping and describing these shifts in the global economy (for example, Dicken, 1992; Barff and Austen, 1993), although until recently little attention was paid to the gendered dimensions of the new economic realities. But a gendered division of labor is deeply embedded in the global economy. Indeed, it's hard to explain how the global economy functions without paying attention to the gendered division of labor that sustains the new world order. The EPZ and *maquiladora* heartlands are feminized places. The "global assembly line" of export-oriented industry (whether in an EPZ or not) runs largely on women's labor. Most of the workers sewing Nike sneakers in China, cleaning microchips in Malaysia, or assembling blue jeans in the Philippines are women. Figures 2.2 and 2.3 capture the typical EPZ factory scene. Recent surveys show that women constitute more than eighty percent of the industrial workforce in EPZs in Mexico, Taiwan, Sri Lanka, Malaysia, and the Philippines, and more than seventy percent of the workforce in South Korea and Guatemala. More particularly, the global assembly line runs on the labor of *young, unmarried* women.

FIGURE 2.2. Photograph of women on the assembly line. Cheap, flexible, replaceable: Women have become the ideal labor pool in the new global economy.

Why women? Employment practices vary from EPZ to EPZ, within and between countries, so generalizations need to be constantly checked out on the ground, but there is a "package" of gender assumptions and stereotypes that typifies employment practices in export-oriented industries. Precisely because of all the ambivalence around women and "work," women have been construed as the ideal flexible labor force in the new industrial regime. Because work is not considered to be primary in women's lives, they can be paid less than men. In economies where formal-sector jobs are scarce, and where women are excluded from many of the nonfactory jobs that might be available, there is a vast pool of women workers eager for employment in the new factories of the Third World. Under these conditions, the female labor force can be continually renewed, such that older (and more expensive) workers are replaced with fresh, cheaper, recruits (reminiscent of the Lowell system). Young, single women are assumed to have fewer family responsibilities that would distract them from their jobs, but also will be more likely to have high rates of voluntary turnover due to the demands imposed when they get married or have children. Women are considered to be a "disposable" labor force: they can be hired or fired at will because a job is not supposed to be a permanent feature of women's lives, and employment is not supposed to be for a lifetime. Cheap, flexible, and replaceable, women have become the ideal labor pool in the new global economy.

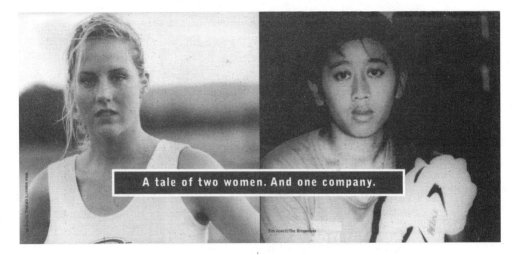

American.

College educated.

Works hard to stay in shape
and maintain her health. Eats well.

Nike's slick ad campaigns encourage
her to take control and demand
more from life.

Indonesian.

Elementary-level education.

Works full-time in a factory, but
is paid so little she is malnourished.

Her boss tells her she is worthless
and if she demands more she'll
have no job at all.

FIGURE 2.3. Brochure about women in the global economy. There is room for feminist debate about the extent to which women's work in the factories of the global economy represents an opportunity for women, or unremitting exploitation of them.

There is also an even more distinctive rationale often touted by managers for hiring women to work the assembly lines, especially in electronics production: their "nimble fingers." Many managers claim that women have smaller fingers than men, greater dexterity, more patience and are more tolerant of tedium—and are thus naturally good at jobs requiring the delicate assembly of small parts (Chant and McIlwaine, 1995). The "nimble fingers" explanation for global investment also clearly plays on racial stereotypes. In the 1970s, just as the global economy was poised for lift-off, an official Malaysian brochure to entice foreign investment proclaimed: "The manual dexterity of the Oriental female is famous the world over. Her hands are small and she works with extreme care. Who therefore could be better qualified by nature and inheritance to contribute to the efficiency of a production line than the Oriental girl?" (quoted in Elson, 1983: 5–6). The convergence of racist and sexist stereotypes is a powerful factor in explaining the particular geography of multinational footlooseness—and it may explain, in part, why assembly production first went to Asia, and not, for example, to Africa. (The representation of Asian women as bright, docile, pliable, and eager to please is a palpable cultural presence in the Western "orientalist" imagination; there is no comparable imagining of African women in which they would be constructed in the Western view as an "ideal" factory workforce.)

A close ideological relative to the "nimble fingers" explanation for why women are preferred workers on electronics assembly lines is another explanation that garment-factory managers often invoke: that sewing comes "naturally" to women, or is one of their "traditional" activities. The "natural tendencies" argument is a key rationale for labor exploitation: managers can pay workers less for a skill that is merely "natural" (as opposed to an acquired skill, one that is the result of training and learning and application, for which workers will need to be rewarded).

There is room for feminist debate about the extent to which women's work in the EPZs and factories of the global economy represents an opportunity for women, or unremitting exploitation of them. The new global economy has brought new jobs to places where none previously existed; factory work offers women opportunities to escape narrow social and economic confines, it gives women some discretionary income, and it allows women to extend their social and political networks through workplace contacts. As feminist geographers have pointed out, "Waged work spaces . . . create opportunities for gender identities to be renegotiated, perhaps even to be reconstituted, and in which new forms of femininity might emerge" (Women and Geography Study Group, 1997: 124). In many instances, women have "found their voices" and have developed skills and confidence through organizing and collaborating with fellow workers.

HOMEWORK

Even at the most frenzied factory-building peak of the Industrial Revolution, industrial production never entirely left the home. In the late-nineteenth-century United States, for example, while hundreds of thousands of workers toiled in the new factories in cities such as Chicago and New York, a second industrial workforce toiled at home: such tasks as piece-production sewing, cigar rolling, finish tailoring, shoe making, and lace making took place in the homes of the working classes. Behind the doors of the home, this industrial production was almost invisible. As Figure 2.4 shows, whole families

FIGURE 2.4. 1910 Riis photographs of home-based production. Behind the doors of the home, industrial production was almost invisible.

were involved, but overall, homework was women's work. Homework was the most exploitative kind of work—labor standards, wage standards, and environmental regulations, to the extent they existed, were almost impossible to impose and enforce in micro-production sites scattered among thousands of living rooms. U.S. social workers of the nineteenth century documented the misery of domestic industrial production, and photographic exposes of homework sites by reformers such as Lewis Hines and Jacob Riis led to limits on homework and legislation that attempted to curb the excesses of exploitation.

But homework never went away. In fact, it is now on the increase again. "Modern" jobs such as white-collar office work, clerical work, and data-entry jobs are being farmed out to homeworkers, a fragmentation of labor made possible by the computer, the fax machine, and the Internet. But white-collar professionals or information workers represent a relatively small slice of the homework population. The core of homework remains industrial piecework production, especially in the garment and toy industries. Homework accounts for a considerable proportion of industrial production in the contemporary global industrial economy—both in the Third World and in the First.

An increasing number of Western garment manufacturers are trying to beat overseas cheap labor competition by turning to home-based production systems in their own country. Marks & Spencer, for example, a British retailer which in the 1980s sold one-fifth of all garments in Great Britain, decided to become "manufacturers without factories," farming out work to small contractors who often subcontract to even smaller producers (Enloe, 1989). Benetton, the avant-garde Italian garment manufacturer, developed a production strategy that relies heavily on the use of Italian family-based subcontractors who hire women to work in their homes or in small non-unionized shops; by the late 1980s, such subcontractors produced forty percent of Benetton's knitting, and sixty percent of garment assembly (Enloe, 1989: 156).

On the one hand, homework can represent an empowering and appealing way for women (or men) to combine domestic and work responsibilities—they can be at home to take care of their children, for example, and still earn money. At its best, homework resolves time/space conflicts for women trying to reconcile family responsibilities with the need or desire to earn income. As one geographer says, it certainly eliminates the "journey to work" (Christensen, 1993)! Potentially, the adjustment of time and space relationships offered by homework could have implications for a broader restructuring of the relation between home and work, and between women and men (Mackenzie, 1989: 48). The "telecommuting" revolution is often heralded for eliminating the "drag" of place. For high-end professionals (like their home-sewing sisters), homework compresses geography. However, despite the hype about the "wireless E-age," only a minute proportion of the workforce in advanced industrial economies actually "telecommute," and most of these are men.

Homework can give women control over their social and work environments simultaneously, including, for example, protection from unpleasant encounters in the workplace. Cynthia Enloe points to Asian women in Great Britain who find that homework affords them protection from racist encounters:

> I want to remain invisible, literally. Also . . . I am a widow and I really do not know what my legal status is. . . . At the moment, my uncle brings machining work to my home. It works out to be 50 pence per hour, not great! But I earn and I feed my children somehow. Most of all, I do not have to deal with the fear of racist abuse in this white world. (1989: 154)

In Great Britain, the United States, and Canada, most homeworkers are recent immigrants or minority women. For these groups, particularly, homework allows a measure of protection from state scrutiny and racism, and may provide a least-resistance entree into waged work.

The flip side of the coin is that with homework, home and work merge. For homeworkers, there is no time or place when they are not (or could not be) "at work," and the waged homework often expands to fill all available time and space. As feminist geographers have shown, the microgeography of the home is seldom designed to accommodate wage-earning work. In a study of contemporary homeworking women in the United States, Kathleen Christensen (1993) found that work space typically either impinged upon or doubled up with rooms that had other domestic and personal functions. Ann Oberhauser (1997), in her study of women homeworkers in Appalachia, similarly found that spatial constraints and limited resources often made it difficult for homeworkers to negotiate demands on family time and household space. Many of the women whom Oberhauser interviewed admitted that they faced resistance from family members who resented the time and space taken up by their homework activities. One of the women put it this way: "I hate to say this, but my husband, he's not real encouraging, because he feels that its a kind of waste of time. You know, that I should be doing other household chores" (quoted in Oberhauser, 1997: 175).

Many of the perils of homework first identified by nineteenth-century labor reformers remain salient. Work in the home remains hard to regulate, it is subject to wage and environmental abuses, it is poorly paid (with the exception of the elite tele-professionals, a small minority of all homeworkers), and it creates a work structure that isolates women in the home. Homework tips the balance in favor of employers (Bullock, 1994: 64): they can pay homeworkers less than factory-based workers, often by piece rates; overhead costs (such as electricity, cleaning, and so on) are absorbed by the worker; employers can ignore health and safety standards that apply in formal workplaces; and homeworkers, isolated from one another, are the least likely sector of the workforce to unionize. Homework also serves to consolidate patriarchal control of women by confining not only women's *domestic* life but also their *work* life to a single male-dominated household structure and space.

THE RETURN OF THE SWEATSHOP

The reemergence of home-based industrial production is not unrelated to the reemergence of sweatshops in advanced industrial economies such as the United States and Great Britain. Western consumers are now accustomed to exposes of shocking sweatshop conditions in Third World factories, but fewer realize that the sweatshop has returned "home" too. The same forces that have encouraged the resurgence of homework also propel the return of "local" sweatshops. In the 1980s and 1990s, sweatshops made a return with a vengeance in the United States, particularly in the garment and toy industries. Sweatshops, whether overseas or "at home," are the dark underbelly of the global economy: the overarching concern in global industrial production is the search for ever-cheaper labor, and many manufacturers don't ask—or feel they can't afford to ask—why the labor is so cheap. Whether in Los Angeles or Jakarta or Beijing, the cheapest labor is the labor of women and children, and especially the most vulnerable women and children, recent immigrants and racial minorities.

Highly publicized raids on sweatshops in Los Angeles in the mid-1990s threw light on the extent to which the global economy, for many women, has become an economy of terror. For example, in a raid on a garment factory in El Monte, just outside Los Angeles, in 1995, the police found a workforce of almost a hundred Thai women, all illegal immigrants, who had been kept in virtual slavery in the factory. The sweatshop owners in El Monte had recruited women in Thailand by promising them jobs and safe passage to the United States. In return, the women were to work in the factory to pay off the costs of their trip—an illegal arrangement called "indentured servitude." Once in El Monte, they were not allowed outside the factory walls (which were topped with barbed wire), and they were beaten if they tried to escape. The invisibility of the new sweatshops

in the landscape of contemporary cities allows these abuses to go un-
noticed; the El Monte factory was a modest anonymous building
tucked away in a warehouse district, far from pedestrian traffic. The
women confined inside the El Monte factory worked seventeen-hour
days to pay off their "debt," by sewing women's and children's ap-
parel at piecework rates amounting to as little as sixty cents an hour.
In their attempts to draw attention to their plight, they had dropped
notes out the factory windows calling for help—notes that went unno-
ticed or unheeded for months. They tried to convey secret "help"
messages to the driver of an ice cream truck who sometimes stopped
outside the factory. Finally, something drew attention to the sweatshop and the women worker/prisoners were finally rescued The El
Monte case is just the tip of the iceberg; as Robert Reich, then labor
secretary for the United States said, "There are many other El
Montes waiting to be exposed."

BETWEEN THE STICKY FLOOR AND THE GLASS CEILING

Most women workers, of course, are not trapped in sweatshops. Indeed, in virtually every country, *some* women have reached the highest echelons of prestige and pay in the waged work world. Almost
everywhere, some women have broken through the glass ceiling to
become surgeons, lawyers, stockbrokers, diplomats, ministers, and
politicians. Women can be found on the annual lists of multimillion-
aires and wheelers-and-dealers. Some of the hottest Internet entrepreneurs are women—including, in the United States, the CEO of
eBay, the powerhouse on-line auction website. Spatially, we might say
that at least a few women can now be found "on the upper floors and
in the corner offices."

Most women workers, however, are *neither* in sweatshops nor in
the corner office. They are somewhere in between, caught "between
the sticky floor and the glass ceiling." But no matter where they are
on the spectrum of waged work, most women earn less than their
male counterparts. The majority of women work in the low-wage sec-
tors of the workforce. In the most feminized jobs, where women predominate and few men are found, pay levels tend to be especially
low. But even when women do similar work and are employed in the
same places as men, they earn less. Statistics on wages are hard to
come by, but a reliable generalization for most countries is that
women in waged work earn about twenty to forty percent less than
men. A recent international sample of manufacturing wages showed

that in 1990 women earned less than fifty percent of what men earned in Japan; about seventy percent of what men earned in several countries including the United States, the United Kingdom, and Switzerland; and about eighty percent of what men earned in Norway, Denmark, and Sri Lanka. Table 2.4 provides a fuller list of the ratio of female-to-male earnings. Overall, the wage gap is slowly narrowing in most, but not all, countries in the world. In some cases, such as the United States, the pay gap is narrowing primarily because men's wages have dropped, not because women's wages have risen. In a few countries, notably Japan and South Korea, the wage gap between men and women has actually *widened* since the 1970s.

The gender pay gap can be attributed to several factors including outright wage discrimination, the fact that women are segregated and concentrated in lower paying female-dominated fields, and the high percentage of women working part-time. These gender differences are magnified and refracted by racial and ethnic discrimination. In the United States, for example, in the early 1990s, white women earned sixty-five percent of what white men earned, while black women earned fifty-eight percent and Hispanic women fifty-three percent. Lower pay on the job has lifelong ripple effects, including lower pensions, diminished access to credit, and limited purchasing power in all domains. Lower pay directly limits women's ability to secure access to services, to transportation (as we will discuss later), and to housing.

Housing statistics make the "purchasing power" discrepancy between men and women particularly evident. In most countries, the majority of women still only have access to home ownership through partnership with a man. Recent statistics for the United States illustrate the intersection of race, gender, and income (see Table 2.5).

GENDER IN THE WORK*PLACE*

Equal pay legislation exists in many countries, and in some is quite aggressively enforced. Women *are* working their way up the occupational ladder. But the gender wage gap persists. Why? Probably the single most important explanation is the segregation of the labor force. Most women work in jobs where the workforce is predominantly female, and women work in a far narrower range of occupations than do men. The majority of women do not work in the same jobs as men, nor in the same places, nor do they have men as direct ("equal") coworkers. Under these conditions, demands for "equal pay" are relatively toothless—"equal pay" only protects women who are doing the same job as men in the same workplace. For example,

TABLE 2.4. Women's Average Wages in Manufacturing as Percentage of Men's, 1970, 1980, and 1990

	1970	1980	1990
Developed regions			
Australia	57	79	82
Belgium	68	70	76
Czechoslovakia	—	68	68
Denmark	74	86	85
Finland	70	75	77
France	—	77	79
Germany (Federal Rep. of)	70	73	73
Greece	68	68	76
Hungary	—	—	72
Ireland	56	69	69
Italy	—	83	—
Japan	—	44	41
Luxembourg	55	61	65
Netherlands	72	80	77
New Zealand	—	71	75
Norway	75	82	86
Portugal	—	—	72
Spain	—	—	72
Sweden	80	90	89
Switzerland	65	66	68
United Kingdom	58	69	68
United States	—	—	68
Africa			
Egypt	64	62	68
Kenya	—	62	74
Swaziland	—	55	54
Zambia	—	—	73
Latin America and Caribbean			
Costa Rica	—	70	74
El Salvador	82	81	94
Netherlands Antilles	—	51	65
Paraguay	—	79	66
Asia and the Pacific			
Cyprus	—	50	58
Guam	—	50	51
Hong Kong	—	78	69
Korea, Republic of	—	45	50
Myanmar	84	86	97
Singapore	—	—	55
Sri Lanka	—	75	88

Source: United Nations, 1995, p. 128.

TABLE 2.5. Home Ownership Rates in the United States, 1993: Percentage Who Own Their Own Homes

All married couples	79%	All women-headed households	44%
White	81%	White	51%
Black	64%	Black	30%
Hispanic	53%	Hispanic	24%

Source: Costello and Krimgold (1996).

two secretaries with the same skills and seniority, one male and one female, must be paid the same, but in a workforce where the majority of women do not work in the same jobs as men, "equal pay" legislation is of limited efficacy. Table 2.6 shows the interlinkages between wages (and other benefits) and occupational segregation: women in female-dominated jobs have the lowest wages and fewest benefits of all workers in the U.S. workforce.

Understanding occupational segregation is therefore crucial to explaining the divergent workplace experiences of men and women. Economists and sociologists have long debated the origins of and the mechanisms that sustain occupational segregation. What geographers contribute to this discussion is an understanding of the role of geography in the creation and persistence of occupational segregation.

Geographers Susan Hanson and Gerry Pratt (1995) argue that distance helps to create a sex-differentiated job market because men and women do not have equal resources to overcome the "friction" of distance. In other words, finding jobs and getting to work is usually more difficult for women than for men. This helps explain the segregation of jobs. Hanson and Pratt also focus attention on the role of job-information networks in employment: while many economists

TABLE 2.6. The Costs of Labor Market Segregation, Worcester (Massachusetts) Case Study

	Women in occupations that are:		
	Female-dominated	Gender-integrated	Male-dominated
Average hourly wage	$8.70	$9.79	$11.70
Percentage with job-provided health insurance	47.3%	57.3%	60.3%
Percentage with job-provided retirement benefits	42.5%	53.2%	46.7%

Source: Hanson and Pratt (1995).

suggest that the job search is a rational and linear purposeful activity, Hanson and Pratt (1991) find that most people find jobs through informal social contacts and "accidents of place." Job information circulates through local geographies and networks. To the extent that men's and women's daily geographies are different, so will be their job search process and access to information about jobs. In particular, Hanson and Pratt (1995) found that women who learn about jobs from other women are more likely to end up in female-dominated jobs. Concomitantly, they found that women who have broken into male-dominated jobs learned about those jobs through *male* family members. This geographical network-based analysis illuminates the ways in which sex-based occupational patterns are created and perpetuated.

Geography is important in other ways (both literally and metaphorically) in the segregation of men's and women's work. In most cultures, there are work*places* from which women are prohibited—sometimes by law, sometimes by "social policing." In the recent labor history of the United States and Great Britain, for example, women have been excluded by law from working in mines, piloting commercial airplanes, driving tanks in the army, and doing most maritime jobs. Around the world, in industrial economies, social and cultural policing has kept women out of the dockyards, off oil rigs, out of the ranks of orchestra conductors, off the stock market trading floor, on the fringes of most industrial trades (plumbing, electrical work, printing, machine tooling), and out of most scientific and engineering professions.

It is important—and not coincidental—to note that many of these men-only (or mostly male) occupations are among the highest paying. On the flip side of the coin, most women-dominated occupations (which includes nursing, teaching in primary schools, bank telling, or clerical work [in the United States]) are neither high-prestige nor high-paying jobs. Men who breach gender barriers to take up "women's work" face real social penalties—male nurses, child-care workers, or secretaries often find their masculinity called into question, or their motives suspected. Women who step into men's workplaces are subjected to the same social scrutiny, but additionally face sexual harassment, violence or threats of violence, and daily on-the-job hostility—sometimes of the severest sort.

Women's presence in workplaces that are deemed to be men's is disquieting—to individual men, to a collective (heterosexual) masculine identity, and to a broader sense of social order. In her study of the exclusion of women from merchant banking in Britain, geographer Linda McDowell makes the point that the very presence of women in the banking profession forces men "to face their preconceptions and privileged position and to deal with issues they define as 'private'" (1995: 81). McDowell suggests that as we enter the twenty-first century, an *increasing* share of jobs involve the marketing of personal attributes—the smile of the airline attendant, for example—and that this is especially true of women's jobs. It is still the case—and perhaps increasingly so—that women have to present a particular "look" and body performance for job success. Especially when women enter men's occupations and workplaces, they have to walk a fine line: between making a convincing display of their commitment to conventional feminine and heterosexual attributes on the one hand (to avoid being accused of being lesbians, man haters, or "ball-busters") and, on the other hand, suppressing feminine traits and activities that may make their male colleagues especially uncomfortable (not breastfeeding infants in the workplace, not crying or being too "emotional," adopting a masculinist version of self on the job). This often means that women have to accept a high level of "teasing" on the job; they have to fine-tune their dress code (the woman lawyer's standard scarf-tie, for example, resembling closely enough a male tie to signify professional decorum, but floppy and bow-like enough to be feminine); and they have to not stand up too often for "women's issues." If women sometimes have a difficult time constructing a stable and appropriate sexual and gender identity in the workplace it is usually because they are not "supposed" to be there.

Gender, race, and class create different spatial experiences for people in the workplace, even in the same environmental setting. For example, architect Leslie Weisman (1992) "deconstructs" a typical U.S. office skyscraper. From top to bottom, the white-collar office workers and the blue-collar maintenance workers inhabit distinct, barely touching, zones of the tower. The assignment of private space reflects hierarchy: secretaries (mostly female) typically are assigned to "open" floor-plan space, while executives (mostly male) are buffered by receptionists, doors, and locks. The assignment of space and light is similarly indexed to one's gender-based occupational status: interior, windowless, fluorescent-lit space is invariably allocated to clerical workers (predominantly women), exterior offices with natural light and views to executives (mostly men). Weisman quotes a study from the 1970s that showed that women receive the same proportion of office space as they do pay, about twenty to fifty percent less than men doing the same work in the same office (1992: 38). In 1999, a group of female scientists at the Massachusetts Institute of Technology forced the administration there to admit to years of discrimination against women. The discrimination took several forms, but closely twinned were the same space:pay continuum that Weisman noticed: women on the science faculties were paid less than their male counterparts and were allocated smaller laboratory space—in about the same proportions!

Because of work*place* segregation of men and women, legislation that mandates equal pay between men and women has a limited effect on closing the earnings gap. In the 1980s, feminists crafted an alternative legislative and conceptual approach to this problem, focusing on "equity" rather than "equality." Rather than simply saying, for example, that male secretaries and female secretaries must be paid equally, the "comparable worth" approach assigns equivalent value to jobs across gender-segregated categories—assigning "equal worth," for example, to secretaries (mostly women) and to painters (mostly men), or comparing the worth of librarians (mostly women) to that of sports coaches (mostly men). Comparable worth legislation exists in only a handful of countries, but in 1999 the Canadian government took a bold step forward in making comparable worth a workplace reality. "Equal pay for work of equal value" is written into Canada's Human Rights Act, but it had languished there for almost two decades until legal action by a group of women federal workers forced the hand of the government. In late 1999, the Canadian government agreed to pay back wages (in the amount of more than $2 billion) to redress the gender inequity caused by occupational segregation and by the failures of equal pay legislation to achieve gender equity.

MAPPING THE TERRAIN OF POVERTY

On-the-job wage inequities and the segregation of women workers into lower paying and lower prestige occupations are directly linked to the "feminization of poverty," a global trend first identified in the 1960s. Everywhere, women constitute a disproportionate share of people in poverty, and in most countries a growing share—thus its "feminization." Women's poverty is not due to job–wage inequities alone, of course, but this is a core factor. In a macroview, to explain poverty globally, one needs to examine larger systems of imbalances in the distribution of resources across societies; in many countries, great poverty has been caused and exacerbated by economic "structural adjustment" programs imposed by Western banks and governments. In Eastern Europe, for example, the transition to a "free market" economy has plunged millions of people into dire poverty. Colonial and neocolonial patterns of resource exploitation create and extend poverty. All these forces affect women and men differently, and almost everywhere women represent a disproportionate share of people in poverty. In the United States, for example, in the mid-1990s, fifteen percent of women were "poor" (using official government measures), while the poverty rate for men was ten percent.

In most Western industrial countries, there are, on average, 120–130 poor women for every 100 men. Women's poverty in the United States, as elsewhere, shows the feminization process (the growth of women's poverty) and the intersection of changes in family structure with changes in poverty: in 1959, twenty percent of all poor families were maintained by women alone; in 1992, this figure had grown to fifty-two percent (Folbre, 1995).

Poverty is universal, but it is not literally found everywhere. In fact, poverty is found in *particular* places, and in most instances this geography is predictable. In most U.S. cities, for example, poverty is concentrated in certain central neighborhoods, as Table 2.7 shows. nPoverty has a particular distribution. Geography and space—understood literally—play a central role in creating and reinforcing poverty. Although it might be stretching the point to say that "you are where you live," this is not too far off the mark. Rich people and poor people in most Western cities do not live in the same places; class distinctions are reflected in—and propped up by—particular spatial distributions. When poverty is concentrated in particular places, this has a snowball effect of multiplying disadvantage. Poor neighborhoods are the least served by public transportation, they often lack basic services such as water or electricity, and they have the most impoverished educational facilities. Thus these areas offer the fewest opportunities for residents to extricate themselves from poverty. Poor neighborhoods are characterized by patterns of "disinvestment." Disinvestment leads to property neglect and abandonment, which leads to further disinvestment. Geographically, poverty thus spirals in on itself to become a spatial trap.

The isolation of the poor from the social and economic mainstream in the United States is increasing, not decreasing. This is a function of economic shifts, especially deindustrialization, and of geographic shifts, especially the movement of jobs out of city cores. But it is also a function of "upping the ante" of spatial strategies that keep class lines tautly drawn. For example, as the downtown functions in many cities have been usurped by suburban malls, this means that people spend more and more of their "public" lives not in public

TABLE 2.7. U.S. Poverty Rates by Residential Location, 1993

	Children	Women	Men
City	35%	21%	12%
Suburb	15%	10%	7%
Rural	22%	18%	11%

Source: Albeda and Tilley (1998).

civic spaces but in privately owned (mall) spaces; the privatized spaces of malls have quite different rules of public and civic engagement than do civic public spaces. Malls can regulate who is allowed in to these spaces (excluding the homeless, for example) and what activities are permitted there (excluding political rallies or the passing out of leaflets, for example). Further, across the United States, a recent proliferation of anti-homeless laws is aimed at removing homeless people from *public* spaces—cities from New York to San Francisco have passed laws designed to sweep the homeless and displaced out of view (Mitchell, 1997). Concomitantly, the profusion of gated communities for the wealthy ensures the complete segregation of the classes. Urban enclaves of the poor, in the United States as elsewhere, are highly feminized places: adult women are the primary householders, adult women are the primary income earners, and adult women are the primary guardians of the community.

Poverty is also the issue that demonstrates most clearly the ways that race and gender intersect in mapping the terrain of relative advantage and disadvantage. Indeed, one of the critiques of the "feminization of poverty" analysis is that it often essentializes "women" without taking account of the significant differences in disadvantage—and in survival strategies—among women. Women's poverty in the United States—as elsewhere—cannot be explained solely by gender. Race and class must be taken into account. As Table 2.8 shows, poverty rates vary widely between men and women, and among men and women of different racial groups.

In the United States, residential segregation is aligned by race as well as by class. One study recently suggested that African Americans living in segregated neighborhoods in U.S. cities are so marginalized that they might well be considered among the most isolated people in the world (Massey and Denton, 1993). This did not occur haphazardly—rather, it was intentionally woven into the fabric of modern cities through real estate practices, banking and investment practices,

TABLE 2.8. U.S. Poverty Rates by Race and Gender, 1999

	Women	Men
White	19%	9%
Black	39%	15%
Asian/Pacific Islander	23%	11%
Hispanic (all races)	39%	17%

Rates are for female and male "householders," with no spouse present.
Source: U.S. Census, 1999.

white violence, government codes, and explicitly racially restrictive housing accords.

It is unlikely that many of my students—the eager class of 2000—will end up trapped in poor inner cities or in segregated neighborhoods. As middle-class, white university graduates, they are far more likely to be the gentrifiers of the old inner cities, or to be the next wave of gated-community suburbanites. Nonetheless, the rosy picture of harmonious relationships between home, work, and gender that they predicted for themselves is equally unlikely to be realized—at least in the short run. Although the world of work and of gender expectations that they will graduate into is dramatically different from that of their parents, many of the massive social structures that have produced the uneven gender landscape remain stolidly in place.

Chapter 3

THE CITY

$\mathbf{A}$lly McBeal, the angst-ridden heroine of the TV show of the same name, manages to do much of her soul searching while fearlessly strolling the moonlit streets of downtown Boston alone. A latter-day Mary Tyler Moore, Ally and her other single, female, lawyer friends take to the city streets (and bars, restaurants, and clubs) unabashedly and with aplomb: they shout in celebration, step in tune to a "theme" song, or use the city's anonymity to gather their thoughts. The city is their playground and their site of redemption from emotional distress.

Fantasy? Well, of course it is—*Ally McBeal* is a TV sitcom. But the romantic imagery of cities as sites of rumination and pleasure is long-standing, perhaps dating back to the beginnings of modernism—to the poetry of Baudelaire or Whitman and the celebration of the lone man wandering the streets of nineteenth-century Paris or New York, commenting and reflecting on the rough-and-tumble lives being lived out around him. The city has often been portrayed as risqué and exciting. Historically, it has most often been men who are able to enjoy those pleasures. But Ally too is a flaneur and a voyeur—she wanders the streets seemingly without purpose and stares longingly at lovers kissing under streetlamps. Does it tell us anything about changing gender roles and/or about postmodern cities that a single woman is now portrayed as the hero of the street? Are our early-twenty-first-century cities qualitatively different from the nineteenth-century city of Baudelaire and Whitman? And what about the suburbs, those safe but sometimes dull places that have often been portrayed as domestic and therefore suitable for women and children. Neither Ally nor any of her friends live in or visit the suburbs (though presumably after they are married and have children, they will move into single-family houses in Newton or Burlington, Massachusetts), nor did Baudelaire or Whitman excite us with tales of the countryside.

The urban imagery of *Ally McBeal* (as well as other recent sitcoms like *Friends* and *Seinfeld*) is certainly different from the urban image on the TV news that follows the show on the Fox network: drug shootings on the streets, assaults, rapes, carjackings. The city here is depicted as the site of threatening behavior, particularly for women, and particularly for lone women at night wandering the streets. And yet there's Ally, alone with her thoughts, at night, strolling the streets!

We seem to be caught between two opposed images of the city: one offers the city as an exciting and fulfilling place for women (and hence "good" for women), and the other offers a potentially dangerous place (and thus "bad" for women). Suburbs, too, are portrayed in contradictory ways: on the one hand, they are portrayed as more safe than cities, and therefore "better" for women; on the other hand, they are presented as spatial traps, where women get stuck in domestic roles with no way to escape (and therefore "bad" for women). How can we make sense of these contradictions? In reality, the contemporary urban landscape contains all facets of these images: it presents the possibilities of economic advancement and social excitement that we see in *Ally McBeal*, but it also constricts the physical and social movement of many women. The suburbs are environments in which some women thrive, but in which others are stifled. Our cities are complex environments, in which various neighborhoods resonate with different gendered and often racialized meanings. The twenty- and thirty-story office buildings that mark our downtowns express the corporate and masculine dominance of our political economy; our decaying inner-city cores, home to many working-class and minority citizens, are imagined as dangerous, most especially off limits to middle-class white women; gentrified neighborhoods, marked by rehabilitated historical structures and trendy restaurants, are often home to gay and lesbian communities. Homeless people wake up in an urban park while "yuppie" businessmen and businesswomen jog by on their morning exercise route. In a gentrified neighborhood, Jamaican nannies with strollers take their white "charges" (babies) to the nearby grocery store. Middle-class women in the suburbs ply the roads back and forth to the shopping mall. Our cities are varied and vibrant places, with opportunities for economic and social success, but they are also sites that restrict and enclose possibilities.

How can we make sense of this somewhat chaotic scene? How do feminist geographers "read" the contemporary urban landscape?

To start, we need to understand that contemporary cities are constructed from layers of past structures, traditions, ideologies, and beliefs, and that any explanation of urban patterns and processes must take into account their historical contexts. Many of us live in cities that formerly were great industrial powers; their landscapes are littered with decaying built forms that once facilitated the movement of raw materials and their transformation into finished manufactured products. Others of us are surrounded by "postindustrial" landscapes: office parks and shopping centers, interlinked with highways. Still others navigate walkways that may date to the late medieval era. Each of these landscapes tells us something about the gendered relationships and gender roles that were played out in the times they were built. Those pasts continue to shape our contemporary social scene. In addition, some of our most powerful assumptions about cities and gender are rooted in a distant past. One of the most powerful of these is the assumption that the city is somehow more masculine, that it is men who are allowed to enjoy its pleasures (although Ally is telling us things may have changed, at least for a few women), while the suburbs are more feminine. Where do these associations come from? What do they tell us about the contemporary worlds in which we live?

MASCULINE CITY, FEMININE COUNTRY?

In the Euro-American tradition, we can trace the historical roots of this powerful association at least as far back as the Renaissance. Urbanist Elizabeth Wilson (1991) suggests that it was during this period (roughly 1400–1650) that the city came to be seen as masculine, in distinction to a feminine countryside. During the Renaissance, the city was envisioned as an arena where the ideals of the mind—coded as masculine—could be expressed literally and symbolically. Renaissance urban thinkers and designers thought of the city as a unified, visual whole, that should reflect rational, geometric principles, as Figure 3.1 demonstrates. The plan of Palma Nuova, designed by Vitruvius, showcases the geometric regularities that were thought to create ideal forms for urban life. These principles were exactly the ones assigned by Renaissance thinkers to the male sphere. Other qualities of human life, for example, those that pertained to the body and to the organic, were assigned to the female sphere. The countryside (with its more earthy connotations) and the older medieval city were seen as the realm of the feminine. This association of the city

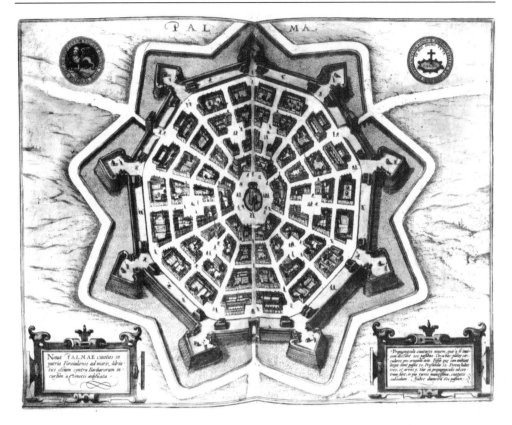

FIGURE 3.1. The ideal, planned Renaissance city of Palma Nuova, designed by Vitruvius. This plan depicts the value given to the rational principles of geometry, principles that in the Renaissance were assigned to men.

with the masculine and the rational served to align the power of the new city with men.

Medieval cities were portrayed by Renaissance commentators as feminine since they represented many of the qualities that the new order disdained. Medieval European cities grew without central planning or authority, that is, they developed organically. As population expanded in the medieval city, or as trade increased, new buildings were simply added next to the old ones. Walkways and roadways appeared haphazardly, as the need arose. From an aerial perspective, medieval cities appear chaotic, resembling a series of congeries or clusters of development appended to each other, as Figure 3.2 illustrates. This is not to suggest that there was no logic to these urban forms. On the contrary, as urban geographers have demonstrated (Vance, 1990; Carter, 1983), the form of medieval cities was well suited to the demands of medieval society and economy.

The early forms of capitalism that characterized the Renais-

FIGURE 3.2. A 1569 depiction of Paris. As a typical medieval city, Paris's plan appears rather chaotic since it grew organically, without centralized planning.

sance, however, brought new class formations and new demands to the city. One of those demands was for better circulation within the city and between the city and the countryside. The urban forms that were idealized by such Renaissance urban commentators as Leon Battista Alberti and Thomas More in the fifteenth and sixteenth centuries were set in distinction to the medieval organic form. The new cities of the Renaissance could be visualized from afar as rational wholes, not as organic patches attached to each other in haphazard and unplanned ways.

Americans have inherited from the European intellectual tradition a way of conceptualizing the city that dates from the Renaissance. The modern U.S. city is rational, planned, orderly; in other words, it is masculine. The countryside on which the city is imposed is represented as feminine. The city is seen as the expression of the human intellect's dominance over nature—man controls nature. Elizabeth Wilson (1991) argues, therefore, that the feminine in the city has always represented a challenge to that rational world; the feminine represents the disorderly, the chaotic, the unknowable. And although this may seem a rather abstract idea, it has real implications:

the presence of women on the streets of the city has invariably been seen as problematic, as we will argue throughout this chapter.

THE EARLY MODERN CITY

Most Renaissance cities had medieval (or even older) antecedents. Only a few Renaissance cities were built from scratch. Palma Nova, completed in 1593 in northern Italy, shows this ideal form. For the most part, the ideals of rational urban planning with grand visual spectacles were limited by reality—most societies lacked the financial and technological means to completely reconstruct medieval urban forms. The changes that occurred in urban infrastructure happened slowly and incrementally. Most urban dwellers in the early modern period (1500s–1700s) occupied dwellings and worked in structures dating from the medieval period. Yet the changes in social and economic power wrought by early forms of capitalism during this period were both reflected in and comprised of changes in the spatial layout and three-dimensional forms of the city.

We can see some of these forces shaping London, for example, a city that rose to dominance during this time period. In medieval London, most craftspeople and merchants lived above their shops, combining in one location work and home. Women were typically engaged in productive labor with their fathers or husbands, or were involved in their own forms of commerce such as selling produce, making and selling cloth, or brewing and selling beer.

Yet as England's control over seagoing trade increased during the early modern period, production and sales activities expanded. A London merchant who traded in woolen cloths, for example, would find both the supply of wool and demand for his cloth on the increase. He needed a place to store his inventory close to the docks where his ship was moored, and perhaps a separate location close to the main market and banking facilities in the center of London for his office. Finding space on the first floor of his residence no longer useful for business, he might convert it into larger and more elegant living quarters for his family. Or, as his business became more successful, he might decide that his family should move out of its old and now unstylish medieval dwelling to a house in one of the newer areas of the city.

Those new residential districts were located on the western edges of medieval London, close to Westminster, home to the royal court, and therefore close to the aristocracy. This lent an air of nobility to this new class of merchants, and helped legitimize their newfound wealth and power. Merchant residential areas, such as

Covent Garden and Bloomsbury Square, were now important symbols of the wealth and status of the families who resided in them.

In modernizing London, not only did work and home become physically separated from each other in the city, but each became important indicators of new identities and values. As we mentioned in Chapter 1, it was during this time period, the fifteenth to the seventeenth centuries, that the values associated with the private realm of home and those with the public realm of work came to be defined in distinction to each other. The new masculine, public sphere was defined by values of egalitarianism and economic utility, while the feminine, private sphere was governed by the value of familial deference and emotional ties. These distinct value systems were expressed and reinforced in space. The workplace for the new merchant expressed his business acumen, while his home expressed his culture and style. Although still involved in work in their homes, the wives of these merchants were now increasingly in charge of representing their family's new cultural identity—that is, their jobs now included home decoration, knowing and using correct manners and etiquette, creating ornamental and beautiful gardens, and clothing their families in appropriate styles.

These immense spatial and ideological changes did not happen quickly, nor did these changes affect everyone in the same way. Nevertheless, cities like London were massively reorganized both physically and symbolically, as they emerged from medievalism into modernism (Bowden, 1975). Recent scholarship on London has revealed the ways in which masculine and feminine identities were expressed in the public spaces of early modern cities (Solkin, 1992; Habermas, 1991; Ogborn, 1998). New retailing and residential areas circumscribed an emerging feminine sensibility. In London in the eighteenth century, as in many other large European cities at the same time, shops were moved indoors and clustered in areas near their former outdoor market sites. Previously, when goods needed to be placed indoors, they were often moved to the first floor of houses that lined the outdoor market space, not to spaces specifically set aside for selling and buying. The new shops of the eighteenth century, however, were devoted to the processes of consumption—to the ritualized bartering process that was now moved from the public marketplace into the semiprivate interior space of the shop.

According to Elizabeth Kowaleski-Wallace (1997), this development of interior spaces designed for selling went hand in hand with the evolution of gendered roles and "performances" within the stores: the business of selling was "figured" in masculine terms, while the activities associated with buying were "figured" as feminine. Behavior in the shops were regulated by certain codes of respectability borrowed from established gender roles: "Thus, in the modern shop, the interiorized processes of salesmanship are borrowed from preexisting ideological definitions of gender. . . . The seller was most often cast in the dominant, or masculine role of the seducer and the buyer, characterized either by her malleability or by her disruptive desires, as feminine. In the parlance of the time, the buyer became the one to be 'seduced' as well as mastered" (86–87). Appropriate feminine behavior was reflected by and reinforced through the activities of the bourgeois woman as she visited, viewed, bargained for, and purchased goods in the new shops in central London. Masculine behavior took shape around the figure of the seller.

Other spaces in the city were designed to reform the "inappropriate" woman. One such space in London was the Magdalen Hospital that opened near the city's eastern border in 1758. The institution was meant to reform prostitutes who, in mid-eighteenth-century London, were figured as fallen women, yet believed to be malleable enough to be remade into respectable women through the power of individual meditation and prayer. The reformatory process required particular spaces where prostitutes could be afforded a sense of privacy and solitude—in these closed interior spaces they could meditate on their past sins and remake themselves into rational and self-controlled women. According to geographer Miles Ogborn (1998), the Magdalen Hospital was designed to effect this transformation: the ground plan was open enough that women's daily rituals of work, prayer, and meditation were constantly under scrutiny, although each woman did have space for private meditation in the form of a separate bed with curtains. At the end of three years in the hospital, following this strict regime of work and prayer, a woman could be considered reformed, that is, able to control her base instincts and resist temptation. She could now return to her family, to continue her reformatory process by applying the appropriate, self-controlled, feminine behavior that she had learned in the hospital to the serving of tea and other feminized rituals of the domestic spaces, and to the buying of goods in the new shopping areas of the city.

Masculine identities were reflected and reinforced in the taverns, coffeehouses, and clubs of the city. Coffeehouses, for example, emerged in London in the mid-seventeenth century, and became important social institutions for England's merchant classes (Figure 3.3). Coffee was originally an expensive import into England, reserved for the nobility. But mercantilism made coffee affordable for the English middle classes by the late seventeenth century, even while it retained its association with the nobility. Drinking coffee, then, was a sign of rising class status, as it not only connoted aristocratic aspirations, but served to distinguish its adherents from those who drank beer and whiskey in taverns. It also connoted a masculine identity. Most coffeehouses barred women, since they were important sites for political and economic discussions.

FIGURE 3.3. View inside a London coffeehouse, c. 1650. Coffeehouses emerged in early modern London as public spaces for the city's new middle classes, and for the acting out of masculine identities. Notice the lack of women in this view; most coffeehouses at the time barred women from entering.

And these new spaces were not located randomly. Most of London's coffeehouses in the seventeenth century were near Cornhill, and along Fleet Street and the Strand, close to the city's emerging financial, publishing, and legal districts. In this way, men working in these areas could drop in to the coffeehouses frequently. For example, the hypothetical cloth merchant we introduced earlier could easily stop in to a coffeehouse on his way from business dealings near Cornhill, discuss the political and economic news of the day with fellow merchants and other men of the emerging professional classes, and return home to his family in the new West End of the city, perhaps in one of the residential squares. All these activities played important roles in expressing his identities: he was a private business figure while at his office in the city, a political and civic participant in the public life of London while at the coffeehouse, a patriarch when he returned to his home.

And yet the spatial and ideological distinction between the masculine and the feminine was often disrupted. The lives of most men and women crossed the boundaries of those distinctions. One of the most important "crossings" was created by the new (seventeenth- and eighteenth-century) definition of femininity that required bourgeois women to become the main consumers for households. This, of course, required women to enter the spaces of business. In London, this meant that women left their residential enclaves in the West End and ventured close to the city, to the emerging retail district along Cheapside. The women depicted in Figure 3.4 has put on her shopping clothes, and presumably will soon be entering a shop, armed with her desires for goods and her skills at negotiating. She has therefore taken on an active role in the important business of the day—a potentially disruptive fact given prescribed roles of femininity that supposedly separated women from the world of commerce. As Kowaleski-Wallace argues, "Because shopping could be depicted as a disruptive chaotic activity, where retailers could be exhausted by an insatiable female desire to see without buying, women were continually viewed as powerful agents, capable of subverting the retail scene" (1997: 87). This ideological and spatial "border crossing" was economically necessary (because the new consumerism fueled England's mercantilism), but it was socially disruptive since it meant that women had to enter the commercial city and engage in commercial activity. But these crossings only serve to highlight the exceptions to what had already become a rule by the sixteenth and seventeenth centuries: the ideological and increasingly physical separation between the masculine and the feminine spheres. London, and then of course most Western cities, took shape around these two worlds: a public masculine world of work, industry, and professionalism, and a private feminine world of home, family, and love.

THE INDUSTRIAL CITY

The ideological division between the masculine and the feminine spheres was given full voice and spatial form in the industrial city. The Industrial Revolution of the eighteenth and nineteenth centuries accelerated the socioeconomic forces that led to a segregation of land uses in European and U.S. cities. With industrialization, entire

The cold, not cruelty makes her weare
In Winter, furrs and Wild beasts haire
Winter
For a smoother skinn at night,
Embraceth her with more delight.

FIGURE 3.4. An etching of a woman walking in Cornhill, by W. Hollar, 1643. Even though the early modern city of London was separated into residential, feminine areas and public, masculine areas, many individuals "crossed" these symbolic borders. As consumers, many middle-class women, such as the one depicted here, came into the city to purchase goods.

sections of cities were taken over for industrial uses: factories, railroads, warehouses, and machine shops. Residential areas too became segregated in relation to industry. The working classes lived in areas close to industry, while the middle and upper classes fled to the other side of town. A social gradient of sorts operated in the typical industrial city, one that was often linked to a topographical gradient: those with enough money lived furthest away (and usually uphill) from the factories and the increasingly noisy downtown, those with fewer means lived wherever they could afford, often close to factories.

The working classes were often caught in the squeeze of competing land uses in the new dynamic industrial city. In nineteenth-century New York City, for example, we know that many working-class
families moved yearly, pushed out as rents increased to keep up with
the city's continually shifting land values (Scherzer, 1992; Blackmar,
1989). Yet many middle- and upper-class families also frequently
moved their places of residence. They were not forced out of rental
property because of high rents, but instead moved because they
found themselves in locations that were shifting from residential to
retail or office uses, or because they realized that newer and therefore more stylish residential areas were located further from the
downtown than their own houses. What we find in nineteenth-century industrial cities, particularly in the United States, is a very unstable urban form, one that was expanding outward at varying rates, at
the same time that its land uses were becoming more dense (Figure
3.5). This simultaneous explosion and implosion of urban growth
was most apparent in those cities that gained the most wealth from
industrialization, such as New York and Chicago, but was also evident to lesser degrees in most other cities.

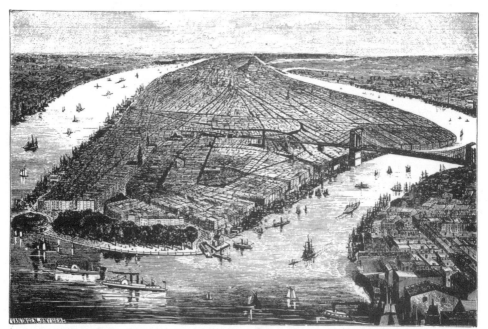

GENERAL VIEW OF NEW YORK CITY, SHOWING THE BRIDGE CONNECTING IT WITH BROOKLYN.

FIGURE 3.5. View of New York City, c. 1872. Industrialization fueled New York City's
growth north up Manhattan, east across the Brooklyn Bridge to Brooklyn, and west to
New Jersey.

New types of spaces were created in the U.S. industrial city. Some, such as a men's "club row," were developed out of impulses similar to those active in the early modern city—that is, to provide social spaces for the city's leading male citizens to gather and form economic and political allegiances. In mid-nineteenth century New York City, for example, this club row was located along several blocks of Fifth Avenue just north of the major shopping area of the city. In the elegant interior spaces of these clubs, men could exchange important economic and political news of the day while sipping sherry and chatting socially. Women returning from their shopping to their upper-class enclaves uptown were often subject to the gaze of these clubmen as they watched the passing parade along Fifth Avenue, though oftentimes shopping women paid little heed to the attention as they proceeded with their own business and socializing. Other masculine spaces in the city served solely social, and more explicitly predatory, purposes: saloons, gambling houses, and male-only restaurants such as oyster houses. In these places, men partook of the pleasures of the city only open to them and to "unrespectable" women: drink, dancing, gambling, and sex. An entire genre of guidebooks to the city, called "Gentlemen's Guides," directed newcomers and locals alike to the hidden doorways and underground cellars where male prerogative guided behavior.

Other types of new spaces were created in reaction to industrialism. Most U.S. cities developed a public park system, providing open space, leisure activities, and aesthetic oases in the middle of industrial, congested areas. Often the impetus behind the development of these parks was a desire by the city's dominant classes to visibly express their civic commitment and to provide a more refined cultural image of their city. Cities openly competed with each other to have the largest, or the most stylish, park or park system. For a while in late nineteenth century, the noted landscape architect F. L. Olmsted was a much-sought-after man. The parks also produced social, leisure spaces for women and the working classes. In fact, as historian Roy Rosenzwieg (1983) has shown, many urban parks were designed specifically for the working classes, in an attempt to create "better" workers by providing them with controlled and "safe" forms of leisure activities. And for some middle- and upper-class women, the new park spaces provided a "legitimate" way for them to socialize outside of the house (Figure 3.6).

In addition, as we will explore in more detail later, industrial cities were further segregated into consumer districts and office districts. By the late nineteenth century most cities could boast of a consumer district downtown comprised of department stores, smaller boutiques, restaurants, theaters, and bars (Figure 3.7). Construction of office buildings began in earnest in the late nineteenth

THE DRIVE IN THE CENTRAL PARK, NEW YORK, SEPTEMBER, 1860.

FIGURE 3.6. A Winslow Homer drawing, *The Drive in Central Park, New York, September, 1860*, that appeared in *Harper's Weekly*. Partly as a reaction to industrialism, many cities invested in park areas. New York's Central Park was one of the most grand. Many middle- and upper-class women of the city found it a prime space to socialize outside of the home.

century, to house new industries such as life insurance that employed large numbers of white-collar workers. So the industrial city of the nineteenth century had a downtown divided between a consumer/leisure district and an office district, other social spaces on the edges of middle-class districts, and a public park system located throughout. The creation of these geographically distinct activities spawned demand for different forms of transportation. As cities expanded, foot traffic, streetcars, carriages, and wagons all jockeyed for space on the busy and often congested streets of the city.

On the one hand, we could imagine that this dynamic urban form would lead to more opportunities and spaces for women, and in some senses, as we will see, it did. Yet on the other hand, such unstable socioeconomic and spatial conditions created social anxiety, especially among economic and political elites. One way of assuaging those anxieties was to attempt to regulate the seemingly chaotic forces that threatened the stability of society. All groups of people

FIGURE 3.7. Photograph of T. E. Fitzgerald's Bar, 1912. Many of the new masculine spaces of the industrial city were little different from the taverns of previous centuries: places for men to congregate, discuss public events, and act out masculine identities.

not of the dominant order—women, people of color, the working classes—were subject to varying forms of regulations regarding their appearance, their behavior, their housing, their sexuality, and their jobs in nineteenth-century cities. These behaviors and regulations were both social and spatial at the same time. For example, in mid-nineteenth-century New York, bourgeois women were allowed access to the public streets of the city, but only if they were accompanied by other women or men, and only at certain hours of the day. Women who disobeyed these social rules risked losing their status as "proper" women.

The industrial city presents a rich palette for thinking about gender and space. Its instability created possibilities for new gender identities, and at the same time challenged traditional identities. We will structure our discussion, then, around these two sides of the same coin.

Working Women

The industrial city in Europe and the United States presented expanded economic opportunities for all those women in need of waged labor: single women, women who supported their families, immigrant women whose wages were sent to another country or to rural areas within the United States. The textile industry, one of the booming industries of both Great Britain and the United States, was a particularly important source of women's jobs (Figure 3.8). The industrial production of cloth and other textiles had a long and intimate association with women's labor, dating back at least to the medieval period. In the United States the first to work in textile factories were women, recruited as cheap and available labor from rural New England.

Not all women in the textile industry worked in factories. As Christine Stansell (1987) demonstrates, for example, most women in the cloth industry in New York City before 1850 worked at home. The form of the city precluded large factories, and the nature of the textile industry at this time was such that most clothing was handsewn, not mass-produced. "Outworking," as it was called, took various forms, from entire families including children involved in the en-

THE DRESS MAKER.

FIGURE 3.8. A lithograph of a dressmaker, c. 1860. One of the most feminized jobs in industrial America was that of a dressmaker—a continuation in many ways of "traditional" women's home labor.

terprise at homes, to cooperative groups of single women renting their own space. These forms of waged work offered women opportunities to earn cash while still staying within the traditional female sphere of home. Yet it also merged traditional forms of patriarchy with the capitalist workplace, creating conditions of harsh exploitation for most women workers.

Because of shifting technologies in the textile industry after 1850, work in factories became increasingly common for women. Inside the factory, women had less control over their immediate environment, having to follow the controls and discipline of factory hours and conditions. Yet working outside the home took women away, at least temporarily, from the patriarchies of home (although this moved them into a different form of patriarchy in the factory, see Figure 3.9). The implications of large numbers of women occupying spaces outside of the home—of walking the street and riding the streetcars on the way to work, of walking back home with other women enjoying their small amounts of leisure time, and of working

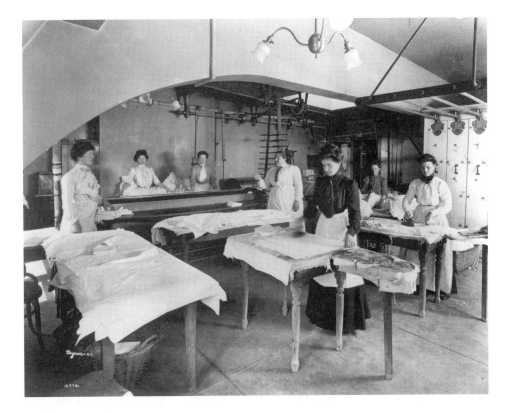

FIGURE 3.9. Photograph of women working in a laundry room, 1902. Women's jobs outside of the home may not have taken place in particularly pleasant surroundings, but they did remove them from the patriarchies at home.

in spaces governed by rules of the masculine workplace—were profound. As Stansell (1987) argues, the "factory girl" became a source of social anxiety in late-nineteenth-century cities. The poverty of a seamstress working at home to support her family was a source of anxiety to bourgeois society, but she at least was feminine, "housebound, deferential and meek" (1987: 129). The factory girl, on the other hand, was often more economically independent, and was "more venturesome and disturbing. In her anti-domesticity, she conjured up threatening possibilities in a society ideologically moored to separate sexual spheres" (1987: 129). And those possibilities led to attempts to control women's behavior in public—as we will soon see. The emerging fashion industry led to other forms of waged labor open to women, and also to possibilities of small business ownership. Many women opened their own hat shops and dress shops in the 1860s and 1870s, or were self-employed as "finishing" seamstresses. According to historian Wendy Gamber, women owned ninety-five percent of the millinery and dressmaking establishments in Boston in 1860; this same percentage also held true in 1890 (1997: 30).

Production was just one aspect of the fashion industry open to women; selling, of course, was another. In most European and U.S. cities, the late 1800s witnessed the development of department stores, large emporiums filled with material fantasies that were staffed by waged salespeople. Originally department store owners hired men for these positions, but as stores expanded and the ranks of salespeople grew, owners shifted to the cheaper labor that women could provide (Figure 3.10). As Susan Porter Benson (1986) has shown, these saleswomen occupied ambivalent positions in society. On the one hand, these new saleswoman had to look fashionable. Thus their appearance indicated that they were bourgeois women. Yet, on the other hand, they were working women, and not earning high wages. These women crossed both gender and class boundaries—they were working women, but could be mistaken for middle-class women, and they occupied spaces of the city thought to be masculine (downtown). Other working women crossed similar boundaries.

Late-nineteenth-century cities in the United States witnessed an incredible growth of financial and other service industries such as insurance and banking. With this growth came an increased need for white-collar workers such as clerical help, accountants, secretaries, and the like. Businesses originally looked to young men to fill these jobs—men who could be trained and then move up the corporate ladder. But the rapid growth of such industries as life insurance required a very large workforce, of whom only a few could be offered the hope of upward movement in the company. Women (primarily young, white, and single) were soon enlisted as workers: they were far

FIGURE 3.10. Photograph of the bargain counter at Siegal Cooper Department Store, New York City, showing the women shoppers and the women clerks. The "counter girls," as they were called, occupied ambivalent positions in society: they were working women, yet were dressed as upper-class women; they appeared feminine, yet occupied masculine positions (previously, most clerks had been men).

less expensive to employ than men, and there were no societal or individual expectations of advancement. Historian Lisa Fine argues that by the turn of the century, most women in office work were hired as stenographer-typists, and that it was "the first clerical job completely dominated by women" (1990: 20).

But women entering sites of male production in large numbers was potentially disruptive: such movement betrayed the "separate spheres" ideology that dominated Victorian society. The presence of women working in offices, mixing with men of different backgrounds and classes in spaces undifferentiated by sex, could be seen as problematic to Victorian sensibilities. One way to ease some of the tensions of women entering a "masculine" world was to "feminize" some aspects of it. Fine (1990) provides an interesting example of this in her discussion of the "feminization" of the typewriter. In the 1870s, as the typewriter was being introduced as a new technology, typewriter companies often chose women to demonstrate the technology because they believed that middle-class women already possessed a skill that predisposed them to mastering the typewriter: playing the piano! It was thought that typing, like piano playing, required manual dexterity, and a certain ease with quick, light movements. Moreover, typewriting did not require too much physical exertion. And since educated women excelled at the piano, they could excel at typing (according to this logic, at least!). Business schools that specialized in typing and stenography targeted middle-class women. An 1880 catalogue for the Bryant and Stratton Business College in Chicago stated that "ordinarily one who has the ability to play well upon the piano and especially one who has practical knowledge of phonography may become an expert typist. This department of industry is exactly suited to women" (quoted in Fine, 1990: 21–22). So the relatively new job of typing became appropriate for women. According to Fine (1990), stenography and shorthand followed suit. Men entering the white-collar workforce were trained and steered into the more prestigious and powerful jobs of middle management, while women were accorded the less prestigious, clerical work.

Reinforcing this gendered differentiation was a spatial separation in office work. Clerical workers were either grouped together in what we today call a "secretary's pool," or were assigned spaces left open for surveillance of their routine work. Women were again placed in their "separate" sphere. So tensions caused by women entering the masculine office space were eased both by making some of the jobs more feminine (for example, typing) and by reconfiguring the site into separate, gendered, workspaces. In this way, the demands of both capitalism and patriarchy were met: cheap labor was provided for a growing industry, but that labor force (middle-class women) worked in conditions and in spaces that reinforced the ideology of separate spheres. This is not to deny, however, that these new jobs provided economic opportunities for many women. The job of stenographer-typist was a fairly prestigious "profession" for women, affording many of them job training, stability, and the opportunity for self-sufficiency. These working women challenged the notion that the commercial city and the professional office were male spaces.

Historian Kathy Peiss (1986) shows how working women not only occupied masculine workplaces, but also masculine places of leisure (Figure 3.11). In New York City, for example, working women ventured to Coney Island to spend their time off, acting as full participants in the pleasures provided there. They could also visit tearooms, museums, theaters, and restaurants, though of course never alone, and most appropriately with their husbands. Women's activities in the city were always circumscribed by what was considered "appropriate" gender behavior. So even though working women began to occupy the city streets, their actions were bumping up against the boundaries of acceptable behavior. The New York City *Real Estate Record and Builders' Guide*, a weekly paper directed at those interested in the real estate and the building trades, remarked in 1881 that there should be special women's cars on the elevated railway so that the "working girls who are forced to patronize" them in the evening hours on their way home will not have to be crammed into cars with working men:

> On the East side, the cars become jammed with men before Canal Street is reached, and the vast swarm of working girls throng the platform up to 23rd Street, unable to get on the cars. They are thrust back by the brakemen, and if they do get in are forced to stand, without even the protection of the straps, which are to be found in the street cars. There ought to be special women's cars starting from Chatham Square, to run during the commission hours. If not special women's cars, then cars in which it is explicitly understood no woman shall stand while there is a man sitting. (April 30, 1881: 421)

FIGURE 3.11. Photograph of women parading along the Boardwalk, Coney Island, c. 1897. Many of New York's working women were able to partake of the city's pleasures, spending their time at Coney Island, a new leisure space of the Victorian city.

Working women, it seemed, presented challenges to the rough-and-tumble atmosphere of urban transport. In many ways, women clerical workers, like the "counter girls" of the department stores, served as lightning rods for many of the anxieties that women in the city created. Yet by challenging Victorian notions of femininity and masculinity, working women helped set the stage for the even more radical challenges of the twentieth century.

Shopping Women

Middle- and upper-class women, whose principal space was the parlor, also ventured into the "masculine" spaces of the city. America's industrial powers required mass consumption to fuel its expanding factories, particularly when military consumption declined dramatically after the Civil War. Mass-production techniques made affordable to the middle classes a range of consumer products previously reserved for the elite. The act of shopping, then, became a distinct activity, as buyers needed to compare the styles and relative worth of the range of goods now available in department stores and other smaller shops. Men were aligned with the world of production, and with the values of hard work and utility; women became aligned with the world of consumption, and the qualities that it required: leisure, playfulness, fantasy. If America's industrial structure required mass consumption to support it, then women could "indulge" in that consumption without fear of contaminating the world of work. Women, after all, were considered "naturally" more moral than men, and therefore could consume wisely, and not overindulge.

This, of course, meant that even proper bourgeois women were supposed to venture downtown and participate in the pleasures of the city. Yet having this class of women stumbling over the cobblestone streets, fighting their way through the crowds, and spending time in drab and unornamented buildings was seen as problematic. How could bourgeois women be in spaces that connoted the masculine workplace? For example, in the 1870s and 1880s, many New Yorkers voiced concerns in the daily newspapers about middle-class women riding the streetcars downtown, rubbing shoulders with men and the working classes. The *Real Estate Record and Builders' Guide* called for legal action to stop men from behaving inappropriately on the elevated cars:

> A man dressed in quite good though half-fitted clothes . . . sat down facing a very genteel and pretty little miss of eleven, and presently drew a newspaper from his pocket, placed his heels on the seat beside her, cocked his hat on one side, and began to read, and very soon, of course, to spit on the floor. The little girl drew her skirts as

far from him as she could, and looked poutingly out of the window instead of chatting gayly with her mother on the seat beside her, as she had been doing. (May 21, 1887: 694)

Clearly, the proximity of "rough" men presented a social crisis for genteel women and their children.

In response to such anxieties, the consumer spaces of downtowns were feminized in the late nineteenth century—that is, stores were made to resemble parlors. They were well organized and lit, ornamental, stylized, and made to appear as cultural, not commercial, institutions. In New York City, for example, a stretch of Broadway, and Fifth and Sixth Avenues between Union and Madison Squares became known as the "Ladies' Mile." This area contained magnificent examples of Renaissance revival stores and restaurants specifically designed to cater to the needs of bourgeois women (Domosh, 1996; Abelson, 1989). If bourgeois women had to occupy spaces in the city, then those spaces had to be feminized.

Stewart's department store, one of the first to be built in New York City, opened in 1851 and started the trend toward ornate design (Figure 3.12). Alexander Stewart, the owner, understood that the standardization of goods and prices ushered in by the factory system of production meant that price was no longer the primary means of distinguishing between goods. So, to encourage sales of goods, he displayed those goods in decorative surroundings, making the whole process of purchasing a pleasant one. Shopping in his store was now suitable for and enticing to women. The exterior of his first store, located on the corner of Broadway and Chambers Street, distinguished itself from its predecessors and all competitors by its expensive white marble façade. Inside, the four-story store centered on a large rotunda topped by a dome, with stairs leading to an encircling gallery so that the shoppers could promenade and visually assess the products available. Such architectural highlights as the white marble façade and the rotunda dome were meant to clearly associate the building with the civic structures of the city, such as City Hall. This association signaled many things: that Stewart had risen above mere merchant status to become a civic benefactor; that purchasing goods was no longer simply an economic necessity, but was now an activity unto itself, almost a civic duty; and that the women who shopped were not actually stepping out of their ordained Victorian roles, but instead were actively participating in the civic duties assigned to their sex.

Stewart's larger and grander store built in 1862 further uptown on Broadway at 10th Street reinforced these associations and set the architectural standard for the other department stores that soon followed. Again, the interior of Stewart's new building was designed as a

FIGURE 3.12. Exterior view of Stewart's 1851 department store in New York City. The white marble facade of this building made the store seem more cultural and civic than commercial, thereby creating an appropriate environment for Victorian, bourgeois women.

series of open encircling galleries, so that women shoppers could view all of the goods on display, as well as each other. Figure 3.13 offers an image of the interior of Stewart's store, depicting a bourgeois woman with her daughter participating in the feminized rituals of shopping.

The growing consumerism of the Victorian era allowed many women to venture downtown and occupy its streets and stores, but this does not necessarily mean that women were "liberated" from the cult of domesticity. What in fact happened, as we have seen, is that the spaces outside the home they were now allowed to occupy were "feminized" so as not to interfere with Victorian definitions of femi-

ninity. In fact, shopping districts served to reinforce those definitions. A woman seen along Broadway in the afternoon, surrounded
by decorative stores, dressed in her finest, greeting other women as
she promenaded on the paved sidewalks, was actively identifying herself as a proper, middle- or upper-class woman, engaged in activities
necessary and important to her family and society.

But even so, a woman downtown alone was potentially disruptive to the masculine values that governed the city. A woman needed
to be ever wary of transgressing the bounds of proper behavior. A
"proper" woman had to confine herself to the prescribed spaces
deemed appropriate for women—usually limited to the shopping district and a few other public spaces. And the timing of her trips into

FIGURE 3.13. Inside view of Stewart's 1862 department store. The design
of the store allowed for natural lighting on all floors, and enabled shoppers to view each other as well as the profusion of displayed goods. Here,
a woman imparts to her daughter the feminized rituals of shopping.

the city was equally important. A woman seen alone on Broadway after dark, for example, was certainly not a proper woman (Figure 3.14). Nor was she meant to go out in the early morning hours, when she ran the risk of sharing the street with working-class men, a particularly inappropriate behavior for middle-class women.

Nevertheless, the culture of consumption afforded middle-class women access to the dynamic city of the late nineteenth century. This offered possibilities of shifting identities, of anonymity, of encountering other cultures. If the industrial city allowed many men to act as flaneurs—that is, as anonymous observers of the dynamic streets and buildings and people of the city—then it also allowed some women, at certain times and in particular circumstances, to act as what Janet Wolff calls the *flaneuse*—the Victorian predecessor of Ally McBeal. For example, the department store itself was designed so that women could visually assess the scene: they could survey not only the goods for sale, but also the other women in the store. The new industrial city provided other new opportunities for women, allowing them to meet each other away from their homes in lunchrooms and teahouses, to travel on streetcars, to take carriage rides in the new parks,

FIGURE 3.14. Lithograph of a woman "walking the gauntlet" on Broadway. The streets of the city were carefully coded by an intricate time–space geography. Women seen alone on particular streets and at certain times found their reputations tarnished.

and to promenade on the streets. Paralleling this movement into the public spaces of the city, middle-class women became more involved in public and even political activities. As historian Mary Ryan (1990) tells us, many middle-class women became engaged in voluntary benevolent institutions, in women's clubs, and in political organzations. Many of these women's clubs extended women's influence into the public sphere, where they took up important civic duties including social work, urban reform, and city beautification. Women became actors in their own right on the downtown streets of nineteenth-century cities. To many, such actions presented a threat to the status quo, a threat that needed to be regulated.

Regulating Women

Although the Victorian cult of domesticity dictated that women's place was in the home, most women, as we have seen, also occupied public areas of the city either as working women or as consuming women. Yet to see a woman promenading alone on the street, or a group of women out for the evening enjoying the pleasures of the city, was problematic to proper bourgeois sensibilities. Such women clearly were out of place; they were not engaged in the activities of the feminine sphere. Women's everyday behavior in the public areas of the city, then, was watched carefully and monitored for propriety; women themselves had to monitor where and when and with whom they were seen. These subtle, personal forms of regulation are difficult to discern from the historical record, although insights can be gleaned from novels. In Edith Wharton's (1984) *The House of Mirth*, published in 1905, for example, Lily Bart makes a fatal error in her rise to social prominence when she allows herself to be seen on the wrong street at the wrong time of day with the wrong man. As Lily thinks to herself, "Why must a girl pay so dearly for her least escape from routine? Why could one never do a natural thing without having to screen it behind a structure of artifice?" (14). Such impropriety condemned her to declining social fortunes. Lily clearly had not read the many etiquette books and women's magazines of the time that directed women in every aspect of their public behavior—for example, how to hold your head and how to look while walking on the street, what to do if you encounter a man you know on the promenade, how (and if!) you could eat in public, and so on.

Behavior on the streets of Victorian cities was governed by strict social codes, for men and women, for the working class and the middle class, for black and white. For those not in power, the penalties for breaking those codes were severe. For women, the implications often revolved around their sexuality. One of the most common terms for prostitution, after all, is "streetwalker." A "woman of the streets" implies a woman whose sexuality is not contained within the home. In the United States and Great Britain, the regulation of prostitution became a focus of social concern during the nineteenth century. Prostitution was seen as the definitive example of the havoc wreaked by the "public" woman. Women in control of their own sexuality and with dominion over the streets were a primary threat to the ideology of separate spheres.

Although prostitution had long been a fact of life in most Western cities, it came to be defined as a "social problem" only in the mid-nineteenth century. Those who set out to reform the evils of prostitution often focused on the health problems of the women involved in prostitution and the threat of the spread of disease. To contain disease, reformers concentrated their energies on identifying and limiting the spatial mobility of prostitutes. In Great Britain, this reform effort culminated in the passage of the Contagious Disease Acts of the late 1860s. These acts created a system for the police to identify, register, and examine prostitutes for venereal disease (VD). Women with VD were locked up in a hospital for up to nine months. Similar types of legislation followed in most parts of the English-speaking world, including those areas under British colonial rule. Interestingly, as Luise White tells us in her study of prostitution in colonial Nairobi, such reform efforts were not taken up in British-controlled Africa, because, she argues, it would have complicated "the business of colonial rule, which consistently saw African sexual behavior as something beyond legislation" (1990: 176)—in other words, because racist stereotypes positioned African women as more "naturally" sexual than white women, African women's promiscuity presented less of a threat than white women's promiscuity to established morality.

So perhaps it was not really disease control that was the issue. Only when prostitution was seen as a threat to particular social orders was it regulated, not when it threatened women's health. And the regulations and concerns over the "fallen woman" bore little relationship to the realities that drove women into the sex trade. As Christine Stansell suggests, "The problem of prostitution as reformers defined it had no necessary relation to the experience of the women involved. For laboring women, prostitution was a particular kind of choice presented by the severities of daily life" (1987: 172). Working-class women had to support themselves and their families. The economic growth that brought them into the city in the first place, as domestic servants or as factory girls, often failed to provide them with a living wage. Prostitution became an option little different from other forms of "dependency on men" (1987: 179) that working-class women faced.

THE MODERN CITY

The most significant urban spatial development of the first half of the twentieth century was the degree to which most American cities became suburbanized. As we have already discussed in chapter 1, by the early twentieth century, living outside the city became both feasible and desirable for those who could afford it. The development of reliable and cheap intraurban transportation via streetcars (and later, the automobile), allowed middle-class people to flee what many considered the noisy and congested city. This movement of the middle and upper classes to the suburbs was followed by the movement of the businesses that relied on them. In the early 1900s, businesses such as small clothing retailers, drugstores, and grocery stores migrated to the avenues that led out of the city and into the suburban developments. As business and money left the city, the value of land in certain downtown areas declined. This decline was further exacerbated by governmental policies that favored the investment of money in the new suburban areas.

For middle-class women, life in the new suburbs was significantly different from what they had experienced in the city. Most importantly, they were now living distant from the city—they were spatially removed from the public spaces of the city. Trips downtown, to go shopping, to visit museums, or simply to see the urban spectacle, were now more difficult, and therefore less frequent. This spatial isolation of women in the suburbs contributed to, and reinforced, a renewed ideal of domesticity. In the early-twentieth-century United States, the prevailing ideology of middle-class life declared the "pastoral" suburbs to be the best environment in which to raise children and care for a family. The city was seen as dirty, chaotic, and immoral, while the suburbs were seen as clean, orderly, and filled with moral promise. That promise centered on the nuclear family, the single-family home they inhabited, and the domestic virtues that the woman of the house embodied.

World War I accelerated the move to the suburbs. Housing demand exceeded supply during the war years, and in the prosperity that followed the war, many Americans found they could afford to buy a home in the new developments on the fringes of their city. As historian Margaret Marsh tells us, the 1920s was the first time that population growth in the suburbs exceeded that of the cities: "The fringe areas of America's cities grew at a rate of 33.2 percent; the inner core at 24.2 percent" (1990: 132). She attributes much of this growth to the middle classes, many of whom could now afford new housing and were looking to escape their old neighborhoods, where

blacks and many European immigrants now lived. The newly liberated woman (the battle for women's suffrage was finally won in 1920)
was free to vote her conscience, but her only real options in life were
to be a wife and mother, and to set up house in the suburbs.

The new suburbs were portrayed as bulwarks of democracy.
Home ownership was seen as a way of combating the rise of bol-
shevism: good American citizens were those who owned their own
homes. As Marsh points out, many popular women's magazines of
the time promoted this ideology. The editor of the *American Home*,
for example, wrote in 1929: "At the back and beginning of [patrio-
tism] is the home. Pride of home, reverence for home, affection for
home, loyalty to home lie at the very foundation of true patrio-
tism. . . . Homeless people make poor citizens" (quoted in Marsh,
1990: 147). Not only was home ownership a symbol of U.S. patrio-
tism, it was also seen as an antidote to class unrest. The early decades
of the twentieth century witnessed significant labor unrest, and in
1919, at the conclusion of World War I, four million people were on
strike in the United States (Hayden, 1984: 32). Spurred on by social
reform efforts, many industrialists began to look not only to providing better wages to keep their workforce content, but also to providing better housing. Encouraging and enabling working-class families
to own their own homes was thought to promote a steady and responsible workforce (for example, long-term mortgages ensured a
commitment to work), at the same time that it provided seemingly
endless possibilities for home consumption (Figure 3.15). Backed by
a decent "family" wage (a wage sufficient enough to allow only the
male head of household to work), working-class families could now
fully participate in the emerging consumer economy. As Dolores
Hayden has argued, "Both union leaders and manufacturers agreed
that a more spacious, mass-produced form of housing was essential
to enable workers and their families to consume" (1984: 33). Those
mass-produced, "spacious" forms of housing were located in the suburbs (Figure 3.16).

As we noted in Chapter 1, the move to the suburbs was accelerated even more after World War II. The domestic ideal centered
around the nuclear family was given a further boost by the postwar
ideology (supported by governmental policies) promoting child rearing. Yet in some important ways the U.S. suburbs of the 1950s
differed from those of the 1920s. First of all, the new technology of
mass housing production, combined with governmental policies that
made financing easy for veterans, made home ownership for the
working classes even more accessible. By the 1950s, then, suburbs
were losing their exclusivity.

Another significant difference between 1920s and 1950s suburbs was that more women worked outside of the home. Having ex-

FIGURE 3.15. The title page of *Good Homes Make Contented Workers*, 1919. Ideals of home ownership that characterized the new suburbs were supported and promoted by industrial corporations, who believed that monthly mortgage payments encouraged a responsible workforce.

GOOD HOMES
MAKE
CONTENTED
WORKERS

FIGURE 3.16. Aerial view of a portion of Levittown, Long Island, New York, 1947. The renewed domesticity of the postwar United States was reflected in, and in turn shaped by, the mass-produced suburban developments like Levittown that made affordable to many the "dream" of single-family home ownership.

perienced the freedom as well as the added income of paid labor during World War II, many women were reluctant to give it up afterward (no matter how energetically they were encouraged to do so). As Marsh tells us, "In 1950, five years after the war had ended, a quarter of married women were still in the paid work force, and the number kept growing" (1990: 186). Suburban women found jobs in the businesses that throughout the 1950s and 1960s were moving out of the city and into the suburban fringe. First retailers, and then other businesses such as branch banks, followed the middle classes as they left the city. These businesses were willing if not eager to employ—at lower wages than most men—the women of the suburbs. By the 1960s, the suburbs, ironically, were becoming urbanized, and in doing so were offering to women many of the same liberating opportunities that their predecessors found in the industrial city.

The ideological and spatial shift in favor of the suburbs had longterm and devastating effect on the centers of U.S. cities. As money poured into the suburbs, it left the inner city, creating a relationship that geographer Neil Smith (1984) has referred to as "uneven development." The flows of capital into the suburbs and out of portions of the city are related—investors sought the greatest return on their money and therefore invested in the suburbs. Cities, no longer valued as good environments for families, and by the 1960s not considered good sites for economic investment, were emptied of much of their tax base and of their symbolic and economic value. In addition, public policies from the late 1940s onward encouraged new, single-family construction in the suburbs over reinvestment in older housing units in the cities, while at the same time federal and local governments chose inner-city locations for subsidized housing. As a result, the "projects," as they came to be known, were built in the central areas at many U.S. cities, where they were surrounded by areas of declining land values. In turn, this led to a perception that conflated these rundown areas and often poorly built structures with the residents who lived there. In most U.S. cities, the residents were primarily black single mothers; in 1978, approximately seventy-three percent of households in public housing were headed by women, and the majority of those women were minorities (Breitbart and Pader, 1995). Black, single mothers therefore became stigmatized as both the cause and result of the "culture of poverty" that seemed to permeate the inner city, while white, nuclear families living in the new suburbs were seen as the embodiments of U.S. affluence and progress.

This perception of cities as dangerous, almost pathological, spaces inhabited by minorities and single mothers, was self-fulfilling—more and more businesses, jobs, and services left the city. Retailing was one of the first to go—shopping centers expanded along the access routes in and out of most major U.S. cities in the

1950s. This development was followed by the creation of the first malls that opened in the early 1960s. Between 1963 and 1972, the share of all retail sales that took place in the suburbs versus the city in the United States went from 48.5 percent to 65 percent (Muller, 1976). At the same time, activities that had always been located in the cities for other reasons—access to transportation, to the labor force, to energy sources, and to capital supply—began to shift their locations to the fringes. In the suburbs, industrial parks and office parks marked these changes; meanwhile, in the cities, empty warehouses, idled factories, and vacant commercial buildings bore witness to these significant changes. For the women and men who could not afford to follow their jobs to the suburbs, or who were prevented from doing so by racism, this decline in economic activity in the cities was devastating. Suburban women, on the other hand, found themselves living in new and economically booming areas—although their participation in that new economy was still limited by their roles as housewives and mothers.

THE POSTMODERN CITY

A generalized portrait of a "typical" contemporary, U.S. city would look something like this: a downtown with skyscrapers representing the power of financial capital, a decaying inner core with patches of gentrified residential areas, middle- and upper-class suburbs surrounding the city and expanding outward, and highways linked by access roads lined with shopping centers. Many Sunbelt cities (cities whose growth has occurred primarily after World War II, such as Miami, Houston, and Los Angeles) don't have much of a traditional downtown, but instead have developed more as a series of clusters at critical junctions in the highway system. Some of the largest cities have managed to maintain an economically viable downtown (for example, New York, Chicago), while some middle-sized cities have not (for example, Detroit, Cleveland). Yet all of these different forms of the contemporary city share certain characteristics typical of the postmodern era: declining industrial and inner-city areas, pockets of gentrification, suburban expansion, the dominance of consumer economies. These new geographies both reflect and shape gender identities.

Crime and Safety

Many women have come to fear the city itself, since they feel that their own physical safety is at risk there. Much of their fear is focused on urban public spaces, such as streets, parks, and subways. Although most violence against women is actually perpetrated in the private spaces of home, it is those spaces defined as "public" that the majority of women fear most.

One of the results of this fear is that most women live under a self-imposed "curfew." They avoid walking in certain places, at particular times, and often will not go out alone. Geographer Gill Valentine has argued that this behavioral response to our fear of crime constitutes a "spatial expression of patriarchy" (1992: 27), since it reflects and reinforces the traditional notion that women belong at home, not on the streets. Given our previous discussion about how the city has been gendered as masculine and the suburb as feminine throughout much of Western history, this is not surprising. Further research demonstrates that this fear of public spaces is true for women of all socioeconomic classes, ages, and stages in the life cycle. Interestingly, one of the few differences that geographer Rachel Pain (1997) found in her study of women's fear of violence was that middle-class women and younger women underestimated to a greater degree the risk of physical assault in their homes—perhaps reflecting their beliefs that domestic violence happens to "other" women and not to themselves. "For middle class women (except for those who have personal experience), knowledge of domestic violence is more often based on what they have read or seen on television and so the threat is more easily distanced from the self" (Pain, 1997: 239).

Women's perceptions of risk from crime in the city, and the gendered association of the city as male, are mutually reinforcing. There are real risks to women who venture into the wrong street at the wrong time, but our culture also tends to exaggerate those risks, thereby keeping women in their "place" (at home).

Homelessness

For some women, there is no home. Homelessness in the United States has reached critical levels in the past thirty years for several reasons. Urban communities have been disrupted and their residents uprooted by urban renewal projects since the 1960s, and more recently by gentrification. The stock of affordable housing has declined, as government housing support has plummeted. In addition, deindustrialization has left many without jobs and without the skills necessary to obtain a job in the new information economies.

Women are susceptible to homelessness in particular ways. They are often the most vulnerable to economic changes and to reductions in government social welfare programs. Rising divorce rates often leave women without adequate resources to provide for themselves and their children. The fact that women earn less than men and often have less access to advanced educational or vocational training leaves them vulnerable to economic shifts. In addition, many thousands of women are made homeless as they flee domestic violence.

Gentrification

Many large Western cities have witnessed in the past thirty years a process known as *gentrification*, the movement of some middle- and upper-class residents into working-class, inner-city neighborhoods. For example, in many U.S. cities, downtown residential areas that in the nineteenth century were desirable to the well-off, became undesirable to them in the early twentieth century. But by the 1970s, however, some members of the new wealthy classes were "rediscovering" these neighborhoods as housing alternatives to the suburbs of their childhood. Gentrification is not just residential. The process of urban decline followed by the reinvestment of money often happens in commercial areas. For example, warehouses along a river that once served an industrial purpose might now be converted into high-tech offices with views out to a waterway that now boasts sailboats, not cargo ships.

The reasons for gentrification are complex. They include deindustrialization (areas of cities once considered unsuitable for middle-class residences because they were close to factories or transportation corridors are now seen as desirable because they have "historical" significance, have water views, and no longer have noisy industries); shifting demographics (some members of the baby-boom generation have come of age with different expectations concerning family life and the roles of men and women, and those new ideals of family life may not be met by the traditional norms embodied in the suburban residence); and changes in public policy (the massive decline in the tax base of many cities spurred on urban policies that encouraged investment in the inner city). The results are new types of neighborhoods, both commercial and residential, within the postmodern city. These new communities accommodate new social identities.

Geographers Liz Bondi and Caroline Mills have analyzed gentrified residential neighborhoods in Edinburgh, Scotland (Bondi, 1998) and Vancouver, Canada (Mills, 1993), highlighting the new socioeconomic class identities that are expressed there. In her study of the gentrified neighborhood of Fairview Slopes, Mills (1993) portrays residents whose social identities are based on conspicuous consumption. This "yuppie" class, where both men and women are employed as professionals, expresses its wealth with elaborate and avant-garde home decor, in a way echoing their Victorian predecessors. Yet changing gender roles have shifted the meaning of this

form of domesticity. For example, the wife in a yuppie couple is typically a full economic partner with her husband, and her identity is expressed and reinforced as much in her workplace as in her home.
The gentrified home that Mills describes, then, is less an expression
of ideals of femininity, and more an expression of the couple's joint
economic status.

This is not to say that there is not a gendering of gentrification.
As Liz Bondi (1998) points out, many gentrifiers are single women
and single mothers, who move into the city to have better access to
jobs and/or child care. Many gentrified neighborhoods are comprised of a majority of women. Their very presence within the city re-
makes our notions about its purported masculinity. Gentrification,
in a surprising twist, has thus led in some instances to a "feminization" of the city: a renewed presence of women, children, and the
domestic within the public spaces of the city. And yet, because of the
fear of violent crime, women's relationship to the public spaces of
the city are still different from that of men. As Bondi has reported in
a recent study, even middle-class, professional women, living in "desirable," gentrified neighborhoods, feel constrained in their behavior on the streets.

Yet gentrification takes many forms, and in some instances can
create streets and public spaces that are considered more safe than
before. For example, the revival of nightlife that has occurred in one
section of Manchester, England, the result of a gentrified, gay social
space called the "Village," has created an area that is widely considered safe (Quilley, 1997) (Figure 3.17). This is particularly true for
women, since gay nightlife on the streets does not carry with it an un-
dertone of heterosexual predation that forms so much a part of
straight nightclubs and bars.

This association of gentrification with gay neighborhoods is
common. In fact, gay and lesbian communities have been key actors
in the gentrification process in most cities. Suburban social codes
hold little appeal for most gay men and lesbians, who, from the turn
of the century onward (and most likely earlier) have looked to the
heterogeneity and anonymity of the modern city to provide them
with alternative spaces. And since gentrification originally occurred
in portions of the city that were no longer important spaces for the
mainstream, this left such spaces "open" to a flow of gay and lesbian
culture and capital. Urban scholars have identified lesbians and gay
men as key actors (for example, as realtors, investors, designers, and
entrepreneurs) in the process of residential and commercial gentrification in many Western cities, from Melbourne to Manchester, from
Amsterdam to New Orleans (Knopp, 1990; Binnie, 1995).

And although gay men seem to predominate as actors in the urban land market, Tamar Rothenberg's (1995) study of Park Slope in

FIGURE 3.17. Photograph of a festival in the "Village" of Manchester, England. Gay men are often at the forefront of gentrification, seeking alternative spaces within the city. As a result, many public spaces, such as this city street, are now considered "safe" for women.

Brooklyn, New York, highlights the role of lesbians in creating their own social spaces as part of the gentrification process. Lesbians were originally attracted to Park Slope because of its old and attractive housing stock, but also because of the area's reputation as a center of leftist political activism. That the community grew and developed, however, was due to social networking and a feeling on the part of lesbians that it was a safe place to outwardly express their identities. As Rothenberg states, the community of Park Slope "provides a respite from an incessantly heterosexist society, and enables them to be themselves and to meet other women as friends or potential lovers" (1995: 179).

Relationships between gentrified gay culture, urban politics, and large-scale socioeconomic change are complex. Quilley's (1997) analysis of the creation of the gay Village in Manchester portrays a case study of this complex relationship. The rise of gay-identified spaces in Manchester coincided with two important developments: the rise to prominence in city politics of the "new urban left," which created a ruling class that was far more tolerant of gay and lesbian culture, and the transformation of Manchester from an industrial city into one geared more to consumption and display. By the late 1980s, Quilley argues, the political powers in Manchester had realized that the only way forward for their deindustrialized (and struggling) city was to promote a new identity as a postindustrial, culturally diverse, European showpiece. The gay Village was seen as a major asset in that development, and is now "incorporated into a marketing exercise in which Manchester is presented as a progressive, tolerant, and above all interesting patchwork of diverse districts and quarters" (Quilley, 1997: 287). Ironically, the Village has almost become mainstream, since it is used in the city's promotional brochures as a sign of Manchester's sophistication and diversity.

Diverse Suburbs

While U.S. suburbs continue to be perceived as the bastions of class and racial exclusivity, this is no longer an accurate portrayal. As we suggested earlier, the suburbs have become increasingly urbanized, containing nodes of new economic activity—large corporate office parks, high-tech research centers, warehouses, restaurants, retail centers, and the like—and are now often referred to as "edge cities." In many metropolitan areas, these businesses are providing the jobs for America's new immigrants, a process in some ways similar to the large numbers of people who immigrated to the United States in the nineteenth century to work in U.S. factories. Instead of inhabiting five-story tenements in the heart of downtown, however, many of America's new immigrants are living in small houses or apartments on the outskirts of the city, working primarily in low-wage jobs that spin off from the new industries (particularly high-tech ones), but also in some highly skilled jobs. Roberto Suro argues that this transformation in the workforce and the location of new industries in the suburbs is equal in magnitude to the changes that swept through nineteenth-century industrializing America: "Today, another transformation of potentially equal magnitude is taking place. The high-tech revolution is fueling the growth of America's suburbs, drawing immigrants from Latin America and Asia to fill the demand for highly qualified technicians as well as low-skilled servants" (1999: 57). In Montgomery County, Maryland, for example, a suburb of Washington, DC, nearly a quarter of all households are headed by someone who is foreign-born, or whose spouse was born abroad. The incomes in these new households tend to be skewed to either end of the socioeconomic spectrum: some highly educated people, particularly from India or Pakistan or other areas of Asia, are drawn to the US to work in high-tech labs and computer-related industries; other people, primarily from Latin America, are coming to the United States without even a high school education, and the jobs they find are in the low-paying service sector or in such jobs as domestic service for women and construction for men. Suro refers to these people as the "suburban proletariat," new immigrants who are making suburbs their first port of entry into the U.S. economy.

What does this urbanization and diversification of the suburbs portend for the lives of women? For many women immigrants it may simply suggest more of the same: the impoverished lives they led in El Salvador, for example, are replicated or made worse by their new situations removed from the context of family and community. But at the same time the promise of a booming suburban economy combined with some opportunities for education may signal a different future for these women than what they could have expected at "home": a chance, primarily through education, to attain skilled jobs and professional careers that move them out of the narrowly defined "feminine" roles of domestic work.

The impact of this "urbanization of the suburbs" on native-born suburban dwellers is difficult to discern. Many white, middle-class suburbanites have fled into gated housing communities, partly in reaction to the new diversity of the suburbs, and partly to avoid what they perceive as the crime associated with urban activities. But unlike the flight into the suburbs of the postwar era, when women were isolated at home, in today's exclusive suburban enclaves many working women need only drive out of the gates, past the guard, to go to work, shop, attend the theater, or have dinner out. And many may choose to dine at the local Thai restaurant, taking advantage of what the diversified suburbs now offer—albeit at a safe distance and in a commodified form.

The Culture of Shopping

Women have a complex and ambivalent relationship with the consumer economy that characterizes the postmodern city. On the one hand, consumerism, with its attendant focus on appearance, reinforces women's insecurities, at the same time that it exacts an economic toll. Yet, on the other hand, consumerism allows for the expression of new identities, and often allows women to appropriate new spaces.

For example, as geographer Jon Goss (1996) concludes, even spaces such as "festival marketplaces" (gentrified shopping areas) and shopping malls that are manipulated and controlled by large corporations allow women opportunities for many different kinds of public interactions. This is because malls are no longer (if they ever were) just about shopping. They have grown larger and more diversified throughout the 1980s and 1990s, so that now we have superregional malls with two and even three hundred stores, cinemas, offices, restaurants—even churches. Malls like the Mall of America outside of Minneapolis have become tourist attractions all to themselves, almost mini-Disneylands, since they include amusement parks, hotels, and circuses. In the United States, shopping malls stand in fourth place for places to spend time, after home, work, and school.

Even smaller, more local malls have taken on a character that is not strictly about retailing. In many towns, they are the place where teenagers go to "hang out," where middle-class women go to socialize, where young people go out for a date, and where seniors come for their daily walk (Figure 3.18). Malls have become, in essence, our new "downtowns." And, as controlled and surveilled spaces, they are considered safe environments for women. Women's fear of violence on the streets of the city is in contrast to the relative sense of security that the mall creates. In ways similar to the Victorian department store owners, mall designers and developers deliberately create

FIGURE 3.18. View of the interior of the Fashion Mall, Plantation, Florida. Malls are no longer just about shopping—they are, for many, centers of social interaction and leisure activities. They also cater to women and children, providing "safe" and convenient spaces for them to shop and socialize.

spaces that cater to our prescribed notions of femininity: well-lit spaces that are visually attractive and that act as sites of fantasy and desire. At the same time, of course, designers and developers create spaces that lead to the most sales. Jon Goss (1993) reveals the often insidious ways that mall design and packaging are meant to stimulate us to buy—from the location of escalators, to the colors of the entrance displays. Femininity and consumption are again brought together, reinforcing the association between the two that, as we have seen, dates back to the nineteenth century.

The nightlife in many postmodern cities focuses around gentrified consumer districts, such as Baltimore's Inner Harbor or Miami's Bayside. In many ways, these urban showpieces are simply adaptations of the suburban mall—they use the design motifs and organizational patterns of an enclosed mall to make shoppers more comfortable, and to give at least the illusion of safety for women. Margaret Crawford (1992) argues that the motif of the shopping mall even informs our new cultural institutions, particularly museums. These civic spaces, she argues, have become commodified, and are designed in ways similar to malls: they are well-organized, "safe," visually attractive settings that are meant to stimulate sales. For example, the new additions to the Metropolitan Museum of Art in New York City resemble the look and feel of shopping malls. Museum presentation of art objects is combined with ministores dispersed throughout the gallery areas, providing opportunities for patrons to purchase objects connected to the art. Again we can see here the aligning of traditional notions of femininity, culture, and consumption.

Downtown

If the shopping mall has taken on many of the functions and meaning of the city, what has happened to U.S. downtowns? Portions of the downtowns of some cities have become gentrified, while other sections continue to deteriorate. The Boston of Ally McBeal and friends is the gentrified Boston—its sites of consumption and leisure, not its homeless population and run-down housing. In Sunbelt cities whose major growth period was after World War II (and therefore after the automobile), the relatively small downtowns are simply abandoned by residents and consumers altogether, and only house the prestige office spaces for banking and financial industry. After 5 P.M., these downtowns are almost like ghost towns, with few people willing to venture along the wind tunnels that are created by the competing skyscrapers. These skyscrapers are examples of, in Leslie Weisman's words, "architectural machismo" (1992: 41). They contain thousands of cubicles (for those workers low on the corporate ladder, typically women), and several hundred offices (for those high on the corporate ladder, typically men). At 5:00 or 5:30 or 6:00 P.M., the workers file out of their spaces, go down in the elevators, and enter the parking garage—each to ride off in his or her car to a home in the suburbs.

In these Sunbelt cities, the effects of global, corporate capitalism are easy to see: tall office buildings, linked electronically to centers of economic power around the world, jut out on the skyline, while at street level few local interactions are visible. But almost all European and U.S. cities have felt the effects of the new globally linked corporate capital that characterizes our contemporary economy. In older cities, bank and corporate headquarter buildings are superimposed on the preexistent industrial patterns. London and New York, for example, combine both the pedestrian activity at the street level with corporate and global activity on the 30th floor. And even though the business world is still coded as masculine, many women are now at work in it. They may have to act as men sometimes, or "masquerade" as geographer Linda McDowell (1995) calls it, but many women executives have managed to retain their "feminine" identity in these buildings of "machismo."

In the end, however, despite the fact that women have gained power and prestige (often through their femininity), even our contemporary work worlds are structured in such a way as to promote inequality. As McDowell argues in her study of the merchant banking industry in the City of London, an industry that is characteristic of the new financial service sector of our economy, jobs and careers are still segregated by gender: "Occupational sex stereotyping and the institutional and everyday structures of workplace interactions have maintained and reproduced patterns of inequality at work" (1997: 204).

We began this chapter by tracing the historical roots of the distinction between the city and the countryside, by thinking about how and why the city became gendered as masculine and the country and suburb as feminine. As we argued, associating the distinctions between city and suburb, commerce and culture, with that of masculine and feminine has lent legitimacy to the belief that these distinctions are inevitable, natural, and essential. These spatial and gender distinctions continue even today, in our global, informational cities.

Yet it is also clear that postmodern urbanism is ushering in a blurring of these distinctions. Parts of cities have been turned into suburban-style shopping malls; spaces of consumption (malls) are increasingly taking over civic functions; and many suburbs are becoming densely settled and almost urban in appearance. This transition into the postmodern city could be interpreted as a triumph of the female over the male—of suburbs over cities, and of enclosed, safe spaces over raw and uncontained urbanism. Some observers caution, however, that the prospect of the overturn of the "old urban order" is a double-edged sword for women. The heterogeneity of the industrial city—for all its masculinity and rough-and-tumble—has also provided women with many opportunities, releasing them from the straitjackets of domesticity. However fantastical Ally McBeal's adventures may be, they do resonate as possibilities for many young women—women who may look to the city as their own proving grounds. Elizabeth Wilson (1991) argues that women have fared pretty well amid that urban heterogeneity, and the prospect of losing that now (by endorsing the "safety" that comes with commodified spaces), when women have more political and economic power than ever before and thus can take advantage of that heterogeneity, is certainly unsettling.

Chapter 4

ON THE MOVE

It's not easy to move through space. The ability of people to move around—to overcome the "friction of distance," as geographers say—varies wildly. The ability to "get around" is shaped by physical capacity, but it is also deeply intertwined with social status. Getting from one place to another takes time, money, confidence, and often machinery of some kind—and it can also take sheer endurance and will.

Mobility is greatest at the extreme ends of the socioeconomic spectrum. The mobility of the destitute is a hardship-induced rootlessness: the homeless, refugees, people on the margins of job markets, and people pushed into migration out of need or crisis are all clustered at this end of the mobility curve. At the opposite end of the spectrum are the highflyers (literally and metaphorically). In contemporary societies, increasing wealth is attended by increasing mobility, and, reciprocally, increasing mobility increases privilege.

These mobility distinctions are also deeply gendered. Men and women have quite different experiences of rootlessness and fixity, of the hardships of forced movement and of the privileges of free movement.

THE BODY IN SPACE

We might start our consideration of mobility at the most intimate scale, that of the body. As geographer Glenda Laws points out, "Both the conceptualization and material construction of bodies *make a dif-*

ference to our experience of places" (1997: 49, emphasis in original). Men and women literally embody norms of masculinity and femininity—or are *assumed* to embody or are *expected* to embody them. The body that navigates the geography of daily life bears a visible mark of being female or male—and thus its appropriate match to certain spaces is easily "read" by even a casual observer. When the "wrong" bodies are in the "wrong" places—when women walk into male spaces or vice versa—this is often translated into a challenge to norms of feminine or masculine behavior. These norms are also challenged when there is ambiguity about whether the physical form is female or male, or ambiguity about the match between the physical form and the gender identity: people who present themselves androgynously, or who crossdress, are typically met with harassment or hostility.

Similarly, bodies are "marked" by racial and, in some cases, ethnic identities. As with gender and sex markers, racial identifiers have geographical correlates. In U.S. cities, for example, urban order has long been predicated on the demarcation of "different places for different races." Mona Domosh's (1998) study of nineteenth-century New York City, for example, demonstrates that the incursion of African Americans into the mostly white, upper-class promenades of the city represented a challenge to conventions of urban decorum as Figure 4.1 shows. Recent exposés have revealed the extent to which police departments in the United States rely on "racial profiling," that is, the practice of stopping cars on the sole basis that the occupants are African American, or stopping black pedestrians who are walking in white neighborhoods. Many African Americans, especially men, complain that they are put under heightened scrutiny and surveillance in all sorts of places, from shopping malls to white suburbs.

Continuing our consideration of the geography of the body, we can observe that mobility through space is clearly affected directly by physical (bodily) ability or disability and the match or mismatch between that and the constructed environment. Most of the world's people live in built environments that are designed—unrealistically—for a physically unimpaired population. Everyone on crutches or in a wheelchair, anyone dealing with the infirmities of age or the frailties of illness, is at a severe disadvantage in day-to-day mobility. Some social roles impose similar constraints: a parent maneuvering a baby carriage through the contemporary city will encounter many of the same limitations and built-in obstacles, as Figure 4.2 illustrates. The design of public spaces, facilities, and transportation clearly favors the most physically fit, nonchildbearing, nonchild-caretaking segment of the population.

Geographer Reginald Golledge reminds us that the experiences of navigating or encountering any given geography vary from person to person and vary considerably with degree and nature of "disability":

FIGURE 4.1. "Our Best Society."

The disabled live in a transformed space. . . . For the disabled persons, the ordinary obstacles and barriers not only are multiplied but are expanded well beyond the normal range; gutters become chasms, sidewalks and streets become treacherous paths, stairs may be impossible cliffs, distinctive size shapes or colors may lose their significance, layout becomes a maze, maps and models may be uninterpretable. Space can become wildly distorted either by incomplete knowledge (for example in the case of the blind or the retarded), or laboriously transformed (as in the case of the wheelchair bound). (1993: 64)

Social norms, and the spaces constructed to hold those norms, shape what we think a body can and cannot do (Laws, 1997: 50). In all societies there is an intertwined reciprocity between space, bodies, and the social construction of both—neither "space" nor "bodies" exist independently of a social imprint. Feminist geographer Vera Chouinard, who uses a motorized wheelchair, writes of her experience in this way:

It is hard to think of any facet of my life which has been untouched by ableism and by struggles to occupy body-spaces on my own terms. For example, as a professor, my workplace, the university, has been a very significant site of my oppression. . . . One form of exclusion is very visible: after four years, I still lack physical access to my office. Two entrances which appeared as scooter and wheelchair

FIGURE 4.2. Photograph of a woman with a baby carriage. The design of public spaces and facilities seldom accommodates roles such as child-bearing and child caretaking; the built environment reflects notions of who "should" and who "shouldn't" be in particular places.

accessible on our official map for disabled staff and students turned out to be nothing of the sort. . . . So, although I have acquired a scooter I still cannot get into my office independently. This situation sends out strong signals that my presence, and the presence of disabled colleagues and students is not important: that we are not valued in an academic setting. (Chouinard and Grant, 1996: 172)

GETTING AROUND: FIRST PRINCIPLES

Moving outward from body-based dimensions of mobility, we encounter other socially structured factors that determine differences in mobility. To answer the question of why *some* groups of people are more able to "overcome the friction of distance" than others requires a curiosity about systems of control, privilege, and hierarchy—and of gender, class, and race.

Economic status is obviously important in determining who "gets around" and the ways in which they do so. Transportation choices reflect, symbolically and really, class and income differences (an observation on which the car, plane, and travel advertising industries depend). Wealthier people move through space more easily than their poorer counterparts: simply put, wealthy people fly, poor people take the bus. "Upward mobility" is not just a metaphor: as personal income increases, choices of transportation expand. Reliability, speed, and choice of modes of transportation all improve with income. Moreover, people in middle- and upper-income brackets usually control their *own* means of transportation: it's not the upper classes who are left at the curb waiting for a bus that never comes.

While the most destitute members of society may be the most rootless, the "ordinary poor" are at the bottom of the slope of mobility. They face daily struggles just to get around. It takes more effort, more time, more thought, more commitment, and proportionally more money for a person in poverty to "get around" than for their middle-class or wealthy peers to do so. The friction of distance is thickest at the bottom of the social ladder. The difficulties of mobility that accompany poverty, in turn, perpetuate that poverty. It is hard to climb out of poverty if jobs, health care, or decent housing are literally beyond reach. In public policy debates in the United States, poor people are often stereotyped by conservatives as "unreliable" (that is, late to work, unable to coordinate family/work demands, missing appointments with the welfare officer, and the like). A closer examination suggests that in societies where the smooth functioning of daily work and home life requires complicated navigation (literally), "unreliability" is hardwired into poverty. In the mid-1990s, "welfare reform" was vigorously pursued in the United States. One of the stumbling blocks that state bureaucrats encountered as they tried to move people off the welfare rolls and into jobs is that to get to most jobs requires a car—and poor people are the least likely to have a car, or to have a reliable one. In 1989, in the United States, ninety-seven percent of families with incomes over $50,000 had a car (or more than one), while only fifty-two percent of the poorest families, those with incomes under $10,000, had a car (Laws, 1997: 57).

Almost everywhere in the world, women constitute the largest constituency of all people in poverty. To the extent, then, that mobility may be framed as a poverty issue, it is also disproportionately a women's issue. Low incomes restrict women's mobility in all societies, and especially in societies that depend on private transportation. But, as we will see, transportation and mobility are "women's issues" for other reasons as well.

Often, differences in mobility among certain social groups are the result of deliberate public policy. After all, as Dolores Hayden reminds us, restricting access to and through space has been one of "the consistent ways to limit the economic and political rights of groups" (1995: 22). It is not unusual to find central authorities (from parents to governments) relying on restrictions on movement/ mobility as an explicit strategy of social control. Many governments employ confinement and mobility-restriction strategies—whether keeping some people in place or others out—as a way of creating or maintaining a desired social order. Prisoners might come first to mind as a group intentionally confined in the name of a greater good. Similarly, militaries everywhere maintain discipline in the ranks by controlling the movement of its members—being "AWOL" (absent without leave) is a punishable offense in all militaries.

But mobility control is even more widely exercised. Indeed, there are few modern governments that have not attempted to exercise overt social control through spatial control. In myriad places, legally encoded and socially tolerated racial and ethnic segregation systems (in schools, housing, public facilities, transportation, and so on) have been designed to separate "first class" citizens from "lesser" groups. South African apartheid was predicated on a series of "pass laws" that restricted the daily movement of nonwhites, and on residential control laws that established zones of race-specific residential separation. The contemporary internal security system in Israel depends on monitoring and restricting the movement of Palestinians. Australian, American, and Canadian governments (among others) perfected reservation systems of different types to control "natives" in the nineteenth century. In the twentieth century, governments in Sudan, Malaysia, Kenya, and Canada, among others, have attempted to bring nomadic populations under central control by forcing them to settle in villages. Governments in China and the former Soviet Union employed residential-permit requirements to control where people lived and moved. Once you start to look, efforts to exercise social control through mobility control are in evidence almost everywhere.

But one need not look only to such ornate and explicit systems of control to see that differential access in mobility is deeply structured into the prevailing social order. *Gendered* differences in mobility and access to transportation are among the more ubiquitous—and "ordinary"—of spatial/social controls.

KEEPING WOMEN IN THEIR PLACE

The control of women's movement has long preoccupied governments, families, households, and individual men. It is hard to maintain patriarchal control over women if they have unfettered freedom of movement through space. Sometimes this control is exercised bluntly and brutally. For example, the foot binding of young women, widely practiced in some regions of China from the tenth century to the early twentieth century to prevent them from moving more than a few paces at a time, is one of the more horrifying examples of gendered mobility restriction. As Figure 4.3 shows, upper-class women in Europe and the United States adopted foot binding as a cosmetic practice in the nineteenth century to make their feet appear small and feminine. However, foot binding is just one practice of many on a continuum of historical and contemporary norms and prescriptions that impose restrictions on women's mobility. Tight corseting, high heels, hobble skirts, the veil, prohibitions against women riding bicycles or horses, restrictions (legal or social) on women driving cars—all suggest the extent to which "keeping women in their place" is often a literal undertaking.

Epidemic rates of sexual violence keep women in a state of spatial uncertainty and geographic disadvantage; many women feel as though they live under a virtual time and space curfew. Geographers Gill Valentine (1989) and Rachel Pain (1997) write that women seldom feel that they "own" the streets, nor that they can move freely

WOMEN OF FASHION HAVING THEIR FEET BANDAGED TO MAKE THEM SMALL.

FIGURE 4.3. Nineteenth-century footbinding in New York. Sometimes "keeping women in their place" is a literal undertaking.

through them. It is no coincidence that women's anti-violence campaigns in many countries center on "Take Back the Streets" rallies. The ubiquitous street harassment that women encounter on an almost daily basis is a not-so-subtle reminder that women in public are considered to be "out of place."

Violence against women in the family or the household—or the credible threat of it—is one of the most common methods used to keep women confined to a house and marriage. Crime statistics from the United States and elsewhere show that women face the greatest likelihood of being killed by their male partner when they leave or try to leave the "marital" house. Violence is one of the most common and powerful tools to sustain particular sexual, family, and household structures and to keep women spatially restricted to them.

In many countries, restrictions on women's spatial behaviors and movements are written into law. For example, in dozens of countries today (including Nicaragua, the Dominican Republic, Morocco, and Zimbabwe) "marital domicile" laws are still in effect that give men the sole right to determine where the family lives—these laws require married women to follow their husbands wherever they go. Even in other countries where domicile laws have been repealed, such assumptions about who will lead and who will follow—geographically—are still the norm. In the late 1990s, there were more than two dozen countries in which women faced specific legal restrictions on their daily movements—restrictions such as requiring permission from a husband, father, or male guardian to travel outside the country (for example, Libya, Zaire, Iran), restrictions on their presence in public (for example, Saudi Arabia, Afghanistan), restrictions on their presence on public transportation vehicles (for example, Sudan), or restrictions on their rights to drive cars or ride bicycles (for example, Qatar, Saudi Arabia) (see Seager, 1997a).

Even in the absence of legally encoded restrictions, in virtually every country of the world women face *de facto* restrictions on their movements and public presence. Feminist poet Adrienne Rich, in an essay on "compulsory heterosexuality," enumerates some of the ways in which men exercise power over women's mobility through: "means of rape as terrorism, keeping women off the streets; purdah; foot binding; atrophying of women's athletic abilities; high heels and 'feminine' dress codes in fashion; the veil; sexual harassment on the streets; prescriptions for 'full-time' mothering at home; enforced economic dependence of wives" (1986: 37–38). Geographer Shirley Ardener (1993) adds two more things to this list: ideologies that encourage women to be physically frail, and the lack of public support for child care or for elder care, responsibilities that typically fall to women.

ROAMING AND "HOMING"

Thelma and Louise made a splash in the theaters in the 1990s—and inspired many U.S. women to think that the open road *could* beckon for them—but the freedom to roam without fear or accountability has mostly been associated with masculinity. Women on the loose are almost never valorized—in any culture. Indeed, geographical "looseness" in women is assumed to be a universal marker for sexual wantonness—or at least cause for concern about their respectability. In contrast, "footlooseness" is often held up as a signifier of "real" manhood. Western popular culture is saturated with the association of mobility and masculinity: in country and western songs, in children's stories, in coming-of-age sagas, in romance novels, and in the cinema, it is the manly man who moves on, the woman (or the henpecked male) who stays behind. In lore and literature, mobility is understood as a male expression of rebellion and resistance. The outlaw, the outcast, the cowboy, and the hobo are stock characters in a masculinized drama of resistance to "the establishment."

More often then not, such resistance is couched as a "flight from commitment," an explicit rejection of home, family, and feminized control. "The road" offers an escape for men from sexual commitment and from the marital demands of women. However, it may be easy to take too seriously the literary posturing on male mobility. For example, a close reading of Jack Kerouac's 1957 novel *On the Road*, often enshrined as a seminal force in the creation of the U.S. countercultural male geographic imagination, suggests that much of the genre of male wandering was as much rooted in a search for home as in a rejection of it (Creswell, 1993; McDowell, 1993). Some critics suggest that it is possible to read *On the Road* as a search by Kerouac and his buddies for *new* home communities. Nonetheless, the association of manliness and mobility remains potent in configurations of cultural and countercultural identity.

In a recent extension of this classically heterosexual portrayal, some gay male theorists argue for an embrace and celebration of "anti-rootedness" as a marker of genuine gay maleness. In a series of letters and editorials in the *Nation* in the fall of 1997, for example, several gay male writers denounced the "mainstreaming" of gay culture, the defining characteristic of which they identified as a feminized (lesbian-identified) domesticity. The core signifier of gay male culture, several of these writers argued, is a resistance to domesticity, to rootedness, to constancy, and to fixed-place social and sexual relationships. Similarly, many gay men argue that their appropriation of public spaces for cruising, sexualized display, or sex sub-

FIGURE 4.4. Pleasure Park. Some gay men suggest that their appropriation of public space represents a radical challenge to the dominant (hetero) norm. Women may not necessarily view a male claim to public spaces as new or radical.

verts the dominant norms (the "heteronormativity") of those spaces. Women, however, may not necessarily view this homosexual male claim to public spaces as either new or radical. For women, male appropriation of space is an old story.

Stereotypes of the "fixedness" of women are not entirely fictitious. Indeed, the daily lives of women almost everywhere do tend to be more homebound or home-centered than those of their male counterparts (see Chapter 1). Symbolic ties to home tend to keep many women on a shorter geographic tether, as do functional ties: in the United States (and elsewhere), male liberation aside, women still have primary responsibility for child care and household upkeep.

The "real world" effect of the home-centeredness of women's lives shows up in commuting and "journey-to-work" patterns. In a recent U.S. job preference survey, all women, across race and ethnicity, prioritized "closeness to home" as an important attribute in weighing job decisions (Hanson and Pratt, 1995). This geographical "anchoring" of women puts them at a disadvantage in competition for jobs and even contributes to the creation and persistence of occupational segregation.

These daily mobility patterns of men and women, especially in the urban United States and Canada, have been extensively studied by feminist geographers. Most of these studies uncover significant gender differences in trip distance and the patterns—although there are equally significant findings of racial differences *among* women in work–home relations (see, for example, Johnston-Anumonwo [1995], Hanson [1992], Pratt [1992], Rutherford [1998], and Preston, McLafferty, and Hamilton, 1993). Specifically, surveys suggest that in their daily lives, white women in the United States tend to travel less frequently, over shorter distances, and via different means than white men. African American women, however, do not have shorter job commutes than their male counterparts, and have longer commutes than white women. In a recent study, the commuting times of white women were found to be shaped by marital status and the presence of children, but the same was not found for African American or Latina women. This rather intriguing finding of racial difference is explained in one study in this way: "Family status effects for minority women are small . . . not because they have freedom from household responsibilities, but because they have fewer employment alternatives nearby and poor access to transportation" (Preston, McLafferty, and Hamilton, 1993: 247).

The spatial boundedness of women is not only—and not always—a constraint. Just as mobility is not inherently a path to power, so immobility is not always a disadvantage. Recent work by feminist geographers provides a reminder that mobility is not the only path to social security: networks based on "localness" and "fixedness" can and do provide deep reservoirs of resources, reciprocity, assistance, and comfort, especially for women, who often are the anchors of such local communities. As Janice Monk and Cindi Katz's work suggests, "Rootedness offers many women personal satisfaction and rewards, as well as the possibilities for social life and the sharing of [work and child-care] burdens" (Katz and Monk, 1993a: 271). Melissa Gilbert's (1998) research suggests that for many poor women in the United States, spatial boundedness can provide security. In a study of

African American and white working poor women, Gilbert found that place-based personal networks played a crucial role in the survival strategy of all poor women, and especially so for African Americans. For many women, stable place-based networks are crucial in finding jobs, housing, child care, and health care.

In most cultures, the assumption (and reality) of the rootedness of women bestows upon them a distinctive role in the maintenance of the culture—a role that can be both a burden and an honor, that can be both trivialized and valorized. In an insightful community study of a village in France in the 1960s, anthropologist Rayna Reiter (1975) details the centrality of women's role as cultural "anchors." The women of Colpied seldom leave the village, but within the village they maintain the social ties, history, information, and even house inheritances, that sustain the life of the village: "[Women sustain] the set of life expectations and a body of knowledge that is centered around the family. . . . Houses as well as families are identified with women. In the women's discussions, it is as if men are simply stand-ins in the world of the family, semi-autonomous additions whose presence allows for the establishment of a household and the birth of children" (1975: 265). Communities such as the one described by Reiter "work" only to the extent that everyone plays their appointed role. They are easily destabilized by changes, especially changes in gender roles or sexual relations—which is one of the reasons why women's liberation movements are especially feared and demonized in communities with the most entrenched gender regimes.

Changes in the *mobility* balance of power can disrupt communities and liberate women almost as quickly as any other social transformation. The patriarchal grip slips when women get cars of their own, or bicycles, or wings—which is why those advances are often fiercely resisted. In Reiter's (1975) village study of France, for example, social stability was anchored in the fact that it was mostly the men who drove cars and traveled with any frequency, and who therefore had contacts outside the village. The boundaries of the domain of women were tightly drawn around home and village, such that women had few external contacts. Women were thus less likely than men to be directly influenced by the social changes and trends of the "outside" world, or to have access to the resources of the world beyond the village. As Reiter says, "Regions, as defined by how people use them, break sharply along lines of sex: men have cars and colleagues, women have families" (1975: 256). Reiter noted, however, in her last visit to the village that change in the social order of Colpied was heralded by the fact that younger women were starting to establish independent households outside the village, and were starting to drive, commute, and to own cars.

BREAKING THE BONDS OF SPACE AND SEX

As Reiter (1975) chronicled in Colpied, despite the pressures in every culture to impose a geographical "fixedness" on women, women are increasingly on the move: for work, for pleasure, or for its own sake. In reality, women have always been more mobile—or have sought to be—than cultural norms would suggest. Like men, women have yearned for geographical freedom, and have found liberation in mobility. Historically, we discover that even in the most restrictive societies some women have found the ability to travel, to explore, to wander. For women of means, travel for leisure or adventure has almost always been one option to loosen the bonds of daily life—as evidenced by the crop of Victorian Great Britain's "lady travelers" whom we discuss in the next chapter. Most of these women reported a palpable sense of release as they left behind the sex roles and "proper places" they occupied as middle- or upper-class women in their home countries. For example, Gertrude Bell, a British traveler who explored the Syrian desert in the early 1900s, expressed the feelings of most of the women travelers when she wrote of the joys of travel: "The gates of the enclosed garden are thrown open, the chain at the sanctuary is lowered, with a wary glance to right and left you step forth, and behold! the immeasurable world. . . . You feel the bands break that were riveted about your heart as you enter the path that stretches across the rounded shoulder of the earth" (quoted in Birkett, 1989: 48).

For many upper-class women in North America and Europe in the late 1800s, travel was "respectable" only when supervised by an older (preferably spinsterish) female companion; the European "grand tour" was the epitome of this sort of contained adventure. The genius of Thomas Cook was to commercialize this sort of travel for women and yet still keep it "respectable." An 1855 testimonial from four sisters with an urge to see the world sparked this revolution:

> How could ladies alone and unprotected, go 600 or 700 miles away from home? However after many pros and cons, the idea grew on us and we found ourselves consulting guides, hunting in guide-books, reading descriptions, making notes, and corresponding with Mr. Cook [a temperance activist who had developed liquor-free travel trips for families and single men]. . . . Tis true, we encountered some opposition—one friend declaring that it was improper for ladies to go alone. . . . But somehow or other, one interview with Mr. Cook removed all our hesitation and we forthwith placed ourselves under his care. Many of our friends thought us too independent and adventurous to leave the shores of old England, and thus

plunge into foreign lands not beneath Victoria's sway with no protecting relative, but we can only say that we hope this will not be our
last Excursion of the kind. (quoted in Enloe, 1989: 29)

Following the success of this trip, Cook quickly expanded his operations, developing package tours for middle-class British women that
offered the promise of chaperoned travel—safe and supervised—but
without the spinster aunt.

Other women, some of whom have become modern heroes,
crossdressed their way out of the narrow confines of their sex-as-
signed places. The Spanish-speaking world, for example, has long
been entranced by tales of the "Lieutenant Nun," a Basque nun who
fled a convent in 1599 disguised as a man and swashbuckled her way
through the New World as a soldier (de Erauso, 1996). In the U.S.
Civil War, literally hundreds of women shed their dress and identities to sign up as male soldiers. The remarkable letters of one,
Rosetta Wakeman, who served with the Union Army as "Lyons
Wakeman," record her determination to "quit home and never live
there again," to dress as she pleased, and to make new friends wherever she went (Burgess, 1994: 10).

Contemporary women, too, have geographical boundaries to
cross. In the 1970s the first women explorers and scientists went to
Antarctica, but to do so they had to battle fierce resistance and undis-
guised misogyny from the men who had claimed the continent as
their own (Rothblum, Weinstock, and Morris, 1998; Seager, 1998).
For most nonindigenous peoples, the "wilderness" (or even the "out-
of-doors") has long been defined as men's territory, but today increasing numbers of women are moving into this terrain as forest rangers,
mountaineers, wildlife biologists, wilderness guides, sportswomen,
or adventurers—although often against considerable opposition.

AUTO-MASCULINITY

The car has been an especially powerful vehicle of women's liberation, both literally and metaphorically. And yet, because of that,
women's relationships to cars have been contested and controversial.
The "gendering" of the automobile demonstrates the complex inter-
twining of mobility, the construction (and reconstruction) of masculinity and femininity, and the assignment of "proper" gender roles.

In the United States, the early development of the mass automobile culture was intentionally and thoroughly masculinized. As
historian Virginia Scharff (1991) documents, cars were deemed inappropriate conveyances for women. The speed and freedom prom-

ised by cars were viewed as dangerous for women, invoking images of wantonness and sexual liberation:

> The popular press sometimes treated the woman passenger as a sexually suspect figure all too vulnerable to the erotic power of her driver. "The Wonderful Monster," a 1905 serial syndicated by William Randolph Hearst and published in *Motor* magazine, warned of the power of both cars and male drivers to awaken incendiary urges in women. (1991: 20)

FIGURE 4.5. Road map image of a woman driver. The idea that women might be able to take independent control of their travel—and of powerful machines—was seen by many commentators as a threat to family stability, good social order, and women's sexual purity.

Women drivers were subject to especially harsh social judgments. "Scientific" studies were conducted in the early decades of the twentieth century that "proved" that women were mentally, physically, and biologically incapable of mastering the complexities of driving. The idea that women might be able to take independent control of their travel—and of such powerful machines—was seen by many early American commentators as a threat to family stability, good social order, and women's sexual purity.

Anxieties about women and cars are not just historical (or Western) anomalies; they continue to be potent, shaping popular culture and actual transportation outcomes. In no country are women yet equal participants in the automobile economy and culture; in several, they are still prohibited from driving at all. In the United States, which arguably has the most deeply entrenched social commitment to the car, jokes about "women drivers" still resonate; automobile makers and dealers still treat women as secondary car consumers; women are still outsiders at garages, auto shows, racetracks, and car dealerships—all consummate "men's spaces."

In terms of transportation realities, women still fall far behind men in owning, driving, or controlling access to cars. As Table 4.1 shows, there are significant gaps in the United States (as elsewhere) in the proportion of women and men licensed drivers. The gap dramatically widens for the fifty-plus age groups, reflecting, perhaps, the imprint of a generation raised before "auto lib" for women, but also reflecting the economics of car ownership: elderly women are much poorer than their male cohorts. Another way to look at the gender mobility gap is in "miles driven": again, data from the United States show that in no age group do women drive more than sixty percent of the miles driven by their male counterparts (Rosenbloom, 1993: 232).

Differences in access to cars are not inconsequential—indeed, they produce deep inequities in cultures and economies that are highly car-dependent. In most industrialized, urban countries, full political, economic, and cultural participation is only possible with a car. In these economies, getting to the shops or to work, or moving goods and people, is really only efficiently possible with a car. Women's urban planning initiatives—for example, in London in the 1980s and in Toronto in the 1990s—have focused attention on these transportation realities, redefining transportation as a "women's issue." A 1980s British planning manual for women, for example, identifies transportation priorities for women:

> High priority should be given to public transport, pedestrians and cycling, and low priority to private vehicles; public transport ser-

TABLE 4.1. Gender Differences in Driving

Distribution of licensed drivers, United States, 1996

	% drivers in each age group		
	Male	Female	F:M gap
Under age 16	0.4	0.4	0
16–19	62.8	61.4	–1.4
20–24	87.5	86.4	–1.1
25–29	98.1	94.5	–3.6
30–34	95.0	92.2	–2.8
35–39	93.4	92.2	–1.2
40–44	94.8	92.8	–2.0
45–49	96.6	92.9	–3.7
50–54	100	94.5	–5.5
55–59	97.9	89.0	–8.9
60–64	96.9	84.8	–12.1
65–69	93.9	78.6	–15.3
70–74	94.4	75.6	–18.8
75–79	90.9	67.0	–23.9
80–84	84.1	52.4	–31.7
85+	71.7	28.5	–43.2
Total	92.1	84.4	–7.7

Annual average miles per driver, United States

	Male	Female	F as % of M
1969	11,352	5,411	47.6%
1977	13,563	5,943	43.8%
1983	13,962	6,381	45.7%
1990	16,632	9,543	57.3%

Sources: Federal Highway Administration, *1990 and 1996 Highway Statistics*.

vices should meet the needs for women: buses designed for parents travelling with children or heavy shopping, for people with disabilities; bus stops and bus stations should be well lit; timing and cost of services should be accessible and geared to journeys made by women; direct, well-lit pedestrian routes should be given high priority. (London Planning Aid Service, 1985: 20)

In most industrialized countries, the largest constituencies of public transportation users are the poor, women, and the elderly. There are direct budgetary and policy trade-offs between public and private transportation systems: the privileging of car-based systems comes at the expense of public systems. Cutbacks in public transpor-

tation services or government subsidies—whether in the 1980s in
Great Britain under the Thatcher administration, or in 1990s Mexico
under International Monetary Fund (IMF) imposed government
spending limits—have gender- and class-specific effects. The extent to
which women are disadvantaged by car-centered transportation systems varies considerably: low-income and elderly women are obviously the most disadvantaged by these systems. But given that many
women gain access to transportation only through a male member of
their household, then single women and lesbians may also be disproportionately affected. Dolores Hayden points to the economic
knock-on economic effects of (male) car-based transportation systems:

> Major decisions have also been made about public investments in
> transportation based on male patterns of movement. . . . By 1980
> [in the United States] one out of seven American workers earned a
> living selling, building, repairing, insuring, driving or servicing vehi-
> cles or highways. Almost all of these workers were male, so it can be
> argued that car culture in the US represents economic development
> for male workers as well as convenience for male consumers. (1984:
> 152–153)

Thus, in places where transportation planning and government ex-
penditures privilege the car (rather than public transportation), this
automobile-centered skew to public policy literally creates a concrete
structure of male privilege and female disadvantage.

Many countries in the world are not yet fully committed to car-
based transportation systems. And yet the realm of the automobile is
expanding rapidly with globalization and the spread of Western cultural norms and economic models. Indeed, embrace of a car culture
is widely accepted as a signifier of "modernization." As countries
such as Russia, China, and Vietnam become integrated into the
global economy, and become dependent on Western economic assistance and guidance, car culture is becoming entrenched in these
countries too. It is in these countries in which the mass diffusion of
cars is a recent phenomenon that we can see most clearly the power
and persistence of gendered assumptions about the car. In most of
the world's newly emerging auto cultures, the same old gendered relationships and assumptions about cars, power, privilege, and masculinity and femininity are being replicated and explicitly adopted. In
Saudi Arabia, women are prohibited from driving cars; in Qatar, they
need permission from a male relative to do so. In most countries,
there are no *legal* prohibitions keeping women out of the driver's
seat, but prohibitive attitudes and social norms have much the same

effect. A recent news report described Calcutta, for example, as a city choked with taxicabs, yet with only one woman taxi driver among the ranks of some twenty thousand drivers; the commentary noted that in India it is "unheard of for a woman to be a chauffeur, a bus or truck driver, or a taxi driver" (Gargan, 1993: A2). In modernizing China, women are barely visible in the new auto elite. In the new Moscow, it's not women who are racing around in the Jeep Cherokees and Chevy Suburbans that have become the signifiers of the new elite.

Many governments in poor countries are not only importing cars, but are also importing the transportation planning models and policies that are already so entrenched in places such as the United States and the United Kingdom. In many developing countries, the same privilege/mobility gap is being created by new transportation policies that give priority to private car transportation at the expense of public transportation systems. Although most of our information about mobility and transportation comes from First World countries, some recent geographical studies from Brazil, Peru, and Kenya show that the gender dynamics of transportation use and priorities familiar in rich countries are becoming the norm in poor countries too (Levy, 1992). For example, a transportation study in Nairobi revealed that while twenty-four percent of male heads of households used a private car, only nine percent of women heads did, and while fifty-six percent of men's trips were made by bus, sixty-six percent of women's trips were by bus. Similarly, in both the Brazil and Kenya studies, for many more women than men walking was the primary means of transportation.

Like cars, bicycles too can be "gendered" (sometimes literally, as in the design of men's and women's bicycles). In nineteenth-century Great Britain and the United States the prospect of women riding bicycles—ushered in by the introduction of bicycling as a mass popular conveyance—was hotly controversial. The design of bicycle seats and the physical pumping required to move the bicycle were decried as sexually inappropriate for women. In turn, many nineteenth-century American and British women explicitly saw the bicycle as a vehicle of independence (which was exactly what conservatives feared). Women seized on the vehicle as a new means of defying tradition; Elizabeth Cady Stanton is reported to have said that "many a woman is riding to the suffrage on a bicycle" (quoted in Atkinson, 1978: 121). It is still the case in many places around the world that bicycle riding for women is viewed as a challenge to the social order. Particularly in economies where the bicycle is the pinnacle transportation mode—parts of rural Kenya or India, for example—bicycle riding is often protected as a male privilege.

GLOBAL MIGRATION

Gender is at work, too, in shaping larger flows of movement such as regional and global migration and immigration. The stereotyped portrayal of migration is of intact families or households migrating in search of better work opportunities, or of whole populations shifting in response to pressures of scarcity, conflict, or disaster. Further, much of the analysis of and reporting on migration assumes that female migration patterns mirror those of male migration, and that men are the initiators of migration while women are the followers (Tyner, 1996a: 405). But recent research by geographers, among others, challenges these views: while women's and men's migration are sometimes linked, just as often we find that men's and women's migration patterns are separate, and that the "push and pull" factors that explain migrations are gender-specific.

Indeed, many geographers have conducted field studies that suggest that "migration in the third world [especially labor migration] is *usually* gender differentiated" (Radcliffe, 1993: 279). Throughout Central and South America, for example, the labor stream from rural to urban areas is often predominantly female: in these economies, women are more likely than men to find waged work in expanding urban areas, especially in the "informal" sector and most especially in domestic service (Radcliffe, 1993; Rengert, 1981). In southern Africa, the typical labor migration stream is just the opposite: men predominate in the regional rural-to-urban labor streams, often finding work in heavy industry and mines, while women are left behind to tend the farms and manage the household economy. Indeed, parts of rural South Africa and Zimbabwe have become feminized zones virtually depopulated of men. The labor stream into the oil-producing Middle East states, where demand for oil field workers is high, is heavily male-skewed. The labor stream out of the Caribbean into Canada is heavily female-skewed, fueled by demand for nurses, home carers, and nannies.

The racial and gender fine tuning of labor migration by governments and commercial interests is common. Labor migration streams are seldom haphazard or coincidental. Many governments have national or ethnic immigration quotas, while others try to manipulate migration to achieve specific gendered labor results. For example, women were largely excluded from nineteenth-century Chinese migration flows into the United States and Canada. In the mid-nineteenth century, male Chinese laborers were a favored migrant pool: they were sought after to fill labor shortages in the North American railroad construction and mining industries. Chinese women, on the other hand, were viewed with suspicion because nervous whites assumed that women would ensure that the Chinese presence would become permanent. It was assumed that single men were transient and could be easily returned to China at the end of their labor contracts, while families were more likely to become permanent settlers. Restrictions by the U.S. government prevented Chinese women from migrating alone into the United States or even coming as the wives of male migrants. At the same time, Chinese cultural traditions limited the movement of women out of China (Takaki, 1993). The end result of legal restrictions on one side of the Pacific and cultural restrictions on the other was one of the most gender-skewed migrations in U.S. history: in 1852, of the 11,794 Chinese in California, only 7 were women; eighteen years later, of 63,199 Chinese in the United States, 4,566 were female—a ratio of fourteen to one (Takaki, 1993: 209). The North American creation of the Chinese "laundry*man*" (a usually feminized migrant employment niche) was one of the more peculiar cultural consequences of this gender-specific migration.

Some contemporary global labor flows are so consistently feminized that they have become a widely recognized phenomena—the "maid trade," for example, is one of the largest labor flows in the world. At any one time, an estimated 1 to 1.7 million women are working as domestic servants outside their own country. Table 4.2 provides a glimpse of the magnitude of this trade (see also Figure 4.6).

The single largest number of the global maids-for-hire come from the Philippines (Heyzer, Nijeholt, and Weerakoon, 1994: 40). The Philippines is one of the world's major labor exporters, of both

TABLE 4.2. Global Maid Trade: Average Annual Migration

	Lowest estimates	Highest estimates
Sending countries		
Bangladesh	2,000	15,000
Indonesia	100,000	240,000
Philippines	275,567	275,569
Sri Lanka	100,000	175,000
Receiving countries		
Bahrain	40,383	
Kuwait	28,833	
Saudi Arabia	750,000	
Hong Kong	65, 924	
Singapore	65,000	

Source: Heyzer, Nijeholt, and Weerakoon (1994).

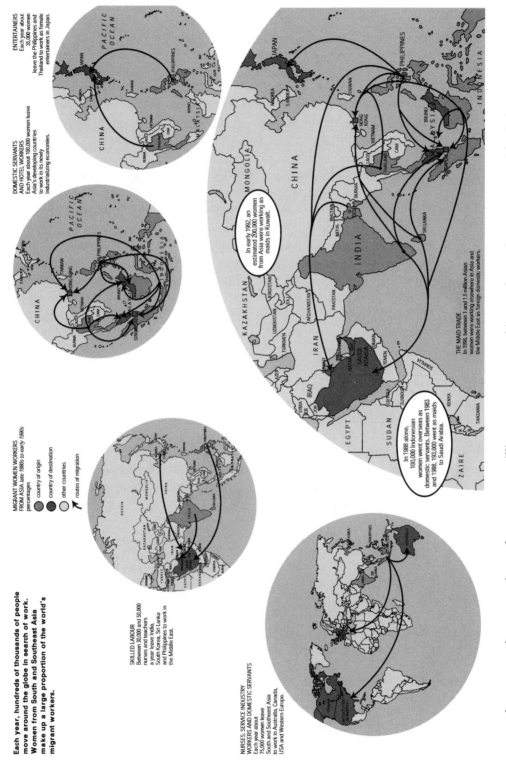

FIGURE 4.6. At any one time, an estimated one to two million women are working as domestic servants outside their own country.

men and women; annually more than a half-million migrant workers leave the Philippines for work overseas, about forty percent of whom are women engaged in service-sector occupations (Tyner, 1996a: 406). Several distinct migration streams of Philippine women workers are identifiable: nurses to Australia, Canada, the United States, and Europe; teachers to the Middle East; and, predominantly, domestic servants to Hong Kong, Malaysia, Japan, and the Middle East (see Seager 1997a; Heyzer et al., 1994).

Like many labor streams, the maid trade is fueled first and foremost by economic disparity. Global labor streams typically flow across the gradient from poorer to wealthier countries. Often the only work available to new migrants in the receiving country is in the "informal" sector (see Chapter 3 for more discussion of this topic). For women migrants, domestic service is the path of least resistance into waged work. The patterns of "sending" and "receiving" countries in the maid trade clearly demonstrate the power of economic push and pull: the countries that are the largest exporters of female labor as domestic workers are Bangladesh, Burma, Indonesia, China, the Philippines, Sri Lanka, and Thailand; the largest importers are Brunei, Canada, the United States, Hong Kong, Malaysia, Pakistan, and Singapore. The income disparities between these sets of countries are striking (Heyzer et al., 1994: 36): the maid trade is clearly a trade between the "have" and the "have not" countries of the world (see Table 4.3).

Although migration streams are usually dictated by economic and social forces beyond the control of individuals, migrants are not just pawns in larger global or political shifts. For many women (and men), migration is a route to expanded opportunities and autonomy. Women migrants often move from regions and cultures of restriction and oppression to places that afford them expanded horizons.

TABLE 4.3. Per Capita Income (U.S.$), Early 1990s

Maid receiving countries	
Canada	20,470
United Arab Emirates	19,860
Hong Kong	11,490
Singapore	11,160
Maid sending countries	
Philippines	730
Indonesia	570
Sri Lanka	470
Bangladesh	210

Source: Heyzer, Nijeholt, and Weerakoon (1994)

The constricting bonds of small, tightly controlled societies can be loosened by flows of people in and out. For individual women, foreign domestic service may be a way "out and up," a move that allows them to escape the strictures of family and home, and to be independent wage earners.

Nonetheless, foreign workers are much more "exploitable" in every way. They are marginalized in a foreign culture, less knowledgeable about labor rights and protection, more dependent on employer largesse, more willing to work for lower wages than the local population. Foreign women domestic servants are especially vulnerable to abuse. Confined to an employer's home, isolated with little contact with friends or other workers, in a foreign culture, and rewarded for being docile and compliant, a woman domestic is especially vulnerable. Rape, sexual harassment, and intimidation of women domestic servants is common. Human rights activists have focused attention on the nearly endemic abuse of foreign women servants in Kuwait and Saudi Arabia, but reports of maltreatment are a constant backdrop to the global maid trade. In an attempt to protect women, some governments have taken steps to stem the outflow of young women workers; some Asian governments, including Bangladesh, India, and Pakistan, have imposed bans or restrictions on the migration of young women.

Indeed, governments are key players in shaping migration flows. Governments in both the sending and the receiving countries enable—and sometimes initiate—labor flows. For example, the migration of women out of the Caribbean to work as domestic servants in Canada is facilitated by a government immigration policy, the Canadian Domestic Worker Program, which encourages this specific labor flow. And the reason why the Philippines is one of the world's largest labor exporters is because out-migration has been seen as a "safety valve" by successive Philippine government regimes. In the face of chronic unemployment and an economy that cannot absorb the increasing working-age population, Philippine governments over several decades have turned to migration to bridge the gap. Remittances—the money that overseas laborers send home—are a major prop of the Philippine economy and provide the largest source of foreign capital. The labor migration stream out of the Philippines is managed by hundreds of government and quasi-government recruitment and placement agencies; fees are paid to these agencies by both the would-be migrants and the would-be foreign employers, providing yet another lucrative incentive to keep the migration stream going.

But the maid trade is not just fueled by economic considerations. Gender imagery and cultural stereotypes play just as big a role. In a recent study of Filipina maids in Hong Kong, anthropologist Nicole Constable (1997) explores the ways in which Filipina women became constructed as the perfect "docile" workforce. All the major players in the Philippine-to-Hong Kong maid trade—the labor agencies, employers, governments, and the women themselves—had an investment in ensuring that Filipinas were docile and obedient domestic workers. Constable details how Filipinas became the desired domestic servant labor force in the 1970s, replacing the Chinese who earlier filled this role. As the ethnic Chinese domestic servants in Hong Kong became more entrenched—and could command higher wages—they became, and were perceived as becoming, less malleable. Further, unlike the Chinese workers, who by and large shared the same ethnic, racial, and national identity as their Hong Kong employers, "Filipinas are increasingly seen as a group whose differences are not simply class based, or even ethnic or cultural, but racially, biologically, and 'naturally' constituted. . . . To some, the term Filipino has become synonymous with 'domestic worker.' . . . Household work is viewed as logical or "natural" for Filipinos to do" (Constable, 1997: 38–39). By the mid-1990s there were about 150,000 foreign domestic workers in Hong Kong, the vast majority of whom were Filipina, with some small numbers from Indonesia, Thailand, and India.

REFUGEES

Among the most vulnerable of migrants are refugees, who comprise a large and growing share of people on the move around the world. It's often difficult to get a clear picture of the size and status of refugee movements. By definition, they are a population in flux, and many governments are not eager to admit to the scope of their refugee problems. Nonetheless, a rough estimate from the United Nations High Commission on Refugees (the main international agency concerned with the welfare of refugees) suggests that in the mid-1990s there were about twenty-five million refugees in the world; this number has grown sevenfold since the mid-1970s. Refugee populations are created by political upheaval, wars, oppression, environmental catastrophes, severe climate events such as flooding or drought, other natural hazards, and sometimes intentionally as an "ethnic cleansing" strategy.

Whether internally displaced (remaining within their national borders) or international (seeking asylum across national borders), refugee populations are among the most needy and desperate migrant groups. Most refugee flows are between Third World countries: in 1995, for example, the largest global refugee flows were from Afghanistan into Iran (1.6 million) and Pakistan (1 million), and from Rwanda to Zaire (1.3 million). Many of the receiving countries are unable to provide adequate shelter and care for the refugees; often refugees are fleeing from terrible to barely better circumstances, escaping from one state of misery to another.

Women and men are affected differently at all stages of a refugee crisis: by the events that provoke flight, by the circumstances of exile, and by the conditions on their return home (Ogata, 1995: 19). The majority of the world's refugees are women, and in some cases they represent a significantly disproportionate share of populations in crisis (see Table 4.4).

While all refugees experience great hardship, women refugees shoulder particular burdens. Women often find themselves fleeing from one country where their status is low to another where it is no better; as refugees, they sink even lower. Women typically have little say in the development of national and international refugee policies, nor in the administration of refugee camps. With no protection from their family or state, women refugees are chronically vulnerable to abuse, especially rape (often by camp guards or other "protectors"). At the same time, women as refugees are still expected to perform the tasks of child care, cleaning, and cooking, but without resources. Family survival depends on women's ability to be the "shock absorbers" of crisis. Since the early 1990s, the United Nations High Commission on Refugees has developed a priority focus on women refugees, but women still tend to be "second class" sufferers.

A recent development in international refugee law is the recognition of gender-based persecution as a basis for asylum claims. Most Western industrialized nations have highly restrictive legal definitions of "refugees." The United States, for example, will only give asylum to refugees who meet the legal test of "credible fear of political

TABLE 4.4. Women Refugees as a Percentage of All Refugees in Asylum Countries, 1995

Cameroon	45%	Djibouti	53%
Iran	45%	Cote d'Ivoire	53%
Iraq	47%	Central African Republic	53%
Mexico	49%	Benin	55%
Nepal	49%	Mauritania	56%
Bangladesh	51%	Ghana	56%
Burundi	52%	Kenya	58%
Pakistan	53%	Algeria	63%

Source: United Nations High Commission on Refugees (1996).

persecution" if returned to their country of origin. In the past, most refugees who met these criteria were activists or opposition leaders fleeing authoritarian government regimes—student leaders of the 1989 Tiananmen Square uprising who fled China, for example, or democracy activists who fled Nigeria. However, recently, refugee advocates have begun to challenge these narrow interpretations of asylum law, and are arguing that women often face gender-specific persecution. Women may be fleeing countries where practices such as genital mutilation or dowry murders put them at risk, or where they face arrest for violating restrictions on dress or behavior. Persecutions such as these have previously been interpreted as private or cultural problems, not defined as "political" under refugee law.

The most significant shift in recognizing gender-specific persecution has occurred in Canada. In 1991, a Saudi Arabian woman arrived at a Montreal airport requesting political asylum. The basis for her claim was that as a woman in Saudi Arabia she faced constant threats and assaults if she did not adhere to strict restrictions on her dress and movement. One of the immigration commissioners reviewing her case wrote that she "would do well to comply with the laws in her home country" (quoted in Davidson, 1994: 22), and her case was at first denied. However, after several other reviews she was accepted as a bona fide political refugee. In 1993, Canada became the first country in the world to issue guidelines expanding the basis of refugee claims to include gender-related persecution. Similar reforms are now being pressed in the United States and other Western nations.

THE SEX TRADE

The sex trade is one of the most distinctive women-specific "migrations"—it is distinguished, in large part, by its coercive and violent character, but also by its shadowy and complex geography. Every year, millions of women are traded around the world to serve in brothels, private clubs, and entertainment centers. Some of these women are willing participants in this sex migration. For some women, prostitution may be a lucrative and even empowering economic option. The largest share of women and girls caught in the global sex trade, however, are unwilling participants, often sold into sexual slavery by their families, or tricked into the trade by advertisements for legitimate-sounding jobs. International sex trafficking is big business involving millions of women and generating billions in revenue. Prostitutes are traded, girls are bought and exchanged among cartels, and international orders for fresh prostitute recruits are placed through brokers. The international traffic in women and girls is flourishing, fueled by a global economy that has heightened economic disparities between countries.

The geography of the international sex trade traces the contours of economic disparity between men and women at all scales, and between regions on a global scale. The trade in women and girls flows along "core–periphery" gradients: from Nepal to India, from the Philippines to Japan, from the Dominican Republic to the Netherlands, from Ukraine to Israel. New regions and countries enter into the sex trade as their economic fortunes wax or wane. As women's poverty has deepened in Eastern Europe since the early 1990s, for example, this area has become a major source region for prostitutes; as the economy expands in parts of Asia such as China and Malaysia, men in those countries are fueling an increased demand for the traffic in women and girls (see Figure 4.7).

Most trafficking takes one of four forms. First, women who are already prostitutes in one country are often "exchanged" by their pimps to another. Second, girls are often sold into prostitution by poor families who are in some instances aware that they are selling their daughter into prostitution, but more often than not believe that the child will be employed as a domestic servant or a factory worker. Once prostituted, the already low value of girls to their families drops even lower. The AIDS/HIV epidemic appears to be fueling demand for ever younger girls (and boys) as customers try to find "safe" commercial sex partners. Third, women are also lured into the sex trade under false pretenses—they are hired to be waitresses or maids, for example, and then forced into prostitution. The maid trade and the sex trade are thus intertwined. And finally, there is considerable evidence of a literal slave trade that starts with the kidnapping of women or girls, often from regions mired in poverty.

A corollary to the sex trade is sex tourism, which is literally that: hundreds of thousands of men each year flock to various centers for "sex holidays." Sometimes men travel on their own, but more often they travel as part of organized tours typically organized as "package sex tours" by travel agencies in Japan, Australia or Western Europe. The majority of sex tourists come from four regions: Australia and New Zealand; Western Europe, especially Germany and Scandinavia; the United States and Canada; and the Middle East. Sex tourism is big business, an important source of foreign revenue within the host country, and in most instances, as a result, has the implicit (or even direct) support of the host governments.

Sex tourism in many countries started with brothels established to service military bases. In Southeast Asia, for example, a thriving sex tourism business has long existed, largely as the result of the overwhelming U.S. military presence in this region throughout the 1960s, 1970s, and 1980s. What has changed in Southeast Asia is the clien-

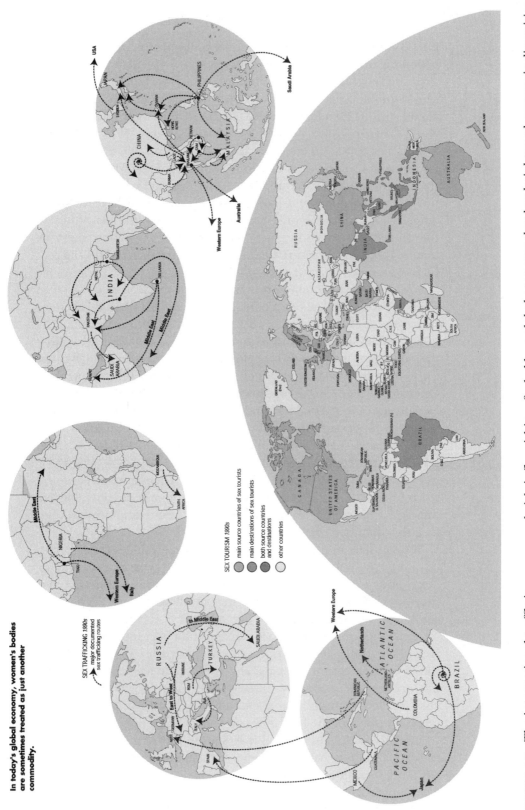

FIGURE 4.7. The international traffic in women and girls is flourishing, fueled by a global economy that has heightened economic disparities between countries.

tele. Reflecting the new integration of China and Vietnam into the global economy, men from those countries are now participating in sex tourism, traveling for sex to Thailand and the Philippines. The women who service the sex tourism industry (often under force) are both "local" women and women and girls imported into these centers through international sex trafficking. The new sex tourism fringe is extending to countries such as Cuba, India, and Hungary

Women's "watch" groups and activist networks have been key to making the sex trade visible. For example, the Philippine-based Third World Movement Against the Exploitation of Women has organized against militarized prostitution in Southeast Asia, and operates shelters and training centers for women who want to leave the sex industry. International feminist groups, most prominently the Coalition Against Trafficking in Women and the Global Network Against Trafficking, have pushed the issue of coerced prostitution (and child prostitution) to the front of human rights agendas.

We started this chapter with the "body in space," and have ended with men on sex holidays. This is not quite the same as coming full circle, but it does underscore the theme that holds the discussion together: simply, that the ways in which women and men get to and through places, and the reasons and the ways in which they do so, vary. These variances are sometimes by-products of other social relations (for example, the political economy of mobility), but they are also more often than not fashioned as intentionally engendered.

Chapter 5

NATIONS AND EMPIRES

At the World's Columbian Exposition held in Chicago in 1893, organized to celebrate the four hundredth anniversary of the European "discovery" of America, visitors could view the material consequences of that discovery in the display cases and exhibits contained within the massive beaux arts buildings (Figure 5.1). They could travel in gondolas along the canals of the White City (so named because its buildings all had white exteriors), re-creating the splendors of Renaissance Venice, or ride the Ferris wheel on the midway. They also could visit the Woman's Building (Figure 5.2), a particularly popular attraction for women because of its tea room, model kitchen, and displays of women's handicrafts (Weimann, 1981).

Prominent among the educational exhibits within the Woman's Building was a display organized by the Smithsonian Institution, highlighting the early historical contribution of women's work to the progress of human "civilization." Called "Women's Work in Savagery," the display cases were filled primarily with examples of Native American women's labor—textile making, tanning, basketweaving—in an attempt to portray the significance of women's work to historical progress. Prominence was given also to displays of women's work throughout the world—or, at least, in the countries that contributed exhibits to the Exposition. Represented here were the imperial powers of the United States, Great Britain, Germany, France, and Spain, and some of their colonies—for example, Ceylon, the East Indies, and Siam. The imperial powers had much grander displays and were

FIGURE 5.1. Bird's-eye view of the World's Columbian Exposition, Chicago, 1893. Meant to showcase America's new prominent economic and cultural position on the world's stage, the Columbian Exposition was designed in the beaux arts style, emphasizing classical and Renaissance motifs. As depicted here, it also included Venetian canals complete with gondolas.

WOMAN'S   BUILDING COST $ 138.000-ARCHITECT MISS SOPHIA G. HAYDEN.

FIGURE 5.2. View of the Woman's Building at the 1893 Chicago Exposition. Designed by a woman architect, Sophia Hayden, the Woman's Building was one of the most popular buildings at the fairgrounds, containing a tearoom, a model kitchen, and displays depicting women's historical contributions to "civilization."

given the prime exhibit space in the building. What was on display was visual proof of the inevitability and progress of imperialism; the visitor could view through time, and across space, evidence of the superiority of white, middle-class Americans and Europeans. This, of course, was not unique to the Woman's Building—it was the primary message of the entire exposition, as well as most other exhibits and fairs held in England and the United States throughout the latter part of the nineteenth and early twentieth centuries (Rydell, 1984).

Yet the imperial displays in the Woman's Building were in some ways different from the others. Many of the women who led the efforts to construct the building, and who helped organize the displays, were explicitly interested in promoting women's rights. The Lady Board of Managers, as they were officially called, included prominent society women, but also middle-class women from around the country who were active in women's clubs and organizations, such as the Women's Christian Temperance Union. Although many of them were not "suffragettes," they did want the building to highlight the value of women's work throughout time and across space. They believed, in accord with the reigning ideology of the time, that women were essentially different from men, and therefore they concluded that the way forward was to show that women's "difference," their civilizing influence, was as important to historical progress as men's work. And so the displays focused on the commonalities of women's contributions across national and cultural borders—whether it was a Sioux basket, or French lace, women's role in the socioeconomic progress of "humankind" was presented as different from, but equally important to, the contributions of men.

To highlight how women served a complementary, but equally important role in society, the Chicago women mobilized exhibits from as many countries as possible. Bertha Palmer, head of the Lady Board of Managers, originally wrote to contacts in more than 50 countries, and twenty-three actually contributed with official exhibits. They also mobilized participation from U.S. women's organizations groups as diverse as the National Council of Women, the Woman's Board of Missions, and the Woman's Industrial Educational Union. The goal of the organizers was to create an impression of a type of universal sisterhood.

This is not to say that the organizers were somehow removed from the imperialist ideology that reigned supreme in the Western world at this time. But they were caught between two positions: while they were white, middle- and upper-class Americans, and enjoyed most of the privileges that came with that position, they were also women, occupying an inferior and "other" status in Victorian America. Both of these positions were represented in the Woman's Building. While the exhibits implicitly suggested that *Western* women's work was the pinnacle of women's contributions to society, they also celebrated *all* women's work, even that of "savages." By way of contrast, the exhibits at the rest of the Exposition, organized of course by men, had only one political agenda, and that agenda was *not* to promote the equality of all men's contributions to society!

The Woman's Building of 1893, then, provides a fascinating glimpse into the intersection of feminism, racism, imperialism, and nationalism.

VICTORIAN LADY TRAVELERS

On display in the Woman's Building at the World's Columbian Exposition were some of the objects that U.S. explorer May French Sheldon had brought back from her 1891 travels in Africa, objects that women in those countries had made. These objects were given their own case in the exhibits of women's historical contributions to civilization. The clothing and traveling equipment used by Kate Marsden, another U.S. female explorer, in her travels in Siberia in 1891, were also on display. Both displays offered proof of the hardiness of women and their abilities to contribute to geographical knowledge.

The Chicago women organizers were clearly proud of the accomplishments of these intrepid "lady travelers," who, in the late nineteenth century, seemed to be exploring the world almost on a par with men. Indeed, many middle- and upper-class European and U.S. women on their own, or with their husbands, participated in geographical expeditions to Africa, Asia, and South America throughout the exploratory and colonial times of the nineteenth and early twentieth centuries. These women were explorers, imperialists, geographers, and "ladies." Often in positions of power when traveling because of the color of their skin and their attachment to imperial authority, they occupied an inferior and prescribed position when at home because of their sex. Isabella Bird, for example, was often ill when at home in England and Scotland, but seemed robust in her many travels, first in the Rocky Mountains in the United States, and then in Korea, India, and China. When traveling she could escape the strictures of Victorian society, and the act of traveling kept her from thinking about her loneliness and lack of power at home. She wrote to her sister, "I always feel dil [dull and inactive] when I am stationary. . . . When I'm travelling, I don't feel it, but that is why I can never stay anywhere" (quoted in Birkett, 1989: 62). The very act of movement through space, as well as the distance that travel put between them and the strictures of home, freed some Victorian women to explore other sides of their personalities (see also Chapter 4). It also afforded them knowledge of "exotic" places and the authority to speak and write about them, enabling some of them to become "professional" geographers who published the results of their "scientific" surveys in scholarly journals.

Geographers have recently engaged in a critical examination of imperialism, focusing particularly on how the discipline of geography was central to its political and economic agendas (Godlewska and Smith, 1994). In the eighteenth and nineteenth centuries, geographers from the imperial powers of Great Britain, the Netherlands, Germany, and France were sent out to gather information about the resources of other lands, and returned to write about those lands and create the body of knowledge from which political, imperial decisions were made. Although most of these geographers who were sent on official missions by governments were men, a sizable group of women also traveled into colonial regions and returned with information that was used to legitimize and promote colonialism.

It is interesting to consider whether imperial women viewed the world and their travels differently from their male peers. Did it matter that they were women? Did the fact that Euro-American women occupied apparently contradictory positions (that is, they were oppressed at home, but privileged abroad) alter the types of knowledge they gained from their explorations, or the ways that they wrote about that knowledge, or the impact of that knowledge on the course of imperialism? As Sara Mills points out, "Women's position is often rather ambivalent" (1994: 39).

It does appear that women's writings about encounters abroad were different from men's in some important ways. For example, women generally seemed more sensitive to the concerns of women and children in other countries. And they often wrote of their own personal, emotional response to different landscapes and different cultures. Of course, within the corps of women explorers, different women wrote about their experiences differently, depending on their economic class and individual backgrounds.

Part of the explanation for these gender differences lies in the gendering of exploration and imperialism itself. In the nineteenth century, empire was "coded as a place where extreme forms of masculine behavior were expected, even if that is not what happened in reality" (Mills, 1994: 37). This "masculinization" of empire, as Mills calls it, meant that women explorers were always confronting a way of doing and thinking in which they had to "alter" their femininity. For example, most women explorers were not taken seriously as geographers—that is, they were not seen as being capable of making scientific contributions to knowledge. Indeed, few of the women explorers seemed to be interested in naming and claiming new geographical discoveries. Their journeys were not necessarily about conquering and controlling, but were often more about self-discovery. There are, of course, exceptions to this. American Louise Boyd, for example, had several fjords named after her in Greenland, after she "discovered" them (Olds, 1985). But most of the women travelers of the late nineteenth and early twentieth centuries were not sponsored by geographical groups or governments whose explicit intent was discovery of new lands for the imperial powers. Instead, they traveled to escape the strictures of European or U.S. Victorian culture, and to gain a sense of control over their own lives.

Geographer Alison Blunt's (1994a, 1994b) analysis of the travel writing of Mary Kingsley is particularly revealing. An Englishwoman, Kingsley visited and explored West Africa in the 1890s, and published what became a popular book, *Travels in West Africa*, in 1897. Because of the "inherently spatial ambivalence of her identity as a white woman traveling in the context of imperialism" (Blunt, 1994: 52), Kingsley's writing style is different from the style that characterizes most male accounts. In her descriptions of the landscapes of West Africa, Kingsley "mapped" the region in narratives and metaphors, rather than in cartographic precision. She often gave personal accounts of her experiences that emphasized her own aesthetic and emotional responses to the landscape. This style undermined her authority as a scientist, but reinforced her personal authority as an eyewitness. She also provided landscape descriptions that expressed her personal identification with the place, instead of the "monarch-of-all-I-survey" genre of travel writing more characteristic of male accounts. For example, her description of the rapids on the Ogowé River (in present-day Gabon) includes a discussion of how the sight of its natural beauty removed her from her daily worries, and transported her away: "If I have a heaven, that will be mine" (quoted in Blunt, 1994a: 62).

Blunt suggests that this writing style emphasizes the connections between observer and observed, quite different from the standard, male style of providing a panoramic gaze that objectifies landscape. Blunt is not arguing that Kingsley somehow stood outside imperialism or did not participate in furthering its course. Her words and observations certainly formed important parts of the knowledge making that was integral to European imperialism in Africa. But she is arguing that as a Victorian woman, the social context in which Kingsley's words were written and read was different from that of men's words. Blunt argues that Kingsley had to constantly negotiate the demands of establishing herself as an authority of sorts (so, participating in the male world), while not upsetting gender categories so much that she would lose all authority (so, not participating in the male world completely). In other words, she had to gain masculine authority by acting feminine!

A similar ambivalence of voice and identity is evident throughout many accounts of other white women traveling and living in Africa. Geographer Cheryl McEwan (1994) examined how African women were portrayed by white British women in West Africa. She shows that although these women's accounts reveal their own racial prejudices, they also "provided an important counterbalance and complement to those of male travelers" (1994: 95). Mary Kingsley, for example, personally identified with West African women, comparing her own quest to gain scientific knowledge with West African women's attempts to learn the secrets of men's societies. Kingsley wrote of "the inextinguishable thirst for knowledge, so long as that knowledge is forbidden, which characterizes our sex" (McEwan, 1994: 87). Constance Larymore, wife of a colonial military administrator in Nigeria, provided descriptions of African women in her 1908 book *A Resident's Wife in Africa* that refuted the "myth of the oppressed African wife" (McEwan, 1994: 84). Indeed, she came to reverse her earlier held conceptions of harems as sites of immoral and lascivious behavior: she visited harems herself and discovered that they were comprised of women of all ages "laughing, clapping their hands, calling greetings and salutations incessantly" (McEwan, 1994: 85). Such descriptions of African women challenged widely held British assumptions, but, at the same time, those descriptions were only given any credence in Britain because the writers had authority based on their racial difference. As white women, they could be authorities on Africa. Again, we see ambivalent subject positions: as women, these travelers had access to African women and could identify with some of their situations, but the basis of their authority was their whiteness.

WOMEN AND COLONIAL SPACE

Imperial women, of course, didn't just travel through colonized regions of the world, they also lived there. Indeed, they were often sent out deliberately to "civilize" the empire. Geographer Morag Bell (1995) outlines how in the early twentieth century the British government convinced schoolgirls to emigrate to the colonies upon graduation by suggesting that it was their patriotic duty to bring their feminine, "civilizing" influence to those "uncivilized" portions of the empire. As Bell shows, women were thought to be particularly useful as imperial citizens in South Africa after the South African War (1899–1902), when the "culture of empire" (1995: 135) shifted to one that was less militaristic and more conciliatory: "Empire based upon the flexible and voluntary concept of community contrasted sharply with Empire based upon domination and subordination. Women's emigration was central to the creation of this 'new spirit'" (1995: 135). In this new form of empire, women's "natural" spaces of family and community were seen as integral to the maintenance of empire.

Between 1862 and 1914, voluntary societies helped more than twenty thousand women emigrate to British colonies (Ware, 1992: 126). This policy both reflected and reinforced racial and sexist stereotypes. In British policy, the peoples of the empire were considered to occupy inferior positions in the hierarchy of civilization, and therefore were viewed as needing the "civilizing" force represented by British women, the exemplars of white, civilized, Britishness. Thus Victorian notions of femininity were exported to the colonies. Similarly, in the United States, as we mentioned in Chapter 1, the ideal of female domesticity was integral to the U.S. government's early-twentieth-century Native American policy; white women were sent to Native American reservations as exemplars and teachers of "proper" home life. If the actual conquering of the empire was gendered as a masculine process, the civilizing of it was gendered as a feminine process.

Domestic Space on the Frontier

In the United States, the displacement of Native American peoples, and the settlement of whites on the frontier, may have been imagined as a masculine process. For example, Annette Kolodny (1975) details how the land itself was seen and written about as female, so that male "penetration" of it was seen as "natural." But many white women were involved in the process as active agents. The harshness of life on the frontier deterred most white women from venturing forth, but the opportunities and adventure it presented lured some Victorian women from the parlors of the East to the sod houses of the West. Many turn-of-the-century homesteaders on the Great Plains were single women, as homesteading presented the only opportunity for working-class women to own their own land. In North Dakota, for example, sociologist H. Elaine Lindgren found that single women accounted for twelve percent of the homesteaders in nine select counties (1991: 52). In five of the three hundred townships included in those counties, single women homesteaded more than thirty percent of the land! They built their own houses, cultivated the land, and created social worlds for themselves, as we can see in Figure 5.3.

White women who settled the frontier with their husbands were engaged equally in productive labor. They may have been able to bring with them some small reminders of the domestic comfort they left behind, such as curtains or musical instruments, but these were

FIGURE 5.3. Photographs of Amelia and Lena Brennon in front of their sod homes in North Dakota, c. late nineteenth century. Although often envisioned as masculine space, the frontier on the Great Plains was also homesteaded by single women, who built their own homes, cultivated the land, and created feminized social worlds.

true luxury items, not for daily enjoyment. As geographer Jeanne Kay found in her study of Mormon women in Utah, the homestead itself was the site of considerable labor: it was "the location of essential and productive outdoor work in the garden, orchard, poultry coops, and dairy. Many women expected to be largely self-sufficient in foodstuffs they produced on their irrigated one-acre house lots as well as to earn income through a cottage industry within its bounds, such as selling produce, weaving, or hat-making"(1997: 372). Within such a context, the few, feminine luxuries took on particularly important meanings. As a symbol of "civilization," the parlor organ, for example, was often carted out to the Great Plains in the latter half of the nineteenth century, an enormous effort considering the dangerous and lengthy journey (Figure 5.4).

The now famous short story by Elizabeth Glaspell, "A Jury of Her Peers," poignantly evokes the significance of the domestic to women on the frontier. In the story, a sheriff is called out to a remote farmstead where he finds John Wright strangled to death in bed, and his wife, Minnie, behaving strangely. The sheriff arrests Minnie, but after searching the farm and consulting with the county attorney, he can find no evidence of a motive that would point to the wife's guilt. Meanwhile, the sheriff's wife and the wife of a neighbor, who have been called to the farm to fetch items for Mrs. Wright while she is in jail, conduct their own "investigation." By examining the smallest of items, particularly Minnie's changing style of stitching on a quilt, they begin to understand what really happened. Because they know the daily rituals of a farmwife, and therefore know how to "see" the domestic, they begin to uncover clues that help them piece together what had happened. John Wright, they realize, had killed Minnie's canary by wringing its neck. And since they also know that the bird represented her last and only vestige of beauty in an otherwise bleak life of unremitting labor, they immediately understand why this act pushed her over the edge. As the neighbor's wife, Mrs. Hale, says to

FIGURE 5.4. Photograph of Mr. and Mrs. David Hilton and their children, Custer County, Nebraska, 1887. Homesteading in Nebraska was certainly a strenuous life, but it did not preclude participation in the reigning ethos of Victorian domesticity. This parlor organ was so important to this family's self-image that they chose to have their portraits taken around it.

the sheriff's wife: "If there had been years and years of—nothing, then a bird to sing to you, it would be awful—still—after the bird was still" (Edwards and Diamond, 1973: 377). The wives (who constitute a "jury of peers") consider telling their husbands what they have found out, but decide against it. Without saying a word to each other, they look into each other's eyes and conclude that the murder of the husband was justified. They remain silent when the sheriff closes the case and releases Minnie. As the story reminds us, women often worked against all odds to make their own feminine spaces on the frontier, and those little pieces of feminine comfort were dear to them.

Domestic Space in the Colonies

The presence of British women in the empire was marked by specific spatial forms and controls. If it was important to guard a woman's respectability on the streets of London (as we mentioned in Chapter 3), it was doubly important to guard her amid the "uncivilized" people of the empire. In India, the British designed their settlements so that there would always be a clear, visual distinction between the landscapes of the ruler and that of the ruled, and in a way that kept these two separate. Often the British would build an entirely new city, designed along geometric, rational principles, that stood next to, but in direct contrast to, the organic forms of the Indian city. The British colonial city of New Delhi, for example, was built in the first decades of the twentieth century adjacent to the indigenous city of Delhi. New Delhi was designed with long, wide streets and parks and promenade grounds that surround the important government buildings. This city was built in direct contrast to Delhi, a city that had evolved over hundreds of years, and whose streets therefore were winding and narrow. This visual difference served both to materially express and reinforce the differences between the colonizer and the colonized, and to keep separate the world of British women from the world of native culture. As Sara Mills suggests, "colonial town planning was an idealized embodiment of colonial relations" (1996: 137).

And yet, of course, these ideal plans could hardly contain the daily behavior of most people living in these cities. Indian servants often lived within or close to the British areas; often Indian soldiers in the British Indian army were often stationed nearby; British women shopped in the "native" town and performed missionary and other benevolent work there; and some white British even served as prostitutes in the native town. In this "contact zone," as Mary Louise Pratt (1992) calls it, relations between the colonizer and the colonized were complex, and women of both worlds met under varying circumstances, and in varying power relationships.

The possibilities presented by these literal crossings between physical worlds were greatly limited in what were called "hill stations." These were settlements built by the British in the Indian mountains specifically for British women and their families. The mountains provided cooler, and purportedly better air, and of course these settlements were isolated from most of Indian society. As geographer Judith Kenny (1995) reminds us, hill stations such as Ootacamund in Madras (Figure 5.5), were designed in direct imitation of the landscapes of upper-class Britain, complete with elegant homes, gardens, and social clubs. In these settings, British women could retain their proper status without tarnish, while at the same time bringing civilization to the men of the empire.

Although isolated from Indian cities and therefore removed from the explicit power politics that were played out in these colonial settings, hill stations were not immune from those power politics.

FIGURE 5.5. The MacNab family, posed in front of their bungalow in the hill station of Ootacamund in Madras, India, c. 1910. This pastoral setting, reminiscent of upper-class British homes and landscapes, shows how Victorian notions of proper domesticity and domestic spaces were used to legitimize imperial rule. Domesticity "civilized" the "savages" of the empire.

The operation of these British, upper-class enclaves was only possible with Indian labor, in the form of cooks, domestic servants, gardeners, and so on. And so even in these domestic settings colonial power relations were replicated.

Sara Mills (1996) has shown that much of the housing in Indian hill towns was built in a bungalow style, with an open floor plan to provide for cooling; this design meant that behavior inside the house was always on display for the outside world. It was important, therefore, that the everyday behavior of British women would reenact their status—that is, women's everyday activities were on display, so they had to monitor their actions to fit into their roles as proper British women. British women, in essence, were spatially "out of view" in the colonies, and yet were always on display. The domestic world over which they had control, the private spaces of the home and the garden, were indeed the spaces that were constantly on public display. In order for them to perform their civilizing duty, they had to be both protected from, and yet somehow interactive with, "native" peoples. And this was accomplished as they acted out, on a daily basis, the rituals of white rule and white femininity. They were meant to embody—in the way they treated their servants, their husbands, their children, their pianos, their domestic chores—the highest ideals that British "civilization" was bringing to the empire.

In a somewhat related manner, power relationships were played out within the spaces of plantations in the pre-Civil War U.S. South. On most plantations, slave cabins were clustered together, apart from the slave owner's plantation house, but close enough to be under his visual scrutiny. Yet many slave women were assigned positions inside the owner's house as cook, maids, and nurses. Slave girls in particular often spent a good deal of their childhoods in the mistress's quarters. It was more convenient to have servants-in-training close at hand, and also, according to Elizabeth Fox-Genovese, "It was widely believed that the best way to develop good house servants, who were notoriously difficult to come by, was to raise them" (1988: 153). White slaveholding women and black slave women, then, were often occupying the same spaces. And within those spaces power relationships were performed on a daily basis, enacting and reinforcing the racist system that governed the U.S. South. So even in such domestic, private spaces as bedrooms and nurseries, racism was acted out by women.

Bringing the Imperial Home

In the United States and Great Britain, the domestic was made imperial. What we mean by this is that the domestic spaces of home were filled with commodities that were from the empire, or that took on meaning through the empire. Many of the rituals of Victorian middle-class British domestic culture were based on products from the empire: tea and coffee drinking, fashionable clothing, household cleaning products. Anne McClintock (1995), in her book *Imperial Leather*, stresses household soap as a prime example of a commodity that was both derived from colonial exploits (the oils came from plantations overseas) and took on meanings that involved much more than washing up. As she states, "At the beginning of the nineteenth century, soap was a scarce and humdrum item and washing a cursory activity at best. A few decades later, the manufacture of soap had burgeoned into an imperial commerce; Victorian cleaning rituals were peddled globally as the God-given sign of Britain's evolutionary superiority, and soap was invested with magical, fetish powers" (1995: 207).

In a sense, soap had come to stand for Britain's imperial, civilizing mission, as well as for its cult of domesticity. The ideal of cleanliness took on imperial meaning: to be clean was a sign of civilization, and therefore part of imperial duty. In an analysis of a Pear's soap advertisement, McClintock explains the relationship between cleanliness and imperial progress. A black boy is literally "scrubbed clean" of his color by a white boy, showing how soap is an agent of imperial notions of historical progress. Soap, then, becomes a bearer of evolutionary progress: "The magical fetish of soap promises that the commodity can regenerate the Family of Man by washing from the skin the very stigma of racial and class degeneration" (1995: 214). But it was not just soap that became a marker of empire within the home. All sorts of home commodities were packaged with imperial motifs— from biscuits to tea, from toothpaste to bacon. The empire was literally inscribed throughout the British Victorian home (Figure 5.6).

There were other, perhaps less obvious, imperial elements present in middle-class homes. If you had walked into most middle-class parlors in the United States in the 1880s and 1890s, you would have seen, to one degree or another, elements of a style of furnishing called, variously, "oriental," or "Turkish," or "Persian." This "oriental" style was a popular fad in Victorian America and Britain, influencing the design of carpets, wallpaper, and furniture. The style originated in the proliferation of images of the Middle East that flooded into popular pictorial magazines such as *Harper's Weekly* and *Frank Leslie's Illustrated Weekly*. The exoticism of these elaborate designs appealed to Victorian tastes, and became markers of class status.

Department stores were important purveyors of these imported styles, particularly in the way that they created displays to entice shoppers to buy the latest fad. The new marketing expertise of department store merchants was expressed in the way their stores

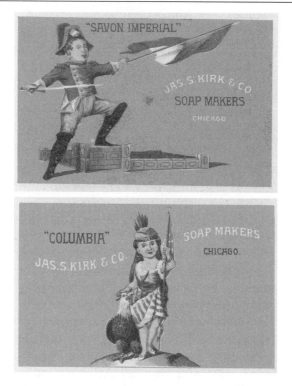

FIGURE 5.6. Victorian trade cards for Kirk soap. Soap was a home commodity that was derived from colonialism, since the oils that went into its production were from overseas plantations, and in addition was given meaning through colonialism. As you can see from these images, soap was often sold through its association with imperialism—soap could be seen as the purveyor of whiteness and "civilization."

were elaborately decorated, often to fit one theme or another. And according to historian William Leach, oriental themes were very popular: " 'An indolent oriental atmosphere'—sheiks, tents, exotically dressed women—'pervaded every nook and corner' of Sanger Brothers' Department Store in Dallas in March 1900" (1993: 83). In this way, images of an exotic "other" of the empire were commodified and made safe to bring home. The empire both made possible many of the commodities that outfitted Victorian homes, and gave the commodities themselves meanings beyond mere economic utility. Biscuits that were served on safaris in Africa, and carpets derived from Persian designs, carried the weight and meaning of empire into the homes, within the "heartland" of the empire.

In the United States, emblems of its internal "empire"—that is, of the Native Americans who by the end of the nineteenth century had been colonialized and displaced onto reservations—were also brought into the home. No longer seen as a military threat by the turn of the century, Native American cultures were represented in newspapers, novels, and museums, and turned into useful domestic symbols for the middle classes (Figure 5.7). Tokens of the so-called warrior-like Plains Indians, such as tomahawks and spears, were hung on walls as symbols of masculinity. As art historian Elizabeth Cromley (1996) argues, this was a particularly common motif in the decoration of boys' rooms. To "assure that there would be nothing 'girly' there," Cromley tells us, "an early twentieth-century author . . . advised that Indian rugs" (265) should be placed in the boy's room. Indian decor could also serve as a reminder of the natural, an element that seemed to be missing from the education of boys in the industrialized East. Navaho rugs on the floor, blankets spread on the bed, or scenes from Native American life on the walls could turn a room into

HISTORICAL CORNERS.   THE
AMERICAN INDIAN CORNER.

FIGURE 5.7. A depiction of a Native American-themed "historical corner," from *Home Decorator and Furnisher*, 1898. America's internal imperialism—its destruction of Native American populations—was literally brought into the middle-class home. Here, images of Native Americans were used to decorate masculine spaces, as they connoted the rough-and-tumble world of "nature" and the frontier.

a masculine and rugged retreat from the industrial, urban, and overcivilized "white" world. And yet, of course, this rugged world was safe, since it symbolized a nature under the control of white culture: "Indian goods were brought into the den, the lodge, and the boy's room to represent nature—a nature both noble and savage yet under the white man's control" (1996: 277). Again, we see here how representations of an exotic "other" are domesticated, and in the process are commodified and made safe for the white world. As Cromley concludes, "For both men and women in mainstream culture, using Indian goods in domestic space for decoration narrowed their encounter with Indians, protecting them from fully connecting with the tragic life Indians endured at the turn of the century" (1996: 280).

FEMINISM AND IMPERIALISM

One of the ideals that the British could share with their imperial subjects was the "proper" treatment of women (Ware, 1992). Many British colonizers suggested that a true test of the degree of civilization of a society was its treatment of women. The rhetoric supporting empire included a strong element of gendered moralism. Many "backward" countries needed the strong moral guidance that British Christian culture could provide, particularly when it came to the treatment of women. As Vron Ware states, the British believed that "the treatment of women by men could be read as an important index of a society's progress on the evolutionary scale of civilization" (1992: 162). Many British reformers, then, set out to study and improve the conditions in which women of the empire lived. Feminists in Britain joined in this effort, seeing an opportunity to help their "sisters" in India and Africa, and an opportunity to exercise their civilizing, patriotic duties. So these women acted as both proponents of women's rights and of imperial duty.

Vron Ware (1992) examined the politics of two such feminists who were concerned with the plight of women in India: Annette Ackroyd and Josephine Butler. Both women were inspired in their work by two impulses: first, a growing awareness by feminists in Great Britain in the mid-nineteenth century of the different forms of subordination of women around the world, as well as at home; and second, a familiarity with the Indian Social Reform movement, a movement that emphasized the role that British women could play in bringing reform and education to their Indian "sisters." As Ware suggests, most of the British public imagined Indian women to be living lives of "intense suffering behind closed doors" (1992: 129). Missionaries had sent back reports describing purdah—the religious strictures that kept women separate from men, and often out of public view—and the spectacle of sati—widow burning—and these had captured reformers' imaginations.

Annette Ackroyd went to Calcutta in the 1870s to set up a school for Hindu girls; Josephine Butler's activities were limited to reform efforts in Great Britain. Ware shows how Ackroyd (Figure 5.8), initially much dismayed by the explicit racism of the British in India, and hopeful of breaking down many of the boundaries separating Indian and British culture, found herself losing any hope that Indian society was able or even willing to change itself. After ten years of taking up various teaching posts in Great Britain and familiarizing herself with the Indian "situation" by attending lectures and taking courses in London, Ackroyd arrived in India in 1872. It took nearly a year after her arrival in India to overcome financial and logistical problems, but in November 1873 she opened her school for girls in Calcutta with five pupils (Ware, 1992: 143). The school remained open for a year and a half, but Ackroyd never considered it a success. She could not understand the way Indian society operated, and she seems to have alienated many of her students. As she wrote in her di-

FIGURE 5.8. Photograph of Annette Ackroyd with her pupils in India, 1875. Feminist Ackroyd left Britain for India, hoping to educate Indian women as part of her imperial duty.

ary in January 1875, after a three-day break, "School, most of the girls not returning" (quoted in Ware, 1992: 145).

In addition to Ackroyd's problematic relationship with her pupils, she was unable to form any close relationships with Indian women, and she came to deeply resent Indian men. She blamed Indian men for not helping "their" women, and therefore found them unworthy of power themselves. As a result, Ackroyd found herself becoming a fervent supporter of imperial rule. As Ware comments, Ackroyd "showed herself to have accepted the dominant ideology of imperialism: that it was only through contact with Western civilization that the 'natives' had any chance of being delivered from their own tyrannical customs" (1992: 147). Here we can see an interesting convergence of feminism and imperialism: to help Indian women, Ackroyd looked to the civilizing mission of British imperialism. Left on its own, Indian society, she believed, would remain barbaric in its treatment of women.

The story of Josephine Butler reveals somewhat different politics. Here we see how the ideology of imperialism helped support feminist politics at "home." Historian Antoinette Burton (1994) convincingly portrays the ways that imperialism created situations that allowed British women to push for equal rights and even suffrage. Two forces were at work. The first was that imperial logic necessitated the creation in British imaginations of an uncivilized "other" (the Indian, or the African) to whom the British were superior, and for whom they had a duty to help civilize. For British feminists, the Indian woman was the "other" who needed their Christian assistance to free her from her backward treatment from both Indian men and British men. The Indian woman, in effect, served as a platform on which British feminists could test their authority as equal citizens in the empire. Second, in the imperial mind, the mission of the British was to civilize and to purify the colonized, the "others." This logic sustained Victorian notions of the role of women in society: they were the civilizers, the ones who brought morality to an increasingly immoral world. So if women were seeking equal citizenship at home, a significant way of proving their worth was to show how they were indispensable to the civilizing effort of the empire. This allowed them to participate as full citizens without giving up their purported femininity. Their feminine duty as the civilizers was integral to the maintenance of a "pure" empire. The cause of empire thus served to give British women authority to speak and act at home on what they hoped would be equal footing with men.

Josephine Butler was an avid crusader for reform efforts on behalf of women in both Great Britain and India. Her writings and activism from the 1860s onward were influential in several important reform movements, including the repeal of the Contagious Disease

Acts (a series of acts passed in the 1860s both in England and in its colonies that enforced registration of prostitutes, and made compulsory their medical examination and treatment). Butler and other reformers considered these acts to be "a violation of personal liberty, a humiliation for the women obliged to submit to them, and, not least, an ineffective solution for reducing venereal disease or eliminating prostitution" (Burton, 1994: 130). After the acts were repealed in Britain in 1886, Butler shifted her attention to the plight of women in India, feeling that it was her duty as a woman and an imperial subject to help Indian women and continue her purification of empire.

Her efforts, as Burton shows, were underpinned by the dual logic of imperialism outlined above: that Indian women needed to be represented by British women, and that only through empire would Indian women be relieved of their oppression. Although Butler saw many imperial policies as corrupt and oppressive for women, particularly the Contagious Disease Acts, she did not envision as a solution the end of imperial rule. Rather, Butler called for the repeal of the Contagious Disease Acts in India as a way of creating a more ethical empire. She imagined that a more ethical empire, under feminine influence, could then improve the status of Indian women. By this logic, then, empire was "not only the cause of but also the solution to social problems in India" (Burton, 1994: 150).

Butler thus made the case for the separate but equal role of women in British society based on their indispensability to empire. This imperial logic, then, gave legitimacy and authority to the British feminist cause. The presumed dependence of Indian women on British women made clear British women's public authority, and the civilizing mission of women in the empire made clear British women's "fitness for citizenship in the imperial nation-state" (Burton, 1994: 17).

Thus, imperialism helped British feminists in their cause at home. It is more difficult to say if the same was true in the United States, partly because empire takes on different meaning in the U.S. context. Certainly the Victorian period did witness in the United States the first great statement of its empire: the purported closing of the frontier, a term that refers to the final elimination of Native Americans as any threat to the white settlement of the continent. The period also witnessed the first military expedition outside the borders of the country: the Spanish-American War and the assumption of territorial control over the Philippines, Puerto Rico, Hawaii, and Guam. Yet the degree to which U.S. feminism developed in relationship to these events is, at this point, difficult to determine. We do know that in the Woman's Building at the 1893 World's Columbian Exposition, there were many visual representations of Native American women, as well as of "natives" from many of the British colonies,

so there certainly was interest among prominent U.S. women in dealing with their "sisters" of the empire.

But in the United States the issue of African American–white relations was more central to feminist discussions. This formed the significant relationship that shaped the ways in which many white
women's political causes were defined. For example, the Lady Board
of Managers of the Woman's Building at the Chicago 1893 World's
Exposition were divided over whether to allow a black woman onto
the board. Many feared that a black woman might undercut the
legitimacy of the board. In the end, the board remained all white
(Weiman, 1981). This controversy echoed the divide within the entire U.S. women's suffrage movement after the Civil War. The align-
ment of the women's rights movement with the abolitionist cause in
the early half of the nineteenth century began to fall apart after slavery was abolished in 1863. Many white women believed that their voting privileges should come before that of black men, and that the
movement for women's rights would be damaged by aligning itself
with racial politics. "At the heart of this belief," Vron Ware tells us,
"was the fear that white women needed protection from black men"
(1992: 201). Many whites believed that allowing black men to vote
and participate equally in politics would place women, particularly
white women, in a dangerously subordinate position. Elizabeth Cady
Stanton, for example, felt that white women would be treated worse
under the rule of black men than under the rule of white men, since
black men would be looking for revenge after years of subjugation
(Ware, 1992). One important strand of U.S. feminism, therefore, developed out of a fear of black men and the presumed need to protect
white women. Thus, some U.S. white feminists actively employed racism to help justify voting rights for white women.

GENDER AND NATIONALISM

Ideas of empire, as we have seen, are suffused with notions of gender. And so too are ideas about "the nation." Not only have nations
often been imagined as masculine or feminine, but women are often
imagined as the signifiers of the "heart" of a nation, so that protecting them from outsiders often becomes integral to nationalist struggles.

To understand how this happens, we first have to realize that nations don't exist naturally, nor have they always existed. Nations, in
the now much-repeated words of Benedict Anderson (1991), are
"imagined communities." A nation is comprised of cultural, socioeconomic, and political systems that converge on some shared con-

ception of community. Women and the feminine represent the part of nation that is unchanging and "natural." In contrast, men and the masculine represent the political and the volatile official apparatus of the nation. The nation is imagined as masculine when it conducts its political affairs, fights its wars, and builds its highways; it is imagined as feminine when it protects its children, tends its land, and maintains its values.

Political scientists distinguish between a *state* and a *nation*. The "state" refers to the political/economic systems that govern a group of people, and the political borders that contain them. The state, then, is often dynamic and changing. The term "nation" refers to people bound together by common culture: history, religion, language, and so on. The sense of nation is often linked with community and homeland and is typically seen as enduring and unchanging. In Jan Pettman's words, the "state is often gendered male, and the nation gendered female" (1996: 49).

But nationalism itself is a complex term, and we can't really understand its relationship to gender without first exploring different types of nationalisms. Jan Pettman (1996) has outlined several different types of nationalism and the role women and gender representation plays in each. "Dominant nationalism" refers to a state that uses power to control and often exclude others. It employs the state apparatuses to identify those who "belong," and often destroys those who are considered "outsiders." Nazi Germany represents an extreme form of such nationalism, but strains of it are evident in many places, including the United States and Great Britain. The notion of women as "mothers of the nation" is often a powerful tool in "dominant nationalisms," as state leaders are concerned with controlling the purity—literally—of the nation. Such governments typically attempt to scrutinize, direct, and control the sexuality and reproduction of "their" women, and often impose policies directed at controlling marriage and reproduction that specifically target women.

"Settler states," the second of Pettman's categories, are those that were formed from colonization and/or immigration, such as the United States, Australia, South Africa, and Israel. Nation building during the settler phase in these contexts requires creating some sense of unity among what is originally a very diverse group of people. As Pettman argues, this usually means that nationalism is constructed in relation to, and often against, "both mother country and indigenous people" (1996: 53). In settler states, commonality needs to be created, often by concocting a common enemy and romanticizing a common past. In the United States, for example, a new robust "Americanness" was explicitly defined as masculine in contrast to an effeminate Britain. The rugged individual on the frontier was always imagined as a white man, whose right to dispossess native peoples from their land was not questioned, as it represented the natural and inevitable course of the progress of civilization. As historian Ronald Takaki tells us, "White 'rebirth' involved Indian death" (1979: 264). The western lands (against which the frontier man tested his might and exerted his will) were imagined in feminine terms, according to Annette Kolodny (1975); either as the "mother" that provides happiness in the form of an ideal, pastoral garden, or as the "virgin" that could be conquered. Women themselves were invisible in representations of the frontier, but were important later in the settlement process, when wilderness was transformed into civilization. Here, women's roles were prescribed as the civilizers and reproducers of white culture. Similarly, in Australia, nationalism was built around the lone white male; white women were "visible only as breeders of the white race" (Pettman, 1996: 53).

Anne McClintock's (1995) discussion of the creation of an Afrikaner nationalism in South Africa is illustrative of the representation of women as the "breeders of the white race." After losing the Anglo–Boer War in 1902, and therefore control over their own land, white Afrikaners (or Boers) began to invent a nationalism that, at least at the level of representation, legitimized their own claims to the nation. A key component in this process was the creation of a male-only secret society of Afrikaners who became the powerful representors of Afrikaner culture. The history of their original settlement of South Africa was re-created to center around "a male national narrative figured as an imperial journey into empty lands" (McClintock, 1995: 369), called "the Great Trek." This created history was vividly re-created in a 1938 spectacle called the "Tweede," or (second) Trek, where Afrikaners dressed up like the early settlers, took to covered wagons, and reconstructed the Great Trek (Figure 5.9). McClintock summarizes it thus:

> Each wagon became the microcosm of colonial society at large: the whip-wielding white patriarch prancing on horseback, black servants toiling alongside, white mother and children sequestered in the wagon—the women's starched white bonnets signifying the purity of the race, the decorous surrender of their sexuality to the patriarch and the invisibility of white female labor. (1995: 371)

The spectacle was wildly popular, and reinforced the idea of the white Afrikaner patriarchal family as the "true" inheritors of South Africa.

Spectacle was also integral to nation building in the United States. Buffalo Bill's Wild West Show was one of the most popular entertainments in the thirty years that it toured both the United States and Europe (1883–1916). The show consisted of a series of elaborate

FIGURE 5.9. Family of seven Afrikaners on and around a covered wagon, reenacting the Great Trek, 1938. Spectacles, such as the Great Trek, replete with images of white patriarchy, created an "invented" history on which to build Afrikaner nationalism.

re-creations of "significant" moments in the settlement of the American West by white Europeans. This included reenactments of the settlement of the original colonies and the Great Plains, buffalo hunts, and Indian attacks on a cabin and a stagecoach. In the wake of massive European immigration into eastern cities, these reenactments were vivid reminders of what was American: the rugged settlers and fighters along the frontier. It was this militant, hardy and masculine nature that characterized the true American spirit. As historian Richard Slotkin argues, "The [Buffalo Bill] Wild West's reenactments of the scenes of 'savage war' were recognized as rituals designed to revive in overcivilized moderns the militant virtues of their frontier ancestors" (1993: 174). Women were almost invisible in the reenactments, appearing as passive victims to be protected by the cavalry (Annie Oakley, however, was an exception, one of the featured performers who displayed her marksmanship in one of the "breaks" between the reenactments). Americanness, in this spectacle, was decidedly masculine.

"Anticolonial nationalisms," to continue Pettman's (1996) typology, characterize former colonies that are attempting to unite themselves, often against the imperial power that once controlled them. To do so, these anti-colonial nationalists often construct an imaginative dualistic geography: an inner country that represents the "true" nation that evaded the influences of the former Western power, and an outer world under Western influence. As the bearers of a country's sacred values and—literally—of its children, women are often constructed as the authentic, inner country, whose purity, sexuality, and traditional roles must be secured.

In Ireland, for example, as geographer Catherine Nash (1994) has shown, this association of women with an "authentic" nationalism took a very particular geographical form. Irish nationalists at the end of the nineteenth century, concerned with distinguishing the "true" Ireland from that which had come under British influence, looked to the "primitive" portions of the country, those areas not urbanized and industrialized, for a source of authentic Irishness. They initially located this "primitive" and "authentic" Irishness of Celtic culture in the rural West region, particularly in the peasant women who lived there.

Yet, as Nash (1994) shows, this initial symbolic gendering was complex and not enduring. The association of women with the West of Ireland was one that relied on images of the "primitiveness" of both: of their untamed, wild nature, removed from English influence. But this wildness meant that the peasant woman was perhaps interpreted as wild sexually and promiscuous, an image that conflicted with the Catholic and nationalist notions of women as the purveyors of morality and innocence. To resolve this conflict, according to Nash, Irish writers and artists in the first decades of the twentieth century reimagined the West as a masculine frontier, the land of the rough-and-tough, masculine Gauls, not of the wild, feminine Celts: "The West of Ireland was redefined as Gaelic, masculine, wholesome, pragmatic, and Catholic in contrast to the femininity and natural spirituality associated with the Celtic" (1994: 236). In this way, the representation of women's sexuality was controlled. This reimagining of women's sexuality in the early twentieth century fit well into the prevailing socioeconomic system in Ireland that was based on family farming, a system that "demanded the regulation of sexuality for the control of inheritance" (Nash, 1994: 236). What this tells us is that the gendering of nationalisms is a complex and changing process, but that it is not capricious: it always relates to, and serves the purposes of, social and economic systems. If the image of a wild and promiscuous woman of the West of Ireland was originally useful in representing Irishness as distinct from Englishness, the threat it presented to the stability of the Irish socioeconomic system led to its replacement by a masculine wildness and a desexualized femininity, represented by a peasant mother on a family farm.

This masculinity that came to represent the nationalist movement in Ireland by the end of the nineteenth century was celebrated and reinforced in statuary constructed to celebrate the one hundredth anniversary of the 1798 Irish rebellion against English rule. Geographer Nuala Johnson (1994) found that all of the celebratory statues found in Ireland, in one way or another, portrayed the nationalist cause and its heroes as larger-than-life men. For example, the monument in Wexford portrays a muscular peasant carrying a pike, with "feet astride and proud" (1994: 88), who stands over seven feet high. The one at New Ross represents a strident, manly rebel, Matthew Furlong. The statue in Wicklow (illustrated in Figure 5.10) is of a local hero of the rebellion, Billy Byrne, with arm upraised and pike in hand. Interestingly, the panel below him is a depiction of the fig-

FIGURE 5.10. Photograph of Billy Byrne Memorial Statue, County Wicklow, Ireland. Statues such as this promoted Irish nationalism through gendered roles, with larger-than-life male heroes (Billy Byrne) on the top, and Erin, a mother figure for Ireland, in a "prayerful pose" beneath.

ure Erin, a mother figure for Ireland, shown in a "prayerful pose" with "arms crossed and head facing slightly downward" (90). She is surrounded by three traditional icons of the Celtic revival. As Johnson argues, the meaning is clear: the active, masculine rebel on top is fighting to protect the saintly, feminine victims. "The sturdy insurgent Byrne, depicted as protector of the saintly and fragile Erin and her landscape of round towers, wolfhounds and crosses, represents martyrdom for the nationalist cause as a gendered discourse where men are active agents, women passive victims" (1994: 90–91).

Similarly, geographer Pyrs Gruffudd (1994) has examined the ways that a masculine, rural notion of Welshness was constructed in the period between World War I and World War II. As a colonized people, the Welsh had been represented by the English as weak and effeminate. But Welsh cultural nationalists in the interwar period, including many geographers at Welsh universities, romanticized the rural common folk—the *gwerin*—as the true bearers of Welshness, and even developed back-to-the-land programs to counter the industrial, metropolitan world of the English. The figure of the robust, masculine peasant became a symbol of the Welsh nationalist movement, while the peasant women, tending the home, was a reminder of the proper, diminutive role of women.

It is interesting to consider that during the same time period (between the two World Wars), portions of the United States were also being represented by images of larger-than-life masculine farmers. Some of the most severe repercussions of the Great Depression were felt in the farming communities of the South, and particularly in areas such as Appalachia. Here, coal mining had destroyed the social fiber of former farming communities, and then left neither jobs nor community nor good land when the mines closed during the depression. Many of the New Deal socioeconomic programs, such as the Tennessee Valley Authority (TVA), were directed at building infrastructure and providing relief to these areas. Such revitalization was often symbolized by the figure of the robust farmer, tilling and tending the land. This is most visually evident in many of the paintings of a school of art called the regionalists. Thomas Hart Benton, for example, often portrayed the spirit of his homeland, the Ozarks of Missouri, through figures of muscular, larger-than-life farmers, such as those in his painting *Cradling Wheat* (reproduced in Figure 5.11).

These representations of active, self-sufficient men were a potent counterweight to the reality of the dependency of these rural areas on outside aid. They were also keen reminders of America's rural past, and its construction of nationalism based on the self-sufficient yeoman farmer. In the 1930s, then, Americanness was being defined by the image of the rugged, masculine farmers of the Appalachians and Ozarks—an image that the government found appealing and pro-

FIGURE 5.11. *Cradling Wheat* by Thomas Hart Benton, 1938. American art of the 1930s often depicted images of robust, male farmers—reenacting the ideal of the yeoman farmer as a symbol of U.S. nationalism. Notice in this image the muscular, larger-than-life arms of the farmers.

moted. The hearty farmer's wife was important to this imagery, but only as a supporting role to her husband.

In nations that are undergoing modernization and/or Westernization, Pettman's (1996) fourth type of nationalism, the image of an authentic, primitive woman from the true "heartland" is often not portrayed in any sort of celebratory way, but instead is seen as a sign of the country's former "backwardness." Geographer Sarah Radcliffe (1996) has shown how in Ecuador, for example, rural, indigenous women of the Andes have come to be used to represent the limits of modernization. Radcliffe argues that in contemporary Ecuador, nationalism is based on approximating all the trappings of Western society: its whiteness, its literacy, its new technologies, and its bourgeois notions of women as guardians of domesticity. The indigenous women of the Andes, according to the Ecudorean popular media, do not participate in any of these forms of modern nationalism. Because of the out-migration of many men from the mountainous areas to work in the cities, women have increasingly taken over agricultural activities by themselves. Most press reports about the backwardness of these rural areas point to the pressing need to modernize agriculture with large-scale projects. Those reports that are meant to promote the "modernity" of Ecuador completely ignore women's participation in agriculture, since that participation is seen as "anti-modern and, by implication, anti-national" (Radcliffe, 1996: 14). The rural women of Ecuador, then, are seen as representatives of the country's "backwardness."

It is the "white" women living in the cities of Quito and Guayaquil who are represented as the national embodiment of femininity. These women are considered modern, and their relative freedoms are represented as evidence of the progress of the nation. In other words, the modern, white, liberated woman is used by the government and the press to show the "progress" of the country. Female suffrage, for example (granted in 1922), is presented as "the (inevitable) part of the (patriarchal) nation's modernity, not as the result of collective female agency" (Radcliffe, 1996: 11).

Yet even these "modern" women are not accorded equal billing to men in the invented history of Ecuador: they are written about as *supporters* of the independence movements (as wives, friends, or mothers of heroic men), not as active agents in their own right. And when the supporting role of these women is discussed, the press reminds readers that these women were active in independence without losing their femininity or their family roles. So in fact there are two distinct and often contrasting images of women in Ecuador's nationalizing discussions: one of "white" women who are models of womanhood, and one of indigenous women who are considered problematic. As Radcliffe (1996) concludes, this divisiveness turns attention away from the inequalities that all women face, and is a considerable obstacle to the formation of any united women's movement in Ecuador today.

WOMEN IN NATIONALIST MOVEMENTS

We can see from the example of Ecuador that women who were involved in independence and nationalist movements often find that their roles in those struggles are refigured when men write history. In Ecuador, these women are not presented as actors in their own right, but only as supporters in traditional family roles. And yet, of course, in all nationalist movements, women's labor, support, and often leadership *is* required. In most nationalist struggles, women are mobilized as soldiers, factory workers, health-care providers, diplomats, and so on. Yet, as geographer Lorraine Dowler (1998) suggests in her study of Northern Ireland, such roles—which often flout conventions of femininity—are typically trivialized as not really aiding the nationalist movement. Further, women who do occupy those roles are often thought to have lost their femininity.

In her interviews with women and men who had been involved in Irish Republican activity in Belfast, Northern Ireland, she found that women active in the Irish Republican Army were not considered really "one of the boys." The way women were supposed to contribute to the nationalist movement was to act as supporters of their husbands and sons, never leaving the domestic space to which society had assigned them. Women could actively support the cause, but only from the living rooms of their houses. Some women did become soldiers, but as Dowler found, they tended to "lose their identities as mothers within this community" (1998: 168).

On the other hand, as Cynthia Enloe has pointed out, helping nationalist movements through traditional feminine activities can be empowering for some women: "Women in many communities trying to assert their sense of national identity find that coming into an emergent nationalist movement through the accepted feminine roles of bearer of the community's memory and children is empowering. Being praised by men in the nationalist movement for bearing more children and raising them well doesn't always feel like being patronized and marginalized" (1989: 55). Yet if those women begin to move outside the home to work in movements that they hope will secure better lives for their children, their husbands often begin to feel threatened. As a result, many women involved in nationalist struggles against foreign powers have recognized that unless domestic relationships change, the nationalist struggle will not improve their daily lives. In making this conceptual link between the larger political struggle and the gendered politics of domestic life, women "active in nationalist movements in the Philippines, Ireland, South Africa, Canada, Sri Lanka, Mexico and Nicaragua," Enloe points out, "are far ahead of those women in industrialized countries who have scarcely glimpsed those political connections" (1989: 56).

But even this recognition may not lead to joint feminist and nationalist struggles, since women's "causes" are often put on the back burner when nationalist struggles begin to heat up. Considered much less important than the masculine business of fighting against imperialism, the fight for women's rights is often set aside until nationalist sovereignty is secured—"after the revolution," as it were. However, after the revolution is over, women's causes are usually forgotten. As Jan Pettman points out, "There is now considerable evidence to suggest that those causes that are marginalized in the struggle are likely to be marginalized in its victories, and especially in the consolidation and institutionalization of victory in the state" (1996: 61).

NATIONALISMS AND SEXUALITIES

We have seen that nations are imagined communities, and that feelings of nationalism are constructed out of particular socioeconomic circumstances. We have also seen that ideas about gender and about race are often integral to these processes of creating a sense of unified community. Turn-of-the-century ideas of Americanness, for example, coalesced around the ideal figure of the white, solitary man, subduing Native American peoples at the same time as he conquers the wild. We know also that this ideal figure is a heterosexual man, even if that identity is assumed without comment.

Traditional histories of the American West have constructed not only an Americanness based on gender (male), but also on sexual preference (heterosexuality). Indeed, the writing and spectacles that created this image of the solitary man use metaphors that position him sexually. As Annette Kolodny (1983) tells us, American identity has been based on "his" penetration into the wilderness, and "his" forceful conquering of native peoples. Nature and native peoples are figured as feminine, the conqueror as a heterosexual man. And when we look at the nationalistic stories of the settlement of the West, we see that its principal characters are those of a heterosexual, patriarchal family. The covered wagon is driven by the male head of household, with his wife at his side, and his children riding in the back. They will tame and domesticate the wilderness, and bring order and civilization to the "savages." So too, the Great Trek that was re-created in the 1930s in South Africa as a nationalistic spectacle was comprised of covered wagons, each representing one heterosexual, patriarchal family. Such "families" were integral to the construction of a Boer sense of South African identity.

Ideas about sexuality, then, in addition to ideas about gender and race, are integral to understanding the historical and contemporary constructions of nationalisms. Nationalisms based on conquest, for example, often contain within them unspoken assumptions about sexuality. Much of eighteenth- and nineteenth-century Western imperialism was legitimized through a way of thinking that envisioned non-Western cultures as the exotic "other" that was naturally submissive to the masculine West. This is most apparent in the Western construction of Asia as the "Orient," a term that came to connote its exotic (hetero)sensuality. Edward Said (1978) calls this attitude "orientalism," and argues that it became the overriding manner of representing Asia in the nineteenth century, thereby making it seem "natural" that Asia would be conquered by the West. Traditional notions of heterosexuality, therefore, have underpinned many Western attitudes and behavior toward nations that they have controlled.

For example, the association of homosexual acts with the "uncivilized" behavior of Native Americans is long lived. Such an association was often used to legitimize imperial rule, as Richard Trexler (1995) makes clear. In his book *Sex and Conquest*, Trexler shows how the Spanish and Portuguese conquerors of Latin America often justified their conquest of native peoples because they had witnessed sodomy among these cultures, and claimed they were therefore bringing them civilization and order:

> As they had from their earliest contacts with Americans, the Iberians . . . claimed the right to conquer native American males once they demonstrated that the latter practiced "sodomy," by which they usually meant homosexual behavior, among themselves. This "nefarious," "unmentionable," and "abominable sin" was, it was said, "against nature." (1995: 1)

Such representations of Native Americans consolidated European beliefs that they threatened the "natural" social order and therefore they had to be destroyed.

On the other hand, in different circumstances, the alleged homosexual activities of those to be conquered is explicitly tolerated. Under the apartheid state of South Africa, for example, black male homosexuality was at times tolerated since it served to make black sexuality less threatening to white culture. As geographer Glen Elder (1995) has shown, the South African state required black male labor to run its gold and silver mines, and housed these workers in hostels built specifically for this purpose. No women or children were allowed to live in these hostels. However, these spatial zones that contained only black men were perceived to be threatening to the white population that surrounded them; fueled by racist assumptions about black male sexuality, whites feared that these pent-up black men would rape white women. Tolerating and even encouraging homosexual activity within the hostels assuaged some of those fears. At the same time it allowed the government to continue to resist "demands on the part of workers to bring their wives and children to the mines on a permanent basis" (Elder, 1995: 60).

Meanwhile, homosexual activity among white South African men was strictly prohibited by the government, as it presented a direct threat to the patriarchal ideology of apartheid. Black male homosexuality was spatially contained within the hostels, and was tolerated as a necessary evil; white homosexuality was potentially uncontainable and far more threatening to a moral order that was based on white, heterosexual norms. South African nationalism, then, was based on the power of white men and white male, heterosexual activity. Black male sexuality was a potential threat that was to be contained, either spatially, through the legislated racial segregation of apartheid, or by deflecting that sexuality by tolerating male homosexual behavior.

Women's sexuality, as we have seen, has often played an important role in defining nation-states. In states that are characterized by "dominant nationalism," women are seen as the "mothers of the country" and therefore their sexuality is heavily monitored and controlled by the state to preserve the "purity" of the nation. Governments that are attempting to unite a country against a former colonial ruler often use women to represent the "true" and "authentic" nation, untouched by imperial powers, and therefore their sexuality is controlled in order to secure national "purity." In these instances, no form of "deviant" sexuality for women is tolerated. In every nationalist imaginary, homosexual women are invisible.

The unity of a nation, therefore, is often created by setting up ideals of what differentiates "us" from "them," and both gender and sexuality play important roles in that differentiating process. At the 1893 Chicago World's Exposition, many of the displays of colonized peoples exaggerated their physical and cultural differences from white Americans, making them exotic and clear markers of what was not Americanness. And in some of those displays, "native" culture was presented as effeminate. In the Woman's Building, for example, the men who formed part of the Ceylonese exhibit were described thus: "They were effeminate in manner, dressed in . . . a cloth wound round the waist and reaching down to the ankles—white jacket, long hair, knotted at the back woman fashion, with a tortoise shell comb, like the round comb usually worn by European children" (Starkweather, 1893). The women in the exhibit were described as "docile, gentle and childlike in appearances" (Starkweather, 1893). Both the men and women are "different" from, and unthreatening to, Americans; the men are effeminate and childlike, dressed in outlandish costumes, the women are passive and childlike.

This "differentiating" process is evident throughout most aspects of imperialism and nation building, whether in nineteenth-century India, or late-twentieth-century Bosnia. Representing nations and peoples in gendered and sexualized terms most often has enabled the dominant powers to maintain and legitimize their power positions. But there are always countertendencies. The displays in the 1893 Woman's Building portrayed the work of Native American women as similar to the work of English ladies; and Mary Kingsley wrote about African women with more insight and respect than her male peers. And it is to those countertendencies that we need look if we want to create, in Iris Marion Young's (1990) words, communities that incorporate diversity and difference instead of excluding it.

Chapter 6

THE ENVIRONMENT

At first consideration, "nature" may seem to be a realm far removed from the frenetic gendering and interpreting (and regendering and reinterpreting) that we find so evident in urban and in suburban landscapes, in nations and in empires. Nature . . . the environment . . . landscape . . . wilderness: in contrast to the urban scene, these seem to be relatively unchangeable places that are not primarily dictated or defined by human fashions and follies. On second look, however, we find many of the same gendered processes at work in shaping nature, and shaping our view of nature.

MOTHERS AND OTHER FORCES OF NATURE

One place to begin is with the notion of nature itself. It is commonplace to talk of nature as female, or, at least, as feminized. "She" is sometimes vengeful (as in the wrath of hurricanes, which in Western climatological convention, until recently, were always assigned-female names), sometimes soothing (as in nature providing for "man's" needs); she is changeable, fickle, powerful, fragile, protecting, and needing protection. The complexity and multiplicity of human views of "nature" are hard to summarize, but in most cultures, and apparently for much of recorded history, one of the consistent characteristics of nature is that it has been conceptualized as a "she."

A number of scholars assert that this construction of nature as female is of consequence. Indeed, it may play a pivotal role in shaping human relations to the environment, in ways that we will explore in this chapter (see Rose, 1993; Fitzsimmons, 1989; Harding, 1986; Nesmith and Radcliffe, 1993; Sparke, 1996; Seager, 1993a). In the first instance, even just characterizing "nature" as female sets it apart from "culture," which is usually characterized as male. The mere fact of conceptualizing the world in these terms sets the stage for conflict—and slyly inserts a hierarchical dichotomy between "man" and the natural world.

While the gendering of nature has roots that are centuries old, and that probably stretch far back into prehistory, the contemporary Western version of this idea is more recent. It was institutionalized by the European "scientific revolution" of the sixteenth and seventeenth centuries. Evidence suggests that prior to the scientific revolution, nature was conceptualized as a living, nurturing organism. Work, culture, nature, and daily life were interwoven in a seamless web, and a nurturing, female-identified earth was considered to be the root of all life. This imagery, historians of science suggest, served to constrain the abuse of nature. It didn't *prevent* the abuse of nature, but it did impose ethical and spiritual responsibilities on humans who would use the earth. As long as the earth was considered to be alive and sensate, it could be considered a grave matter to carry out destructive acts against it: "One does not readily slay a mother, dig into her entrails for gold or mutilate her body," as Carolyn Merchant, one of the most prominent scholars of the history of science, points out (1980: 3).

The scientific revolution that swept through Europe replaced the metaphor of earth as a nurturing organism with a mechanistic worldview. Under the gaze of "modern science," nature was reduced to a set of laws that were presumed to be knowable, and to principles of physical properties, presumed to be universal and monolithic. Scientists set about to discover the "laws of nature," the mysteries of which could be "penetrated" by men of inquiring minds. In this new worldview, culture was sentient, nature was insentient; nature didn't act, it was acted upon. The scientific revolution, shaped largely by the philosophical and scientific writings of Francis Bacon (the "father" of modern science), was predicated on the understanding that "man" could and should control the unruly forces of nature. In tandem, the scientific and industrial revolutions of the seventeenth and eighteenth centuries provided the institutional and technical means for "man's" ownership and control of nature. Science historian Lynn White suggests that these twin forces transformed human relations to the environment thoroughly and rapidly, in character and to a degree never before seen:

The emergence in widespread practice of the Baconian creed that scientific knowledge means technological power over nature can scarcely be dated before about 1850, save in the chemical industries, where it is anticipated in the 18th century. Its acceptance as a normal pattern of action may mark the greatest event in human history since the invention of agriculture, and perhaps in nonhuman terrestrial history as well. (1967: 1205)

The identification of nature as female was not lost with the scientific and industrial revolutions, but it was transformed. In the era of emerging modernism, *both* nature and women were cast as servants for the male scientific spirit. "Man's" newfound interest in (and capacity for) controlling nature was framed explicitly as a gendered contest: the subordination of (female-identified) nature was reconceptualized as a struggle of male consciousness over female. As Merchant (1980) points out, the "scientific method" was designed to be an interrogatory one whose key feature was "man's" constraint of nature in the laboratory and the "penetration of hidden secrets" of nature. The new Baconian men of science struggled to subdue woman/ nature, to know her secrets, to tame her wildness, and to put nature to work in the service of (male) human enterprise. Merchant also makes the startling suggestion that the inquisition of witches (mostly women) paved the way for a scientific "inquisition" of feminized nature. Merchant argues that the "controversy over women" and the inquisition of witches—both present in Bacon's social milieu— permeated his descriptions of nature and were instrumental in his conceptualization of the earth as a source of secrets to be extracted for economic advance. Merchant turns to Baconian language as an example of the inquisitive nature of the modern scientific enterprise:

> [For] the new man of science, Nature must be "bound into service" and made a "slave," put "in constraint" and "molded" by the mechanical arts. The "searchers and spies of nature" are to discover her plots and secrets. . . . Here in bold sexual imagery is the key feature of the modern experimental method—constraint of nature in the laboratory, dissection by hand and mind, and the penetration of hidden secrets—language still used today in praising a scientist's "hard facts," "penetrating mind," or the "thrust of his argument." (1980: 170)

At the same time that nature was being reconceptualized as a feminized terrain for male exploitation and domination, and justified by "rational" science in the service of cultural advance, the notion persisted of the earth as a nurturing mother. This odd dualism is paralleled by the "whore/madonna" dichotomy into which women are cast by men who are nervous about their power: nature (and women) can be capricious, lustful, wild, and uncultured, needing to be tamed, subdued, and mastered (the role of rational man and his culture); nature (and women) can also be nurturing, life-giving, and supportive, out of whom sustenance is to be coaxed, seduced, and wheedled (see Rose, 1993; Fitzsimmons, 1989; Harding, 1986; Nesmith and Radcliffe, 1993; Sparke, 1996; Seager, 1993a).

The "gendering" of nature continues to be ubiquitous in contemporary Western culture. It plays a particularly prominent role in shaping modern environmentalist consciousness. One of the most reproduced icons of modern environmentalism is the image of planet Earth as seen from space, a lonely blue orb floating in a black void, with the caption "Love Your Mother" (see Figure 6.1). The conceptualization of the earth as a mother has a long and honorable history. Earth as mother, as a sacred and honored female life force, is a powerful symbol in the cosmography of many non-Christian, non-Euro-American agricultural cultures. Further, it has rejuvenated a contemporary women-centered spirituality movement, and it inspired a generation of Earth Day activists. But there is good reason for feminists to be cautious about the facile adoption of the gendering of earth by a modern political (and, not unimportantly, male-dominated) environmental movement.

Some feminist environmentalists suggest that one of the problems with the representation of earth as mother is that this offers a weak stimulus for inculcating an ethos of environmental responsibility—indeed, it may even be seen as offering an "excuse" for irresponsibility. In truth, the earth is *not* our mother; there is no warm, nurturing, anthropomorphized earth that will take care of us if only we treat "her" nicely. Moreover, the emotion-laden, conflict-laden, quasi-sexualized mother–child relationship, many argue, is an inappropriate metaphor for environmental consciousness. To cast the earth as "mother" suggests a skewed distribution of power and responsibility: if the earth is really our mother, then we are children, and cannot be held fully accountable for our actions. This imagery obfuscates the real power relations of who's controlling what, and who's responsible for what, in the contemporary global environmental crisis.

Indeed, the idea that we are naughty children and that our "Mother" (Earth) will clean up after us when we make messes has been used as an excuse for complacency in the face of environmental crisis. For example, in 1989, a vice-president of Exxon invoked "Mother Earth" imagery in defending his company's (inadequate) cleanup operations in Alaska after the Valdez oil spill, the biggest spill in U.S. waters. His words suggest the cynical and facile use of the "Mother Earth defense": "I want to point out that water in the [Prince William] Sound replaces itself every 20 days. The Sound flushes itself

FIGURE 6.1. Mother Earth. The ubiquitous icon of the contemporary environmental movement.

out every 20 days. Mother Nature cleans up and does quite a cleaning job" (Charles Sitter, senior vice-president of Exxon, May 19, 1989). But Sitter is not alone; the notion that Mother Nature will "clean up" is a routine part of the discussion that follows many environmental catastrophes.

There may be a broader subtext to the "Mom-will-pick-up-after-us" school of environmental philosophy. In 1989, Linda Weltner, a Boston journalist, gave voice to the suspicions many women harbor:

> Sometimes I think the problem boils down to this: . . . most men have had women to clean up after them. In fact, it wouldn't surprise me one bit to find out that science has been covertly operating on the Mom-Will-Pick-Up-After-Me Assumption. . . . Men are the ones who imagine that clean laundry gets into their drawers as if by magic, that muddy footprints evaporate into thin air, that toilet bowls are self-cleaning. It's these over-indulged and over-aged boys who operate on the assumption that disorder—spilled oil, radioactive wastes, plastic debris—is someone else's worry, whether that someone else is their mother, their wife, or Mother Earth herself. (*Boston Globe*, April 28, 1989)

Feminist environmental ethicists have also raised questions about the philosophical implications of the "mothering" of earth. Many have argued that sex-typing the planet and imposing human imagery on the earth reinforces an anthropomorphism that may be at odds with a broader environmental agenda. To describe the earth in human terms in order to understand or "identify with" it implies that the earth in its *own* terms is neither especially valuable nor knowable.

On a more provocative note, some feminist environmentalists detect an even deeper strain of masculinism embedded in the popular "earth-from-space" imagery of the Mother Earth icon and in similar distant-view images of place now made ubiquitous through geographic information systems (GIS) and satellite technologies. In the view of at least one author, Yaakov Garb, these images might be interpreted as products of a masculinist impulse, creating distanced, voyeuristic, almost "pornographic" representations of place (Garb, 1990; see also Cosgrove, 1994). Garb's argument is that these images situate us as impassive from-a-distance viewers of earth—in a relationship most like that of a voyeur. The one-way gaze and stance of watching (especially watching a desirable and pretty object), silently and from afar, is one of the defining characteristics of pornography. This "distant viewing" is also a favored technique of social control, of course, not unrelated to the surveillance technology that increasingly defines the modern landscape.

CONTROL

In many cultures and over several centuries, human relations to the environment have been characterized by the control or attempted control of nature. Some of these have occurred on a large scale—the diversion of rivers for irrigation in ancient Egypt or the draining of the fens in eleventh century England, for example. However, it wasn't until the European scientific revolution that a reproducible *ideology* of control was developed. With the technological developments of the Industrial Revolution, real control was finally within man's reach.

The control of nature by men—whether men literally, or "man" universally—is made ideologically easier if nature is feminized. The metaphor of "rational man" subduing a female "nature," which the scientific revolution articulated, cannot just be seen as a quirk of the seventeenth century. It certainly remains deeply embedded in the language and the metaphors of modern science, and it is also a broader cultural feature of modern life. The literature of European (male) exploration of new lands, from the fifteenth-century reports to contemporary accounts, is rife with metaphors of raping the wilderness, penetrating virgin lands, conquering a capricious nature, mastering the wild, and subduing untamed lands. Control of nature is also common currency in popular culture, as the recent advertisements reproduced in Figure 6.2 illustrate. An amusing tour through several of the recent massive efforts in different parts of the world to control nature is chronicled by John McPhee (1989), including stupefying efforts combining male hubris and megamachinery to stop lava

FIGURE 6.2. Advertising images. From cars to colognes, advertisements play on the notion that "real men conquer nature."

flows in Iceland and Hawaii. Reduced to a soundbite, the prevailing Western—and perhaps global—ethos is that "real men control nature."

The "necessity" of controlling nature—indeed, man's "right" to do so—was largely unchallenged until recently. Indeed, the extent to which a culture has control over nature is often considered to be a measure of the extent of its modernization or, conversely, of its "backwardness." Vast engineering feats that subdue the forces of nature—the massive dams that hold back the Zuider Zee in the Netherlands, or the Three Gorges Dam in China, or the Hoover Dam in the United States—are widely heralded as triumphs of modernity. Countries or places that still sway to the rhythms or forces of nature are considered to be less "developed," or, at a minimum, less fortunate.

The export of technologies and ideologies of control or "management" of nature was a major part of European colonization around the world; indeed, it is still part of the "neocolonial" project of First World relations with the Third World. In conventional political economy doctrine, "development" is virtually synonymous with the acquisition of technologies to control nature and the adoption of modern ideologies of managing nature.

The control of nature was central to colonial control—and was also seen by the colonial powers as an enlightened export, bringing "modernization" to colonial territories. In truth, such colonial nature management schemes more often than not brought ecological catastrophe. For example, Vandana Shiva (1989, 1993) details the program for "scientific management" of forests that the British brought to India in the 1800s—a program that she characterizes as "patriarchal and reductionist." The colonial forestry model was not established on the basis of actual ecological knowledge about India's forests; rather, it was a bureaucratic model imposed to ensure the continued supply of timber to the empire. Under the British, forests were removed from local use, plantations of commercially valuable (but nonindigenous) trees were planted, forests that were not commercially valued were destroyed, and ecological cycles of sustainability were broken. In the colonial model, trees were not seen as part of living and complex ecosystems, but were conceptualized as commercial wood products; as Shiva (1985) argues, trees seen in this way—in terms of their dead product, wood—exclude the possibility of seeing them in their living function as providers of water, food, or fertilizer. At the same time, and not coincidentally, Indian women's knowledge of forest "management," a knowledge steeped in centuries of living with and from the forests, was entirely dismissed as unimportant. This is "maldevelopment" at its worst, Shiva (1993) points out.

The export of scientific rationality in service of the control of nature continues to characterize neocolonial relationships today (Shiva, 1990). The World Bank, the IMF, and similar international agencies that oversee the "development" of poorer countries typically encourage—or coerce—them to implement Western-style and Western-directed projects to turn natural resources into commodities that can be traded on the global markets. Around the globe, in the name of "development," dam building, road building, forest and mineral-export schemes, and the development of commercialized agriculture monoculture have been undertaken with zeal. In India, the World Bank is pushing controversial dam projects that will displace millions of peasants; in Ethiopia, the displacement of pastoral nomads by foreign commercial agriculture contributed to the massive famines of the 1970s; in Mexico, strawberries grown for foreign export are rapidly displacing beans and corn; and in Senegal, commercial cropping of peanuts is edging out local millet production. Throughout the poorer world, rapid and uncontrolled resource exploitation has brought about the collapse of whole ecosystems and has deepened poverty.

While some of these projects have improved quality of life, others have failed miserably. All of them have wrought significant environmental changes, in some cases environmental disasters. In many instances, the negative knock-on effects have outweighed the positive effects. Dams, for example, will tame floods, but in tropical environments will also spawn raging epidemics of schistosomiasis (a disease that causes severe disability and blindness), caused by snails that flourish in placid dam-contained waters. Road building and forest clearing opens up new agricultural frontiers, but deforestation caused by road building and settlement expansion results in accelerated erosion, which in turn undermines the viability of agriculture and causes widespread habitat deterioration. Women typically bear the larger burden of the poverty and dislocation that follow in the wake of such disasters. As the "shock absorbers" of local communities, it is women's labor that substitutes for a reduced resource base; women are responsible for finding clean water, fuel, or food even in the face of pollution and scarcity.

In the United States too, a country that might be considered to be the hearth of nature-control ideology, the effects of grand schemes of control have, as often as not, backfired. This became painfully apparent in the great Midwest floods of 1993. In the spring of 1993, an unusual shift in the jet stream stalled a weather system over the upper Midwest, dumping two to three times as much rain as normal over a wide region. The Mississippi River and its tributaries flooded ferociously, destroying dozens of towns and leaving tens of thousands of people homeless and jobless. This was a "natural disaster" of grave proportions. But postflood analysis underscored the extent to which this wasn't primarily a "natural" disaster—it was "man-made" as much as anything.

Since the 1930s, the U.S. Army Corps of Engineers has carried out an ambitious program of flood control. To the engineers of the Corps, "flood control" has meant—at least until very recently—massive construction projects to straighten out, contain, channel, and confine rivers. The Corps is a military engineering bureaucracy—an unholy trinity if ever there was one. The history of the Corps is interwoven with the nation-building European American frontier ethic of mighty men subduing a big land (Seager, 1993b). At one time, the official history of the Corps proudly reported that "[corps engineers] were the pathfinders sent out by a determined government at Washington. They guided, surveyed, mapped and fought Indians and nature across the continent." This view of nature as an adversary has remarkable persistence in the Corps specifically, and among engineers generally. In conventional engineering wisdom, the best river is a straight river; rivers are not viewed as living entities but rather as unruly bits of a system that need to be brought into line.

It is this approach to flood control that created the pent-up rivers that burst with a vengeance in the U.S. Midwest in 1993. Not only were the dams ineffective at keeping the rivers in their channels, but once flooding began the dams and levees prevented the floodwaters from receding. The attitude of the Corps, and the paradigm of control that the story of the floods reveals, is not specific to men qua men. Women living in the Midwest benefitted as much as men did from the flood-control schemes of the Corps. Most women, like most men, did not challenge the paradigm of the engineered control of nature.

The reconciliation of people and rivers does not necessarily require the intervention of big men with their big machines, and the technics of control. For example, cities might use floodplains as greenbelts—they can provide urban open space which, in between periods of high water, serve as parks or athletic fields. Permanent settlement structures can be placed on high land. These sorts of accommodations are now being made across the U.S. Midwest as the lessons of the 1993 floods become apparent: several towns have moved uphill, abandoning their previous location. Meanwhile, the Corps is publicly reassessing their engineering focus. But these lessons are hard-won and often seem ephemeral. The notion that "man" can tweak a system with technology holds sway over research agendas and funding priorities. The concrete-and-macho ethos that produced disastrous flood control systems in the Midwest is by no means a thing of the past.

ENCOUNTERS IN THE ENVIRONMENT

In the literature of *urban* geography and sociology, most available evidence suggests that men and women have different experiences of the same environment. As we have illustrated throughout this book, safety and fear of crime, for example, color women's experiences of streets, parks, buildings, and public spaces in different ways than they do for men; women and men prioritize differently urban and suburban amenities and attributes; notions of men's and women's appropriate "place" have shaped geographical and environmental relationships.

It may not be surprising, then, to find that men and women also often view the *natural* environment through somewhat different lenses. Some of the earliest research on this difference derived from studies of the European frontier and settlement experience in the new lands of North America. Until the 1970s, scholars of the "frontier" experience had relied primarily on men's reports to reconstruct what the settlers thought of the land and landscape they encountered; the main sources for these histories were the published works and accounts of public figures, fur traders, religious leaders, and the like. However, with the emerging interest in women's history, some scholars turned to sources such as women's diaries or personal letters, sources that provided a more gender-balanced view of the European encounter with new lands. What emerged from these writings was a surprising gender difference in the encounter experience (see Kolodny, 1975, 1983; Schlissel, 1982; Wilkinson, 1979). While European men tended to focus on the grandeur of the scenery in the American West, for example, and on conquering, subduing, and mastering the wilderness and "virgin lands," many of their women counterparts did not share these visions. Although some women, of course, shared the impulse to tame the new land, many women assessed the new landscape in terms of its prospects for shelter, its potential to be transformed into "home." Annette Kolodny's (1975, 1983) work rewrites the history of the American frontier, establishing that images of "conquering the wilderness," "taming nature," and "mastering the wild"—images that North Americans take to be the standard fare of the European encounter with new lands—were, in fact, male constructions and male imagery, and were not shared by their women counterparts. A recent ambitious study of landscape interpretation across gender, class, race, and ethnicity, *The Desert Is No Lady* (Norwood and Monk, 1987) reinforces the argument made by Kolodny that where European men saw the American West as a virgin land, ready to be raped and exploited, women typically regarded the landscape as "masterless."

In a study of contemporary "pioneers" around the world, geographer Janet Townsend (1995) finds that the encounter with new lands in a contemporary setting, too, is different for men and women. Townsend looked at contemporary government-planned land-settlement schemes in a range of countries, including Brazil, India, Sri Lanka, and Malaysia. These are internal relocation programs whereby governments provide incentives for people to start new permanent agricultural communities in regions previously without agriculture or permanent settlements. What these studies reveal is that women have different interests and needs, and experience different hardships than their male compatriots in these pioneer settings:

> Planned colonisation hardly ever takes account of women. Women tend to have to work harder and longer in worse conditions, lose their rights in land, to lose control over income, to have poorer access to health care, to education and to places to buy goods, and to suffer even more painful isolation than men. There are great differences, of course, between different places and cultures. The surprise is that there is similarity in findings for countries as diverse as Colombia, Sri Lanka, Nigeria, Malaysia, or India and Brazil, perhaps because the planners around the world have had the same training, read the same books and make the same mistakes. (Townsend, 1995: 8–9)

A corollary to landscape-perception studies are studies of attitudes toward animals. In a 1980s study on gender-differentiated attitudes to wildlife in the United States, the authors developed a scale of attitudes toward wildlife and then surveyed Americans to determine how widespread these attitudes were in the general population (Kellert and Berry, 1987). They found that American men's attitudes to wildlife were characterized by utilitarian, "dominionistic," naturalistic, and ecologistic views. Women, on the other hand, knew less about wildlife than men and had more fear of animals, but scored significantly higher than males on moralistic and humanistic attitudes. That is, women were more concerned about animal cruelty and about the welfare of wildlife, and they expressed significantly greater opposition than men to rodeos, to the use of laboratory animals, and to hunting. Men expressed a much greater willingness to use animals for purposes that suited humans, and derived greater personal satisfaction from the mastery and control of animals. The authors of this study concluded that "gender was among the most important demographic factors in determining attitudes about animals in our society" (1987: 370).

Geographer Jody Emel (1995) adds to the literature on gendered attitudes to wildlife with her study of the eradication of wolves in the United States over two centuries. Wolves, once plentiful across the entire United States, were systematically hunted to near-extinction by European settlers. Hunting was initially justified as necessary to protect livestock from wolf attacks, but, as Emel establishes, the scale and ferocity of killing exceeded any utilitarian justification. Much of the hunting was done for sport or for "fun." Wolf killing reached a frenzy in the mid-nineteenth century; estimates suggest that as many as two million wolves may have been slaughtered. Much of the killing was done with extreme cruelty, a feature, Emel suggests, that can only be explained by "the dominant construction of masculinity that is predicated upon mastery and control through the hunt" (720). Hunting and killing fierce animals was (and is) one of the highest forms of male sport, and the wolf was considered an especially noble, fearsome, and intelligent foe—characteristics that led to its demise.

STUDYING NATURE

Women have played an important (but largely overlooked) role in the systematic study of the environment—as botanists, naturalists, illustrators, and nature writers, for example. Historically, they often assumed these roles as amateurs because their access to formal training and entry into the environmental professions was largely blocked. However, some naturalists' pursuits have long been considered appropriate for women. Cheryl McEwan reports that in nineteenth century Britain, for example, "the involvement of leisured women in . . . botany was believed to induce modesty and reverence, encourage domesticity and curtail flightiness" (McEwan, 1998, 217); men could be "scientists," but women could be "naturalists." Indeed, McEwan reports that botany became "stigmatized" as a feminine pursuit in the late nineteenth century and men started to shun the field. In some instances, women's work as naturalists derived from (and was sometimes masked as) gardening, a quintessentially acceptable women's pastime. Historically, women's work as gardeners has played an especially important role in nature conservation. Equally importantly, in the United States and elsewhere, women extended their reach from the garden to the city, playing crucial roles in "city beautiful" movements and in designing sustainable urban environments (Norwood, 1993).

Even when they have been professionals, women's work and their contributions to ecological knowledge and education have often been ignored, scorned, or trivialized. The work of Rachel Carson, who is *now* recognized as a brilliant environmental biologist, was in her own time attacked viciously—and often on the very grounds that because she was a woman she could not possibly have authority in the environmental sciences. Her book on the environmental dangers of pesticides, *Silent Spring,* first appeared as a three-part serial in the *New Yorker* magazine in 1962. An irate letter to the editor in June of that year, in response to Carson's article, is characteristic of the opprobrium with which her work was received:

> Miss Rachel Carson's reference to the selfishness of insecticide manufacturers probably reflects her Communist sympathies, like a lot of our writers these days. We can live without birds and animals but . . . we cannot live without business. As for insects *isn't it just like a woman* [emphasis added] to be scared to death of a few little bugs! As long as we have the H-bomb everything will be OK. (reprinted in the *New Yorker*, February 20 and 27, 1995: 18)

Vera Norwood's (1993) study of women naturalists exposes the complexity and diversity of women's roles in relation to nature. In many instances, women's active participation in the study of nature did nothing to challenge Western norms of nature dominance. For example, many women expressed no more ambivalence than their male counterparts as they went about their—often gruesome— business of specimen collecting or trophy hunting in the wild. In other cases, women did seem to bring a distinct ethos to their encounter with nature. Dian Fossey and Jane Goodall, for example, probably the most important figures of this century in primate studies, consciously challenged the dominant scientific establishment over how to study primates in the wild, bringing intimacy, respect, love, and reciprocity to their relationships with the animals.

Women's role in scientific fieldwork is often complicated by conceptualizations of "the field" in ways that make it no place for a woman (Rose, 1993; Sparke, 1996). In disciplines such as geography and geology that have a field-science tradition, the prevailing conceptualization of "the field" is imbued with masculine associations: sleeping outdoors under the stars, living without modern frills and amenities, working vigorously under rigorous conditions. Fieldwork is often represented as a proving ground for manhood. Gillian Rose (1993) persuasively details the extent to which much of the (male) writing about fieldwork in geography, for example, lauds it as simultaneously a tough and heroic activity and as a distinctively masculine endeavor. Success in "the field" is often construed as a signifier of *manly* achievement, not just of professional accomplishment.

ENVIRONMENTAL PERCEPTION

Recent studies of environmental attitudes and reactions to hazards reveal other interesting—and sometimes contradictory—gender differences in "environmental perception." Although some of these studies do *not* find a gender gap in environmental attitudes (or find only a minor one), the majority do show a gender difference—and sometimes a quite sizable difference. In studies from around the world, available data suggest that in general women favor passing more stringent environmental protection laws and spending more money on environmental protection, and they express more alarm over the state of the environment, than do their male counterparts (Schahn and Holzer, 1990).

Studies of hazards and environmental fears extend these findings. Several studies in the United States and elsewhere have focused on the role of technology in environmental affairs; most conclude that women are more leery of the environmental costs of technological reliance, and are less sanguine about the role of technological innovation in environmental problem solving. This gender gap was particularly apparent in a mid-1980s study on attitudes toward nuclear power in the United States which found that women were significantly less supportive of continued use of nuclear power; compared with men, women believed that nuclear plants were less safe, they evaluated the problems associated with nuclear production as being more serious than did men, and they expressed greater concern about health and safety (Brody, 1984). An early 1990s study in the Netherlands found that women felt more insecure than men in the face of environmental risks and threats, and that they generally assessed all environmental risks to be more threatening than did their male counterparts (Guettling and Wiegman, 1993). A study of men's and women's reactions to a 1989 earthquake in California (the Loma Prieta quake, one of the biggest of this century) found, again, that women experienced greater stress and expressed more fear about the encounter than did men; women also estimated that the quake lasted significantly longer than did men (Anderson and Manuel, 1994).

ENVIRONMENTAL ACTIVISM AND ECOFEMINISM

Explanations vary for such gender gaps in environmental attitudes. Some environmentalists—especially some ecofeminists—argue that findings that suggest that women are more concerned about environmental integrity than men provide evidence of an innate woman–nature connection. Other scholars conclude that these attitudinal and perceptual differences reflect socialization differences, arguing instead that if there is a "women's voice" on the environment it derives from materially grounded facts about women's social location.

As environmental activists, women occupy distinctive niches and have taken on new roles. While most mainstream environmental groups are dominated by male policymakers and power brokers, women have tended to cluster in grassroots organizing. In part, the predominance of women at the grassroots is precisely because many women have found mainstream environmental groups to be inhospitable places. Until very recently, the professional "green" movement has been mostly white and mostly male; almost everywhere that a professional environmental movement exists, women and minorities have been marginalized in that movement (Seager, 1993a). This marginalization is evident in the personnel hierarchy of most mainstream environmental groups (men at the top as decision makers, women at the bottom as volunteers and stamp lickers). It is also evident in the policy priorities of mainstream environmentalism: in most professional environmental groups in the United States, for example, community health and women's health issues have been (until recently) low on the priority agenda, and issues of racial environmental justice and urban environmental health have been all but invisible.

"Radical" environmental groups have not necessarily been any more hospitable to women. Indeed many of the radical environmental groups are infused with male bravado and macho posturing. In its late-1980s heyday, the testosterone-hyped U.S. Earth First! movement typified the best and worst of the radical ecological fringe; a self-ironic portrait, published in the summer 1988 Earth First! newsletter (see Figure 6.3) suggested the extent to which the radicalism of Earth First! was inextricably linked with the image of redneck male bravado. Earth First! disbanded in the early 1990s, and then reemerged as a restructured, less overtly masculinist group. But many feminists inside radical environmental movements still complain about how difficult it is for feminist analysis to be taken seriously, or even just for women's voices to be heard.

By contrast, grassroots organizing provides a local venue for activism, one in which the large-scale institutional power hierarchies that almost always marginalize women are absent. Further, the politics and realities of grassroots organizing resonate well with many women's social roles in household, community, and family. Women's grassroots environmental activism occurs within the context of, and as a result of, their particular socially assigned roles—roles that in many key ways transcend boundaries of race, ethnicity, and class. At the 1991 Global Assembly of Women for a Healthy Planet, held in

FIGURE 6.3. Earth First! cartoon. The new Earth First! is kinder and gentler, but in its heyday it was an unapologetically "he-man" organization.

Miami, Peggy Antrobus outlined the common consciousness that women bring to (and that brings women to) environmental activism (1991):

> We are different women, but women nonetheless. The analysis and the perspectives that we get from women are certainly mediated by, influenced very profoundly, by differences of class, and race, and age, and culture, and physical endowment, and geographic location. But my hope and my optimism lies in the commonalities that we all share as women—a consciousness that many of us have, if we allow ourselves to have it, of the exploitation of our time and labor in unremunerated housework, subsistence agriculture and voluntary work. Our commonality lies in the often conflicting demands of our multiple roles as caretakers, as workers, as community organizers. Our commonalities lie in our primary responsibility for taking care of others. Our commonality lies in our concern about relationships; the commonality that we share is the exploitation of our sexu-

ality by men, by the media and by the economy. The commonality that we share is in our vulnerability to violence. Our commonality finally lies in our otherness, in our alienation and exclusion from decision-making at all levels.

It is the linkage of "women's work" to the environments of lived ordinariness that explains why, globally, it is women who are usually the first to become environmental activists in their community. Everywhere in the world, women are responsible for making sure that their families are fed, housed, and kept healthy. They are, in many cases, responsible for creating the means of subsistence—globally, it is often women's work in the waged workforce and in the family fields that provides the basics for family survival. And in all economies, women take raw materials and income, whether provided by themselves or by others, and fashion it into food, clothing, housing, health care, and child care. In environmental management terms, we could say that women make the primary consumer and resource-use decisions for their families and their communities, that women in all cultures serve as managers of fixed resources.

The ideology and approach to environmentalism that is most identified with women is "ecofeminism." "Ecofeminism" is an umbrella term for a wide variety of approaches to environmental analysis that bridge feminist and environmental concerns. It is both theory and practice, built on the intellectual foundations of ecology and feminism, and on the populist strength of women's rights and women's health movements, peace, anti-nuclear, socialist, labor, ecological, environmental justice, and animal rights movements. There are varying claims about the origin of the term itself, although most attribute it to French author Françoise D'Eaubonne (1980).

A wide range of scholarly and popular writing is often designated as being "ecofeminist." However, there is some ambivalence about the use of this term and not all feminists working on ecological or environmental matters identify their work as ecofeminism. Many prefer to employ such designations such as "ecological feminism" (Warren, 1994), "feminist political ecology" (Rocheleau, Thomas-Slater, and Wangari, 1996), or simply "feminist environmentalism" (Seager, 1993a).

Discussion of the "woman–nature" relationship is a key part of most ecofeminist ideology and activism and it is a touchstone issue that distinguishes various schools of thought in ecofeminism. The notion that women are "closer" to nature is woven into the intellectual, religious, and social fabric of many cultures—but there is considerable disagreement among ecofeminists about how this association is to be interpreted. Much of the *academic* writing on ecofeminism argues that this association is created by patriarchy to distance women from cultural loci of power and to prop up male domination of both women and nature. Much of the *populist* and more spiritually grounded ecofeminist writing, in contrast, embraces a woman–nature connection, interpreting this as a distinctively "womanist" claim to strength, a connection perhaps to a long historical lineage of matriarchal power. This way of seeing the women–nature connection gives women a distinctive voice and position from which to critique the dominant male culture. (see Warren, 1994; Merchant, 1980; Griffin, 1978). A corollary debate among ecofeminists is the extent to which consideration of a woman–nature connection presumes (and promotes) an essentialized view of "women." Many feminists are leery of these claims because they seem to cast women as "naturally" or "essentially" more nurturing (more connected to ecological consciousness), and negate the reality of differences among women.

However, there are common analytical and conceptual interests that cut across the plurality of "ecofeminist" positions. These include the following:

♦ *A commitment to illuminating the role of gender, class, and race in mediating the ways in which people live in and with local environments.* Because ecofeminism is both a political stance and an academic inquiry, much of the literature—even the most theoretical writings—pivot around a central interest in the "real" lives of women and their relationships to the environment. Women everywhere have a different relationship to resources and environmental technics than do their male counterparts. Because of their social location and socially assigned gender roles, women and men seldom have the same environmental relationships or responsibilities, nor do they enjoy the same access to environmentally constituted power and wealth. Women and men live differently in their environments, and are affected differently by ecological change and crisis. In addition, large-scale "development" processes or decisions that affect environmental sustainability reverberate differently in women's and men's lives, and among women and men across divides of class and race.

It was primarily Third World feminist theorists and activists who forged, in the 1980s, a unified ecofeminist theory and praxis around questions such as: How are "resources" defined? Who controls them? How does ecological crisis manifest itself? Who gets to control the definition of environmental "problems"? Who controls the relationships between local environments and global processes? How does women's involvement in environmental movements change them? Who speaks for the environment? Because environmental matters are survival matters—literally—these ecofeminist questions take on a certain urgency (see Agarwal, 1992; Shiva, 1989; Rocheleau et al., 1996; Momsen and Townsend, 1987).

♦ *An interest in examining the ways in which human–environment perceptions and values may be mediated through "gendered" lenses and shaped by gender roles and assumptions.* As we discussed earlier, among feminist geographers this interest has been explored primarily in examinations of the gendered dimensions of environmental perception, landscape assessment, and hazards assessment (Norwood and Monk, 1987; Gutteling, 1993). A related literature explores the extent to which human theorizing *about* nature, ecology, and environment may reflect gendered imprints. It can be argued that the dominant (Western) theorizing about nature, including the discourse of environmental ethics and rights, reflects a gender-embedded consciousness. As many ecofeminists point out, "A heavily masculine presence has inhabited most accounts of environmental philosophy" (Plumwood, 1993: 3). The very distinction between human and nonhuman realms, the creation of the chasm between human and nature, has been interpreted by some ecofeminists as a product of a distinctly "masculinist" culture (Fitzsimmons, 1989; Rose, 1993). More broadly, much of the (Western, contemporary) ethical and philosophical environmental writing is steeped in a masculinist worldview about the hierarchical and utilitarian relationship of humans and nature, or about the role of "management" of nature and wildlife. Much environmental and nature writing presents views of environmental history that reflect only or mostly male activities, thoughts, and priorities. Similarly, priorities and assumptions embedded in the ethos, policies, and activities of many of the large environmental organizations show a gendered imprint.

♦ *An interest in examining the gendered nature of the constellation of political, economic, and ecological power in those institutions that are instrumental players in the state of the environment.* Environmental relations are largely shaped by and mediated by bureaucracies and institutions—on a global scale, by entities such as governments, militaries, multinational corporations, and multilateral organizations such as the World Bank; on a smaller scale, by organizations such as, in the United States, for example, the Forestry Service and the Army Corps of Engineers. A gendered analysis of the institutional logic of, the "culture" of, and the exercise of power by these institutional entities can shed light on environmental agency, causality, and consequences (Seager, 1993a, 1993b; Shiva, 1993; Rocheleau et al., 1996).

♦ *An interest in exploring the interconnectedness of systems of oppression and domination.* Many ecofeminists argue that systems of belief that lead to the abuse and exploitation of "natural" environments are similar to—and perhaps even derivative of-structures of belief that lead to oppression in human relationships (see Merchant, 1980; Warren, 1994; Sturgeon, 1997). For example, ecofeminists point to linkages between environmental oppressions based on "species-ist" hierarchies (valuing humans above other mammals, mammals above fish, and so on) and human social oppressions such as hierarchies based on class, race, gender, or sexuality classifications. The environmental justice movement derives, in part, from such an analysis of multiple and overlapping oppressions. It is also at this point that the interests of environmental feminism converge with animal rights. It is no coincidence that over several centuries, at least in Western Europe and North America, women have been the primary supporters of animal rights movements and among the most influential theorists of the rights of animals. Rough estimates suggest that about three-quarters of animal rights activists are women. Feminists have constructed a broad animal rights agenda that includes consideration of the parallels between the oppression of women and the oppression of animals, and of the parallels in the violence directed against both; consideration of the parallels between the oppression and "ownership" of animals and the oppression and "ownership" of slaves; a rejection of the prevailing rationalist worldview that treats animals as instruments that can be manipulated to further social and economic ends; critiques of hunting and the "normalization" of violence inculcated through hunting; and a close examination of the sexual politics of meat eating and meat production (Spiegel, 1988; Adams, 1990; Donovan, 1990; Seager, 1993a).

Thoughts of meat eating bring us full-circle, back to home. The association of meat eating with masculinity that runs deep through most Western cultures is imprinted in everyday spaces: the carving knife, the carving board, the dining room sideboard, the barbecue pit, the head of the table, the hunt club, the hunting camp, the duck blind, the butcher's shop, the cattle feedlot, and the smokehouse are all sites that are redolent with gendered associations. The intertwinings of gender and space, sex and place may be sometimes deep and complex, or sometimes shallow and funny, but they are always twinned and usually so intimately interleaved that it is difficult to talk about the one without the other.

REFERENCES

Abelson, Elaine, S. 1989. *When Ladies Go a-Thieving: Middle-Class Shoplifters in the Victorian Department Store*. New York: Oxford University Press.

Adams, Carol. 1990. *The Sexual Politics of Meat*. New York: Continuum.

Agarwal, Bina. 1989. Women, land, and ideology in India. In Haleh Afshar and Bina Agarwal, eds., *Women, Poverty, and Ideology in Asia*. London: Macmillan, 70–98.

Agarwal, Bina. 1992. The gender and environment debate: Lessons from India. *Feminist Studies, 18*(1), 119–132.

Ahrentzen, Sherry. 1997. The meaning of home workplaces for women. In John Paul Jones, Heidi Nast, and Susan Roberts, eds., *Thresholds in Feminist Geography*. Lanham, MD: Rowman & Littlefield, 77–92.

Aiken, Susan, et al., eds. 1998. *Making Worlds: Gender, Metaphor, Materiality*. Tucson: University of Arizona Press.

Ainley, Rosa, ed. 1998. *New Frontiers of Space, Bodies, and Gender*. London/New York: Routledge.

Albelda, Randy, and Chris Tilly. 1998. *Glass Ceilings and Bottomless Pits: Women's Work, Women's Poverty*. Boston: South End Press.

Ames, Kenneth. 1992. *Death in the Dining Room and Other Tales of Victorian Culture*. Philadelphia: Temple University Press.

Anderson, Benedict. 1991. *Imagined Communities: Reflections on the Origin and Spread of Nationalism*. London: Verso.

Anderson, Karen, and Gerdenio Manuel. 1994. Gender differences in reported stress response to the Loma Prieta earthquake. *Sex Roles, 30*(9–10), 725–733.

Antrobus, Peggy. 1991. Women and the environment. Audiotape of speech presented at the Global Assembly of Women for a Healthy Planet.

Ardener, Shirley, ed. 1993. *Women and Space: Ground Rules and Social Maps* (rev. ed). Oxford, UK: Berg.

Asia Watch/Human Rights Watch. 1993. *A Modern Form of Slavery: Trafficking of Burmese Women and Girls into Thailand.* New York: Asia Watch.

Asia Watch/Human Rights Watch. 1995. *Rape for Profit: Trafficking of Nepali Girls and Women to India's Brothels.* New York: Human Rights Watch.

Atkinson, Paul. 1978. Fitness, feminism, and schooling. In Sara Delamont and Lorna Duffin, eds., *The Nineteenth-Century Woman.* New York: Barnes & Nobles Books, 92–133.

Bannan, Helen. 1984. *"True Womanhood" on the Reservation: Field Matrons in the United States Indian Service.* Working Paper no. 18. Tucson, AZ: Southwest Institute for Research on Women.

Barff, R., and J. Austen. 1993. "It's gotta be da shoes": Domestic manufacturing, international subcontracting, and the production of athletic footwear. *Environment and Planning A, 25,* 1103–1114.

Barry, Kathleen. 1979. *Female Sexual Slavery.* New York: New York University Press.

Barry, Kathleen. 1995. *The Prostitution of Sexuality.* New York: New York University Press.

Bartram, Rob, and Sarah Shobrook. 1998. You have to be twice as good to be equal: "Placing" women in Plymouth's Devonport Dockyard. *Area, 30*(1), 59–65.

Bell, David, and Gill Valentine, eds. 1995. *Mapping Desire: Geographies of Sexuality.* London/New York: Routledge.

Bell, Morag. 1995. A woman's place in "a white man's country": Rights, duties, and citizenship for the "new" South Africa, c. 1902. *Ecumene: A Journal of Environment, Culture, Meaning, 2*(2), 129–148.

Bennett, Judith M. 1994. Medieval women, modern women: Across the great divide. In Ann-Louise Shapiro, ed., *Feminists Revision History.* New Brunswick, NJ: Rutgers University Press, 47–72.

Benson, Susan Porter. 1986, *Counter Cultures: Saleswomen, Managers, and Customers in American Department Stores, 1890–1940.* Urbana: University of Illinois Press.

Binnie, Jon. 1995. Trading places: Consumption, sexuality, and the production of queer space. In David Bell and Gill Valentine, eds., *Mapping Desire: Geographies of Sexualities.* London: Routledge, 182–199.

Birkett, Dea. 1989. *Spinsters Abroad: Victorian Lady Explorers.* Oxford, UK: Basil Blackwell.

Blackmar, Elizabeth. 1989. *Manhattan for Rent, 1785–1850.* Ithaca, NY: Cornell University Press.

Blunt, Alison, 1994a. Mapping authorship and authority: Reading Mary Kingsley's landscape descriptions. In Alison Blunt and Gillian Rose, eds., *Writing Women and Space: Colonial and Postcolonial Geographies.* New York: Guilford Press, 51–72.

Blunt, Alison. 1994b. *Travel, Gender, and Imperialism: Mary Kingsley and West Africa.* New York: Guilford Press.

Blunt, Alison, and Gillian Rose, eds. 1994. *Writing Women and Space: Colonial and Postcolonial Geographies.* New York: Guilford Press.

Bondi, Liz. 1998. Gender, class, and urban space: Public and private space in contemporary urban landscapes. *Urban Geography, 19*(2), 160–185.

Bowden, Martyn J. 1975. Growth of central districts in large cities. In Leo Schnore, ed., *The New Urban History*. Princeton, NJ: Princeton University Press, 75–109.

Breitbart, Mryna, and Ellen-J. Pader. 1995. Establishing ground: Representing gender and race in a mixed housing development. *Gender, Place and Culture, 2*(1), 5–20.

Brody, Charles. 1984. Differences by sex in support for nuclear power. *Social Forces, 63*(1), 209–228.

Bullock, Susan. 1994. *Women and Work*. London: Zed Books.

Burgess, Lauren Cook. 1994. *An Uncommon Soldier*. New York: Oxford University Press.

Burton, Antoinette. 1994. *Burdens of History: British Feminists. Indian Women, and Imperial Culture, 1865–1915*. Chapel Hill: University of North Carolina Press.

Cahill, Cathleen. 1998, 19–22 March. *Homes on the Range: The Contest over Household Space in United States Indian Policy, 1890–1938*. Paper presented at the Nineteenth-Century Geographies Conference, Houston, TX.

Carter, Harold. 1983. *An Introduction to Urban Historical Geography*. London: Edward Arnold.

Chant, Sylvia, and Cathy McIlwaine. 1995. Gender and export manufacturing in the Philippines: Continuity and change in female employment? *Gender, Place and Culture, 2*(2), 147–173.

Chouinard, Vera, and Ali Grant. 1996. On not even being anywhere near "The Project." In Nancy Duncan, ed., *Bodyspace: Destabilizing Geographies of Gender and Sexuality*. London/ New York: Routledge, 170–197.

Christensen, Kathleen. 1993. Eliminating the journey to work: Home-based work across the life course of women in the United States. In Cindi Katz and Janice Monk, eds., *Full Circles: Geographies of Women over the Life Course*. New York: Routledge, 55–87.

Clarke, Alison. 1997. Tupperware: Suburbia, sociality and mass consumption. In Roger Silverstone, ed., *Visions of Suburbia*. New York: Routledge, 132–160.

Coleman, Debra. 1996. Introduction. In Debra Coleman, Elizabeth Danze, and Carol Henderson, eds., *Architecture and Feminism*. New York: Princeton Architectural Press, ix–xvi.

Connor, Tom. July 18, 1999. For him: The perfect lawn is a status symbol again. *New York Times*, pp. 1–2.

Constable, Nicole. 1997. *Maid to Order in Hong Kong: Stories of Filipina Workers*. Ithaca, NY: Cornell University Press.

Cosgrove, Denis. 1994. Contested global visions: One-world, whole-earth, and the Apollo space photographs. *Annals of the Association of American Geographers, 84*(2), 270–294.

Costello, Cynthia, and Barbara Kivimae Krimgold. 1996. *The American Woman, 1996–97*. New York: Norton.

Cravey, Altha. 1998. *Women and Work in Mexico's Maquiladoras*. Lanham, MD: Rowman & Littlefield.

Crawford, Margaret. 1992. The world in a shopping mall. In Michael Sorkin, ed., *Variations on a Theme Park*. New York: Noonday Press, 3–30.

Creswell, Tim. 1993. Mobility as resistance: A geographical reading of Kerouac's *On the Road*. *Transactions of the Institute of British Geographers*, *18*(2), 249–262.

Cromley, Elizabeth. 1996. Masculine/Indian. *Winterthur Portfolio*, *31*, 265–280.

Davidson, Miriam. 1994, May. Second-class refugees: Persecuted women are denied asylum. *The Progressive*, pp. 22–25.

D'Eaubonne, Françoise. 1980. Feminism or death. In Elaine Marks and Isabelle de Courtivron, eds., *New French Feminisms: An Anthology*. Amherst: University of Massachusetts Press, 64–67.

de Erauso, Catalina. 1996. *Lieutenant Nun: Memoir of a Basque Transvestite in the New World* (Trans. Michele Stepto and Gabriel Stepto). Boston: Beacon Press.

Dicken, Peter. 1998. *Global Shift: Transforming the World Economy* (3rd ed.). New York: Guilford Press.

Domosh, Mona. 1996. *Invented Cities: The Creation of Landscape in Nineteenth-Century New York and Boston*. New Haven, CT: Yale University Press.

Domosh, Mona. 1998. Those "gorgeous incongruities": Polite politics and public space on the streets of nineteeth-century New York City. *Annals of the Association of American Geographers*, *88*(2), 209–226.

Donovan, Josephine. 1990: Animal rights and feminist theory. *Signs: Journal of Women in Culture and Society*, *15*(2), 350–375.

Dowler, Lorraine. 1998. "And they think I'm just a nice old lady": Women and war in Belfast, Northern Ireland. *Gender, Place and Culture*, *5*(2), 159–176.

Duncan, Nancy, ed. 1996. *Bodyspace: Destabilizing Geographies of Gender and Sexuality*. London/New York: Routledge.

Dyck, Isabel. 1990. Space, time and renegotiating motherhood. *Environment and Planning D: Society and Space*, *1*, 459–483.

Elder, Glen. 1995. Of Moffies, kaffirs, and perverts: Male homosexuality and the discourse of moral order in the apartheid state. In David Bell and Gill Valentine, eds., *Mapping Desire: Geographies of Sexualities*. London: Routledge, 56–65.

Elson, Diane. 1983. Nimble fingers and other fables. In Wendy Chapkis and Cynthia Enloe, eds., *Of Common Cloth: Women in the Global Textile Industry*. Amsterdam: Transnational Institute, 5–13.

Emel, Jody, 1995. Are you man enough, big and bad enough? Ecofeminism and wolf eradication in the USA. *Environment & Planning D: Society and Space*, *13*, 707–734.

Enloe, Cynthia. 1989. *Bananas, Beaches, and Bases: Making Feminist Sense of International Politics*. Berkeley and Los Angeles: University of California Press.

Fan, C. Cindy, and Youqin Huang. 1998. Waves of rural brides: Female marriage migration in China. *Annals of the Association of American Geographers*, *88*(2), 227–251.

Federal Highway Administration. 1990, 1996. *Highway Statistics*. Washington, DC: U.S. Government Printing Office.

Fine, Lisa M. 1990. *The Souls of the Skyscraper: Female Clerical Workers in Chicago, 1870–1930.* Philadelphia: Temple University Press.

Fitzsimmons, Margaret. 1989. The matter of nature. *Antipode, 21,* 106–120.

Folbre, Nancy. 1995. *The New Field Guide to the U.S. Economy.* New York: New Press.

Fox-Genovese, Elizabeth. 1988. *Within the Plantation Household: Black and White Women of the Old South.* Chapel Hill: University of North Carolina Press.

Frederick, Christine. 1919. *Household Engineering: Scientific Management in the Home.* Chicago: American School of Home Economics.

French, Marilyn. 1977. *The Women's Room.* New York: Jove Books.

French, Marilyn. 1992. *The War Against Women.* New York: Ballantine Books.

Friedan, Betty. 1983 *The Feminine Mystique.* New York: Dell. (Originally published 1963.)

Gaard, Greta, ed. 1993: *Ecofeminism: Women, Animals, Nature.* Philadelphia: Temple University Press.

Gamber, Wendy. 1997. *The Female Economy: The Millinery and Dressmaking Trades, 1860–1930.* Urbana: University of Illinois Press.

Garb, Yaakov Jerome. 1990. Perspective or escape? Ecofeminist musings on contemporary earth imagery. In Irene Diamond and Gloria Orenstein, eds., *Reweaving the World: The Emergence of Ecofeminism.* San Francisco: Sierra Club Books, 264–278.

Gardner, Carol Brooks. 1995. *Passing By: Gender and Public Harassment.* Berkeley and Los Angeles: University of California Press.

Gargan, Edward. 1993, 30 December. A back seat to nobody in fight against sexism. *New York Times,* p. A2.

Gilbert, Melissa. 1997. Identity, space and politics: A critique of the poverty debates. In John Paul Jones, Heidi Nast, and Susan M. Roberts, eds., *Thresholds in Feminist Geography.* Lanham: Rowman & Littlefield, 29–46.

Gilbert, Melissa. 1998. "Race," space, and power: The survival strategies of working poor women. *Annals of the Association of American Geographers, 88*(4), 595–621.

Glaspell, Susan. 1917, 5 March. A jury of her peers. *Everyweek.* Reprinted in Lee R. Edwards and Arlyn Diamond, eds., *American Voices, American Women.* New York: Avon Press, 359–381.

Godlewska, Anne, and Neil Smith, eds. 1994. *Geography and Empire.* Oxford, UK: Basil Blackwell.

Golledge, Reginald. 1993. Geography and the disabled: A survey with special reference to vision-impaired and blind populations. *Transactions of the Institute of British Geographers, 18,* 63–85.

Goss, Jon. 1993. The "magic of the mall": An analysis of form, function, and meaning in the contemporary retail built environment. *Annals of the Association of American Geographers, 83*(1), 18–47.

Goss, Jon. 1996. Disquiet on the waterfront: Reflections on nostalgia and utopia in the urban archetypes of festival marketplaces. *Urban Geography, 17*(3), 221–247.

Gregson, N., and M. Lowe. 1994. *Servicing the Middle Classes: Class, Gender and Waged Domestic Labour in Contemporary Britain.* London: Routledge.

Grier, Katherine C. 1988. *Culture and Comfort: Parlor Making and Middle-Class Identity, 1850–1930*. Washington, DC: Smithsonian Institution Press.

Griffin, Susan. 1978. *Woman and Nature*. New York: Harper & Row.

Gruffudd, Pyrs. 1994. Back to the land: Historiography, rurality, and the nation in interwar Wales. *Transactions of the Institute of British Geographers*, *19*(1), 61–77.

Gutteling, Jan, and Oene Wiegman. 1993. Gender-specific reactions to environmental hazards in the Netherlands. *Sex Roles*, *28*(7–8), 433–447.

Habermas, Jürgen. 1991. *The Structural Transformation of the Public Sphere: An Enquiry into a Category of Bourgeois Society*. Cambridge, MA: MIT Press.

Hanson, Susan. 1992. Geography and feminism: Worlds in collision?. *Annals of the Association of American Geographers*, *82*(4), 569–586.

Hanson, Susan, and Ibipo Johnston. 1985. Gender differences in work-trip length: Explanations and implications. *Urban Geography*, *6*(3), 193–219.

Hanson, Susan, and Geraldine Pratt. 1991. Job search and the occupational segregation of women. *Annals of the Association of American Geographers*, *81*(2), 229–253.

Hanson, Susan, and Geraldine Pratt. 1995. *Gender, Work, and Space*. New York: Routledge.

Harding, Sandra. 1986. *The Science Question in Feminism*. Ithaca, NY: Cornell University Press.

Hayden, Dolores. 1983. *The Grand Domestic Revolution*. Cambridge, MA: MIT Press.

Hayden, Dolores. 1984. *Redesigning the American Dream*. New York: Norton.

Hayden, Dolores. 1995. *The Power of Place*. Cambridge, MA: MIT Press.

Health. 1999, July/August. "And June Cleaver Seemed So Cheery," p. 18.

Heyzer, Noleen, Geertje Lycklama a Nijeholt, and Nedra Weerakoon, eds. 1994. *The Trade in Domestic Workers*. London: Zed Books.

Hunt, Margaret. 1996. *The Middling Sort: Commerce, Gender, and the Family in England, 1680–1780*. Berkeley and Los Angeles: University of California Press.

Hunter, Jane. 1984. *The Gospel of Gentility: American Women Missionaries in Turn-of-the-Century China*. New Haven, CT: Yale University Press.

Ingram, Gordon Brent, Anne-Marie Bouthillette, and Yvonne Retter, eds. 1997. *Queers in Space: Communities/Public Spaces/Sites of Resistance*. Seattle, WA: Bay Press.

Jackson, Kenneth. 1985. *Crabgrass Frontier: The Suburbanization of the United States*. New York: Oxford University Press.

Jacobs, Jane. 1961. *The Death and Life of Great American Cities*. New York: Vintage Books.

Jennings, Jan. 1996. Controlling passion: The turn-of-the-century wallpaper dilemma. *Winterthur Portfolio*, *31*, 243–264.

Johnson, Nuala. 1994. Sculpting heroic histories: Celebrating the centenary of the 1798 rebellion in Ireland. *Transactions of the Institute of British Geographers*, *19*(1), 78–93.

Johnston, Lynda, and Gill Valentine. 1995. Wherever I lay my girlfriend, that's my home: The performance and surveillance of lesbian identities in domestic environments. In David Bell and Gill Valentine, eds., *Mapping Desire: Geographies of Sexualities*. London: Routledge, 99–113.

Johnston-Anumonwo, Ibipo. 1995. Racial differences in the commuting behavior of women in Buffalo, 1980–1990. *Urban Geography, 16*(1), 23–45.

Jones, John Paul, Heidi Nast, and Susan M. Roberts, eds. 1997. *Thresholds in Feminist Geography*. Lanham, MD: Rowman & Littlefield.

Kamel, Rachel. 1990. *The Global Factory*. Philadelphia: American Friends Service Committee.

Katz, Cindi and Janice Monk. 1993a. Making connections: Space, place, and the life course. In Cindi Katz & Janice Monk, eds. *Full Circles: Geographies of Women over the Life Course*. London/ New York: Routledge, 264–278.

Katz, Cindi, and Janice Monk, eds. 1993b. *Full Circles: Geographies of Women over the Life Course*. London/New York: Routledge, 264–278.

Kay, Jeanne. 1997. Sweet surrender, but what's the gender? Nature and the body in the writings of nineteenth-century Mormon women. In John Paul Jones, Heidi Nast, and Susan Roberts, eds., *Thresholds in Feminist Geography*. Lanham, MD: Rowman & Littlefield, 361–382.

Kellert, Stephen, and Joyce Berry. 1987. Attitudes, knowledge, and behaviors toward wildllife as affected by gender. *Wildlife Society Bulletin, 15*, 363–371.

Kenny, Judith. 1995. Climate, race, and imperial authority: The symbolic landscape of the British hill station in India. *Annals of the Association of American Geographers, 85*(4), 694–714.

Knopp, Larry. 1990. Some theoretical implications of gay involvement in an urban land market. *Political Geography Quarterly, 9*, 337–352.

Kodras, J., and John-Paul Jones III. 1991. A contextual examination of the feminization of poverty. *Geoforum, 22*(2), 159–171.

Kolodny, Annette. 1975. *The Lay of the Land: Metaphor as Experience and History in American Life and Letters*. Chapel Hill: University of North Carolina Press.

Kolodny, Annette. 1983. *The Land before Her: Fantasy and Experience of the American Frontiers, 1630–1860*. Chapel Hill: University of North Carolina Press.

Kowaleski-Wallace, Elizabeth. 1997. *Consuming Subjects: Women, Shopping, and Business in the Eighteenth Century*. New York: Columbia University Press.

Laws, Glenda. 1997. Women's life courses, spatial mobility, and state policies. In John Paul Jones, Heidi Nast, and Susan M. Roberts, eds., *Thresholds in Feminist Geography*. Lanham, MD: Rowman & Littlefield, 47–64.

Lay, Mary, Janice Monk, and Deborah S. Rosenfelt, eds. 2001. *Encompassing Gender: Integrating International Studies and Women Studies*. New York: Feminist Press.

Leach, William. 1993. *Land of Desire: Merchants, Power, and the Rise of a New American Culture*. New York: Vintage Books.

Leuchtag, Alice. 1995, March–April. Merchants of flesh: International prostitution and the war on women's rights. *The Humanist*.

Levy, Caren. 1992. Transport. In Lise Ostergaard, ed., *Gender and Development: A Practical Guide*. London/New York: Routledge, 94–106.

Lindgren, H. Elaine. 1991. *Land in Her Own Name: Women as Homesteaders in North Dakota*. Fargo: North Dakota Institute for Regional Studies.

London Planning Aid Service. 1985. *Planning Advice for Women's Groups*. London: Greater London Council.

Lupton, Ellen, and J. Abbott Miller. 1992. *The Bathroom, the Kitchen, and the Aesthetics of Waste: A Process of Elimination*. Dalton, MA: Studley Press.

Mackenzie, Suzanne. 1989. Restructuring the relations of work and life: Women as environmental actors, feminism as geographic analysis. In Audrey Kobayashi and Suzanne Mackenzie, eds., *Remaking Human Geography*. Boston: Unwin Hyman, 40–61.

Markusen, Ann. 1980. City spatial structure, women's household work, and national urban policy. In Catharine Stimpson, Elsa Dixler, Martha J. Nelson, and Kathryn B. Yatralcis, eds., *Women and the American City*. Chicago: University of Chicago Press, 20–41.

Marsh, Margaret. 1990. *Suburban Lives*. New Brunswick, NJ: Rutgers University Press.

Martin, Susan Forbes. 1991. *Refugee Women*. London: Zed Books.

Massey, Douglas, and Nancy Denton. 1993. *American Apartheid: Segregation and the Making of the Underclass*. Cambridge, MA: Harvard University Press.

Matrix. 1984. *Making Space: Women and the Man-Made Environment*. London: Pluto Press.

Mazey, Mary Ellen, and David Lee. 1983. *Her Space, Her Place*. Washington, DC: Association of American Geographers.

McClintock, Anne. 1995. *Imperial Leather: Race, Gender, and Sexuality in the Colonial Conquest*. New York: Routledge.

McDowell, Linda. 1993. Off the road: alternative views of rebellion, resistance, and "the beats." *Transactions of the Institute of British Geographers, 21*(2), 412–419.

McDowell, Linda. 1995. Body work: Heterosexual gender performances in city workplaces. In David Bell and Gill Valentine, eds., *Mapping Desire: Geographies of Sexualities*. London: Routledge, 75–95.

McDowell, Linda. 1997. *Capital Culture: Gender at Work in the City*. London: Blackwell.

McDowell, Linda, and Joanne P. Sharp, eds. 1997. *Space, Gender, Knowledge: Feminist Readings*. London: Edward Arnold.

McEwan, Cheryl. 1994. Encounters with West African women: Textual representations of difference by white women abroad. In Alison Blunt and Gillian Rose, eds., *Writing Women and Space: Colonial and Postcolonial Geographies*. New York: Guilford Press, 73–100.

McEwan, Cheryl. 1998. Gender, science, and physical geography in nineteenth-century Britain. *Area, 30*(3), 215–223.

McLeod, Mary. 1996. Everyday and "other" spaces. In Debra Coleman, Elizabeth Danze, and Carol Henderson, eds., *Architecture and Feminism*. New York: Princeton Architectural Press, 1–37.

McPhee, John. 1989. *The Control of Nature*. New York: Farrar, Straus, Giroux.

Merchant, Carolyn. 1980. *The Death of Nature: Women, Ecology, and the Scientific Revolution.* New York: Harper & Row.

Mies, Maria, and Vandana Shiva. 1993. *Ecofeminism.* London: Zed Books.

Mills, Caroline. 1993. Myths and meanings of gentrification. In James Duncan and David Ley, eds., *Place/Culture/Representation.* New York: Routledge, 149–172.

Mills, Sara. 1994. Knowledge, gender, and empire. In Alison Blunt and Gillian Rose, eds., *Writing Women and Space: Colonial and Postcolonial Geographies.* New York: Guilford Press, 29–50.

Mills, Sara. 1996. Gender and colonial space. *Gender, Place and Culture, 3*(2), 125–147.

Mitchell, Don. 1997. The annihilation of space by law. *Antipode, 29*(3), 303–336.

Momsen, Janet. 1992. *Women and Development in the Third World.* London: Longman.

Momsen, Janet Henshall, and Vivian Kinnaird, eds. 1993. *Different Places, Different Voices.* London/New York: Routledge.

Momsen, Janet, and Janet Townsend. 1987. *Geography of Gender in the Third World.* London: Hutchinson.

Monk, Janice. 1984. Approaches to the study of women and landscape. *Environmental Review, 8*(1), 23–33.

Monk, Janice. 1988. Engendering a new geographic vision. In John Fien and Rod Gerber, eds., *Teaching Geography for a Better World.* Edinburgh: Oliver & Boyd, 91–103.

Muller, Peter. 1976. *The Outer City: Geographical Consequences of the Urbanization of the Suburbs.* San Francisco: Harper & Row.

Mwaka, Victoria. 1993. Agricultural production and women's time budgets in Uganda. In Janet Henshall Momsen and Vivian Kinnaird, eds., *Different Places, Different Voices.* New York: Routledge, 46–52.

Nash, Catherine. 1994. Remapping the body/land: New cartographies of identity, gender, and landscape in Ireland. In Alison Blunt and Gillian Rose, eds., *Writing Women and Space: Colonial and Postcolonial Geographies.* New York: Guilford Press, 227–250.

Nesmith, C., and S. Radcliffe. 1993. (Re)mapping Mother Earth: A geographical perspective on environmental feminisms. *Environment and Planning D: Society and Space, 11,* 379–394.

Nicholson, Linda. 1986. *Gender and History: The Limits of Social Theory in the Age of the Family.* New York: Columbia University Press.

Norwood, Vera. 1993. *Made from This Earth: American Women and Nature.* Chapel Hill: University of North Carolina Press.

Norwood, Vera, and Janice Monk, eds. 1987. *The Desert Is No Lady: Southwestern Landscapes in Women's Writing and Art.* New Haven, CT: Yale University Press.

Oberhauser, Ann. 1997. The home as "field": Households and homework in rural Appalachia. In John Paul Jones, Heidi Nast, and Susan Roberts, eds., *Thresholds in Feminist Geography.* Lanham, MD: Rowman & Littlefield, 165–182.

Ogata, Sadako. 1995. Refugee women: The forgotten half. *Our Planet, 7*(4), 19–22.

Ogborn, Miles. 1998. *Spaces of Modernity: London's Geographies, 1680–1780.* New York: Guilford Press.

Olds, Elizabeth Fagg. 1985. *Women of the Four Winds.* Boston: Houghton Mifflin.

Pain, Rachel. 1991. Space, sexual violence and social control. *Progress in Human Geography, 15*(4), 415–431.

Pain, Rachel. 1997. Social geographies of women's fear of crime. *Transactions of the Institute of British Geographers, 22*(2), 231–244.

Palm, Risa, and Allen Pred. 1974. *A Time–Geographic Perspective on Problems of Inequality for Women.* Department of Geography Working Paper No. 236. Berkeley and Los Angeles: University University of California Press.

Paul, Bimal Kanti. 1992. Female activity space in rural Bangladesh. *Geographical Review, 82*(1), 1–12.

Peiss, Kathy. 1986. *Cheap Amusements: Working Women and Leisure in Turn-of-the-Century New York.* Philadelphia: Temple University Press.

Pettman, Jan Jindy. 1996. *Worlding Women: A Feminist International Politics.* New York: Routledge.

Plumwood, Val. 1993. *Feminism and the Mastery of Nature.* London/New York: Routledge.

Pratt, Geraldine. 1997. Stereotypes and ambivalence: The construction of domestic workers in Vancouver, British Columbia. *Gender, Place and Culture, 4*(2), 159–178.

Pratt, Mary Louise. 1992. *Imperial Eyes: Travel Writing and Transculturation.* New York: Routledge.

Preston, Valerie, Sara McLafferty, and Ellen Hamilton. 1993. The impact of family status on black, white, and Hispanic women's commuting. *Urban Geography, 14*(3), 228–250.

Quilley, Stephen. 1997. Constructing Manchester's "new urban village": Gay space in the entrepreneurial city. In Gordon Brent Ingram, Anne-Marie Bouthillette, and Yolanda Retter, eds., *Queers in Space.* Seattle, WA: Bay Press, 275–294.

Radcliffe, Sarah. 1993. The role of gender in peasant migration. In Janet Henshall Momsen and Vivian Kinnaird, eds., *Different Places, Different Voices.* London/New York: Routledge, 278–288.

Radcliffe, Sarah. 1996. Gendered nations: Nostalgia, development and territory in Ecuador. *Gender, Place and Culture, 3*(1), 5–22.

Reiter, Rayna. 1975. Men and women in the south of France: Public and private domains. In Rayna Reiter, ed., *Toward an Anthropology of Women.* New York: Monthly Review Press, 150–170.

Rengert, Arlene. 1981. Some socio-cultural aspects of rural out-migration in Latin America. In O. H. Horst, ed., *Papers in Latin American Geography.* Muncie, IN: Conference of Latin American Geographers, 15–27.

Rich, Adrienne. 1986. Compulsory heterosexuality and lesbian existence. In *Blood, Bread, and Poetry: Selected Prose, 1979–1985.* New York: Norton.

Rocheleau, Dianne, Barbara Thomas-Slayter, and Esther Wangari, eds. 1996. *Feminist Political Ecology: Global Issues and Local Experiences.* London/New York: Routledge.

Rose, Gillian. 1993. *Feminism and Geography: The Limits of Geographical Knowledge*. Minneapolis: University of Minnesota Press.

Rosenbloom, Sandra. 1993. Women's travel patterns at various stages of their lives. In Cindi Katz and Janice Monk, eds., *Full Circles: Geographies of Women over the Life Course*. London/New York: Routledge, 208–242.

Rosenzweig, Roy. 1983. *Eight Hours for What We Will: Workers and Leisure in an Industrial City, 1870–1920*. New York: Cambridge University Press.

Ross, Andrew. 1999. *The Celebration Chronicles: Life, Liberty, and the Pursuit of Property Values in Disney's New Town*. New York: Ballantine Books.

Rothblum, Esther, Jacqueline Weinstock, and Jessica Morris, eds. 1998. *Women in the Antarctic*. New York: Haworth Press.

Rothenberg, Tamar. 1995. "And she told two friends": Lesbians Creating Urban Social Space. In David Bell and Gill Valentine, eds., *Mapping Desire: Geographies of Sexualities*. London: Routledge, 165–181.

Rutherford, Brent, and Gerda Wekerle. 1988. Captive rider, captive labor: spatial constraints and women's employment. *Urban Geography, 9*(2), 116–137.

Ryan, Mary. 1990. *Women in Public: Between Banners and Ballots, 1825–1880*. Baltimore: Johns Hopkins University Press.

Rydell, Robert. 1984. *All the World's a Fair: Visions of Empire at American International Expositions, 1876–1916*. Chicago: University of Chicago Press.

Sachs, Patricia. 1993. Old ties: Women, work, and ageing in a coal-mining community in West Virginia. In Cindi Katz and Janice Monk, eds., *Full Circles: Geographies of Women over the Life Course*. New York: Routledge, 156–170.

Said, Edward. 1978. *Orientalism*. New York: Pantheon Books.

Samarasinghe, Vidyamali. 1997. Counting women's work: The intersection of time and space. In John Paul Jones, Heidi Nast, and Susan M. Roberts, eds., *Thresholds in Feminist Geography*. Lanham, MD: Rowman & Littlefield, 129–144.

Sapiro, Virginia. 1994. *Women in American Society*. Mountain View, CA: Mayfield.

Sardar, Ziauddin, ed. 1988. *The Revenge of Athena: Science, Exploitation, and the Third World*. London: Mansell.

Schahn, J., and E. Holzer. 1990. Studies of individual environmental concern: The role of knowledge, gender, and background variables. *Environment and Behavior, 22*, 767–786.

Scharff, Virginia. 1991. *Taking the Wheel: Women and the Coming of the Motor Age*. Albuquerque: University of New Mexico Press.

Scherzer, Kenneth A. 1992. *The Unbounded Community: Neighborhood Life and Social Structure in New York City, 1830–1875*. Durham, NC: Duke University Press.

Schlissel, Lillian. 1982. *Women's Diaries of the Westward Journey*. New York: Schoken Books.

Seager, Joni. 1993a. *Earth Follies: Coming to Feminist Terms with the Global Environmental Crisis*. London/New York: Routledge.

Seager, Joni. 1993b, November–December. A not-so-natural disaster: Militaries, technology, and the floods of 1993. *MS Magazine, 4*(3), 26–27.

Seager, Joni. 1997a. *The State of Women in the World Atlas*. London/New York: Penguin Books.

Seager, Joni. 1997b. Throwing the body out with the bathwater. *Environment and Planning A, 29*(9) 1521–1523.

Seager, Joni. 1998. Women out of place: The gendered geography of Antarctica. In Esther Rothblum, Jacqueline Weinstock, and Jessica Morris, eds., *Women in the Antarctic*. New York: Haworth Press, 211–219.

Shiva, Vandana. 1985. Ecology movements in India. *Development: Seeds of Change, 3*, 22–26.

Shiva, Vandana. 1989. *Staying Alive: Women, Ecology, and Development*. London: Zed Books.

Shiva, Vandana. 1990. Development as a new project of Western patriarchy. In Irene Diamond and Gloria Orenstein, eds., *Reweaving the World: The Emergence of Ecofeminism*. San Francisco: Sierra Club Books, 189–200.

Shiva, Vandana. 1993. Colonialism and the evolution of masculinist forestry. In Sandra Harding, ed., *The Racial Economy of Science*. Bloomington: Indiana University Press, 303–314.

Sklar, Kathryn K. 1995. *Florence Kelley and the Nation's Work: The Rise of Women's Political Culture, 1830–1900*. New Haven, CT: Yale University Press.

Slotkin, Richard. 1993. Buffalo Bill's "Wild West" and the mythologization of the American Empire. In Amy Kaplan and Donald E. Pease, eds., *Cultures of United States Imperialism*. Durham, NC: Duke University Press, 164–181.

Smith, Neil. 1984. *Uneven Development: Nature, Capital, and the Production of Space*. New York: Basil Blackwell.

Solkin, D. 1992. *Painting for Money: The Visual Arts and the Public Sphere in Eighteenth-Century England*. New Haven, CT: Yale University Press.

Spain, Daphne. 1992. *Gendered Spaces*. Chapel Hill: University of North Carolina Press.

Sparke, Matthew. 1996. Displacing the field in fieldwork. In Nancy Duncan. ed., *BodySpace*. New York: Routledge, 212–233.

Sparke, Penny. 1995. *As Long as It's Pink: The Sexual Politics of Taste*. London: Pandora Press.

Spiegel, Marjorie. 1988. *The Dreaded Comparison: Human and Animal Slavery*. Philadelphia: New Society Publishers.

Stansell, Christine. 1987. *City of Women: Sex and Class in New York, 1789–1860*. Urbana: University of Illinois Press.

Starkweather, Amy. 1893. Reports of Amy Starkweather, Superintendent of Installations. *Board of Lady Managers Manuscript Collection*, Vol. 29. Chicago: Chicago Historical Society.

Stiell, Bernadette, and Kim England. 1997. Domestic distinctions: Constructing difference among paid domestic workers in Toronto. *Gender, Place and Culture, 4*(3), 339–359.

Sturgeon, Noel. 1997. *Ecofeminist Natures*. New York: Routledge.

Suro, Roberto. 1999. Crossing the high-tech divide. *American Demographics, 21*(7), 55–60.

Takaki, Ronald. 1979. *Iron Cages: Race and Culture in Nineteenth-Century America.* New York: Knopf.

Takaki, Ronald. 1993. *A Different Mirror: A History of Multicultural America.* Boston: Little Brown & Co.

Thrift, Nigel, and Allen Pred. 1981. Time-geography: A new beginning. *Progress in Human Geography, 5,* 277–286.

Townsend, Janet. 1995. *Women's Voices from the Rainforest.* New York: Routledge.

Trexler, Richard C. 1995. *Sex and Conquest: Gendered Violence, Political Order, and the European Conquest of the Americas.* Ithaca, NY: Cornell University Press.

Tyner, James. 1996a. The gendering of Philippine international labor migration. *Professional Geographer, 48*(4), 405–416.

Tyner, James. 1996b. Constructions of Filipina migrant entertainers. *Gender, Place and Culture, 3*(1), 77–93.

Tyner, James. 1997. Constructing images, constructing policy: The case of Filipina migrant performing artists. *Gender, Place and Culture, 4*(1), 19–35.

United Nations Environment Programme. 1989. *Public and Leadership Attitudes to the Environment in 14 countries.* New York: Lou Harris/United Nations Environment Programme.

United Nations High Commissioner for Refugees. 1996. *The State of the World's Refugees.* New York: Oxford University Press.

United Nations. 1995. *The World's Women, 1995.* New York: United Nations.

Valentine, Gill. 1992. Images of danger: Women's sources of information about the spatial distribution of male violence. *Area, 24*(1), 22–29.

Vance, James E. Jr. 1990. *The Continuing City: Urban Morphology in Western Civilization.* Baltimore: Johns Hopkins University Press.

Varley, Pamela. 1998. *The Sweatshop Quandry: Corporate Responsibility on the Global Frontier.* Washington, DC: Investor Responsibility Research Center.

Ward, Kathryn, ed. 1990. *Women, Workers, and Global Restructuring.* Ithaca, NY: Cornell University Press.

Ware, Vron. 1992. *Beyond the Pale: White Women, Racism, and History.* London: Verso Books.

Waring, Marilyn. 1988. *If Women Counted: A New Feminist Economics.* New York: Harper.

Warren, Karen J., ed. 1994. *Ecological Feminism.* London/New York: Routledge.

Weimann, Jeanne M. 1981. *The Fair Women.* Chicago: Academy Chicago.

Weisman, Leslie. 1992. *Discrimination by Design: A Feminist Critique of the Man-Made Environment.* Urbana: University of Illinois Press.

Wharton, Edith. 1984. *The House of Mirth.* New York: Bantam Books. (Originally published 1905.)

White, Luise. 1990. *The Comforts of Home: Prostitution in Colonial Nairobi.* Chicago: University of Chicago Press.

White, Lynn. 1967. The historical roots of our ecologic crisis. *Science, 155,* 1203–1207.

Wilkinson, Nancy. 1979. Women on the Oregon Trail. *Landscape, 23*, 42–47.

Wilson, Elizabeth. 1991. *The Sphinx in the City: Urban Life, the Control of Disorder, and Women*. Berkeley and Los Angeles: University of California Press.

Wolch, Jennifer, and Jody Emel, eds. 1998. *Animal Geographies: Place, Politics, and Identity in the Nature–Culture Borderlands*. New York: Verso Books.

Wolff, Janet. 1985, The invisible flaneuse: Women and the literature of modernity. *Theory, Culture and Society, 2*, 37–46.

Women and Geography Study Group of the Institute of British Geographers. 1997. *Feminist Geographies: Explorations in Diversity and Difference*. London: Longman.

Wright, Gwendolyn. 1981. *Building the Dream: A Social History of Housing in America*. Cambridge, MA: MIT Press.

Young, Iris Marion. 1990. *Justice and the Politics of Difference*. Princeton, NJ: Princeton University Press.

INDEX

Note: Figures appearing outside the page range of a discussion are indicated by an *f* following the page number.

ABOUT THE AUTHORS

Mona Domosh is a professor of geography at Dartmouth College. She is the author of *Invented Cities: The Creation of Landscape in Nineteenth-Century New York and Boston*, the coauthor of *The Human Mosaic: A Thematic Introduction to Cultural Geography*, and the former co-editor of the journal *Gender, Place and Culture*. Her research lies at the intersection of cultural, feminist, and historical geography.

Joni Seager is a professor of geography at the University of Vermont. She is the author of *The State of Women in the World Atlas* and *Earth Follies: Coming to Feminist Terms with the Global Environmental Crisis*. Her research focuses on feminist geography, global political economy, and environmental analysis.